DISCUSSION:

METHOD OF

DEMOCRACY

Laura Crowell

University of Washington

Scott, Foresman and Company

Chicago, Atlanta, Dallas, Palo Alto, Fair Lawn, N.J.

BF637
D5 C7

4.50

PREFACE

This textbook for the first course in group discussion has two interrelated purposes: to analyze the process of discussion and to suggest means for its more effective use. Such an undertaking is repeatedly necessary in a society seeking by democratic methods the achievement of its democratic goals—among them, the enhancement of the individual within the compass of the general good. This relationship of man and his society is symbolized in the ancient design of the three spheres free within the bounding circle,[1] a symbol used in works of art ranging from banners of the early Tibetans to a Christ of Memling. In the words of former Vice-President Henry A. Wallace, this design suggests "the maximum development of individual diversity within the limitations of the whole."

Basic to this book is the belief that improved discussion requires improved handling of ideas by the group, an activity which can occur only, however, when interpersonal relations are being appropriately handled. For both these processes the book aims to provide explanations and to suggest assignments that will be valuable to new instructors in the discussion method as well as interesting to experienced ones. The first three chapters provide a foundation for study of the discussion process by explaining its uses, its nature, and its appropriate subject matter. The next four chapters deal with suitable preparation for problem-solving and enlightenment discussions through the gathering of information, the employment of critical thinking, and the organization of materials. The following five chapters concern the conduct of discussion—handling ideas and attitudes, communicating effectively, and performing the functions of leadership. Chapter Thirteen suggests the adaptations necessary for *public* discussion. Chapter Fourteen reiterates and further clarifies the assumption made throughout the book that discussion is truly a method of democracy.

Several matters of order and emphasis are worthy of note. In the preparation chapters it is suggested that students give attention to problem-solving discussion before turning to enlightenment discussion.

1. This symbol is used on the cover of this book and at the beginning of each chapter.

Since the problem-solving discussion takes investigators through the total act of thought—from the recognition of the problem to the plan for putting the chosen solution into effect—it exemplifies one of the most important types of discussion; furthermore, it lays the foundation for more specific work on those particular segments of the thought process involved in study and evaluative discussions. Having then studied and practiced the methods of sound thinking and of cooperative interaction, students are prepared to undertake the exploratory form—a form whose very freedom makes it look deceptively easy. To participate successfully in this type of discussion, participants must have acquired appropriate restraints, methods of procedure, and attitudes and, further, must exercise them spontaneously and fittingly; hence, the discipline of the more structured forms of discussion markedly increases the likelihood that students will use the exploratory form well.

The chapters make unmistakably clear that students must not delay their own critical thinking until the time of the discussion but, rather, must also be alert to accuracy of fact, credibility of source, validity of inference, and clarity of statement during their work of investigation and organization. There is extended analysis of the process of idea-development—the slow interaction of partial thoughts, the quick stabs of new ideas forming, the tentative questionings, the final interweavings that are the essence of the discussion process. Emphasis is also placed on the responsibility of participants to give unremitting assistance in the common task, and of the leader to act with sensitivity and skill to preserve individual initiative among the members while marshaling it in cooperative effort. Explanations and recommendations for improvement in the use of the discussion process are solidly grounded in sociological and psychological theory and research, significant studies being made easily available in the various chapters through references within the text and through the readings and problems.

Of special value are the numerous annotated discussion examples that illustrate the explanations of the chapters. Abundant and varied readings and problems are suggested at the end of each chapter to allow the instructor to draw upon them as he wishes in developing his own approach. It is my hope that these suggested assignments will give the instructor substantial assistance in providing his students significant opportunities for developing understanding of and skill in the use of the discussion process and, furthermore, for playing with greater success and satisfaction their continuing roles as individuals and as members of a democratic society.

This book represents most strongly the influences of these persons: my parents, who believed in education and in me; Professors Upton S. Earls and James A. Fitzgerald, who gave me early encouragement; and Professor A. Craig Baird, who introduced me to the joys of scholarship by his inspired teaching and personal example. My grateful appreciation goes to Douglas Ehninger for his perceptive suggestions on the entire manuscript, and to James L. Golden and Orville L. Pence for their thoughtful assistance on particular chapters.

Laura Crowell
University of Washington, 1963

CONTENTS

Chapter one

THE

USES

OF

DISCUSSION

Through the corridors of factories and legislative halls and up in the elevators of large office buildings go men on their way to confer. Through air terminals and hotel lobbies pass men who have crossed a nation or a continent to confer. In schools, business offices, courthouses, churches, hospitals, and homes—men come together to exchange information and opinions in order to solve problems or to try to understand complex matters more fully. They use *discussion,* a method of democracy.

Some are engaged in the work of government. Ideally, in a democratic society the citizens determine the national goals and the means of achieving them. The proper machinery of such determination is free discussion, and the value of the decisions reached depends upon the human worth of the citizens who make them and their skill in cooperative deliberation. Some, on the other hand, are engaged in private concerns. Through discussions with their associates they develop and carry out plans; again, the value of these plans depends upon the human quality and the cooperative skills of the participants.

In everyday conversation the term *discussion* has many different meanings. For example, we say that the Congressman, mending his fences in the home district, *discusses* issues before his constituents in a careful hour-long address, then *discusses* spontaneously the questions they raise in the forum period. After the meeting he *discusses* the political temper of the district with his staff and lays plans for a television *discussion*—in reality, a debate—with his opponent. In public speeches, in forum replies, in face-to-face interchanges with a committee, or in actual debate—in all of these situations, ideas are being formulated, compared, and evaluated. In short, the term *discussion,* even when restricted to its oral forms only, may refer to a variety of types of communication.

The major concern in this textbook, however, is with the committee type of discussion.[1] Examples of this kind of discussion include the Congressman talking with his staff about his chances in the district, a small group of interested citizens meeting to deal with a community problem, or a group of friends gathering to talk over recent political events. You and your fellow students also participate in this kind of discussion when you meet in small groups to prepare joint assign-

1. You will find explanations of the use of discussion before audiences in Chapter 13. The presence of listeners will alter somewhat the conditions referred to for small discussion groups in all the chapters before Chapter 13.

4

ments, to review before an examination, to decide how to improve conditions in your residence halls, or to explore ideas presented by a renowned visiting lecturer. In such groups citizens of a democracy prepare for unified action or seek general enlightenment.

Purposes of discussion

Preparation for action

"We look on discussion as the best preparation for action," said Pericles in 431 B.C. in his oration honoring those who had died in the service of Athens in that first year of the Peloponnesian War. The Athenians that day looked out upon the ravaged fields of Attica and murmured against his conduct of the war with Sparta. Pericles, in his eulogy of the war dead, set forth ringingly his stand on the questions before them; and, as he spoke, he created an unforgettable picture of a democracy in action, of a citizenry who scorned precipitate action and prided themselves on taking counsel among themselves as a guide to action. "We look on discussion as the best preparation for action."

How does preparation for action take place in twentieth-century America? In American government, discussion in small committees, then debate in the larger assembly precedes the decision by majority vote. A committee of community-minded doctors spends long hours in cooperative planning for the memorial hospital before the bids are let. If the publishers of two national magazines wish to affiliate, they hold a series of joint meetings to arrange the pooling of interests. The sponsors of programs for the aging meet regularly to make decisions for improvement and extension of their services. A football coach and his scouts plan together their strategy for playing their traditional rivals. Building upon the suggestions of each member, a research team plots the next stage of its program. You as a college student plan your course of study with your advisers, your recreation with your friends, and your long-term goals with the members of your family.

How do we—in government, the professions, industry, social service, recreation, research, education—prepare for action today? Even after twenty-four hundred years of complex cultural change, we must answer with Pericles: "We look on discussion as the best preparation for action."

5

General enlightenment

But cooperative planning of action is only one of the purposes served by the discussion process in a democracy. Another purpose is the enlightenment and personal growth of the individual who engages in it.

Robert Hutchins (1)[2] declared in 1954,

> It is now necessary for everybody to try to live, as Ortega says, "at the height of his times." The democratic enterprise is imperiled if any one of us says, "I do not have to try to think for myself, or make the most of myself, or become a citizen of the world republic of learning."

As a student you participate in classroom discussions and in seminar and coffee-break exchanges; in such deliberations you discover what sort of person you really are and—something that is perhaps even more important—what you hope to become. In college you have the great ideas, the significant accomplishments, and the continuing problems of the world spread out before you. Discussing these in the classroom, the instructor's office, a friend's apartment—doubles and triples your contact with the world and thus enriches your life and increases your ability to shape it.

In the meantime you are doubtless learning a great deal about human relationships. Nowhere is it easier to see the operation of other persons' thoughts and feelings than in the close contact of the discussion group; here is a laboratory situation for discovering how people's cooperative and creative faculties are either liberated or choked off. You are also learning how to make your ideas and opinions clear to your listeners, how to understand their reactions and ideas, how to cooperate with them in evaluating these contributions. Through such discussions you learn to express yourself effectively—an invaluable skill for future college work and for later professional activity.

Furthermore, as you consider—in your political science classroom, in your microbiology laboratory, or in your Russian literature seminar —the engrossing complexities, the continuing torments of man's igno-

---

2. References given at the end of the chapter are indicated by numbers in parentheses. Footnotes at the bottom of the page are indicated by superscript numbers.

rance or folly, you gain a sense of his compelling desire to stamp out unsatisfactory conditions wherever they are and of your own civic responsibility to play your part in this endeavor. Men are useless to the society of which they are a part and with which their futures are inextricably bound if they do not assume their public responsibility. Pericles declared that his countrymen regarded "the man who takes no part in public affairs not as one who minds his own business, but as good for nothing." And in this shirking of public duties the individual hurts himself most of all, for he deprives himself of the personal growth that comes from, in the late Lyman Bryson's words, "facing the ultimate issues." Only in undertaking them fully does he have a chance of attaining his fullest stature in his society.

This is an age of breakthroughs. Never did man move forward so swiftly as in our own times: out to the reaches of space and deep into the heart of physical matter. And no area is more exciting or more vital than the striving of awakening populations around our globe to find greater dignity for man himself or the struggle of our own country to keep its democratic footing in an economy of abundance. As Christopher Fry (2) wrote,

> Dark and cold we may be, but this
> Is no winter now. The frozen misery
> Of centuries breaks, cracks, begins to move,
> The thunder is the thunder of the floes,
> The thaw, the flood, the upstart Spring.
> Thank God our time is now when wrong
> Comes up to face us everywhere,
> Never to leave us till we take
> The longest stride of soul men ever took.

In such an age we must consult with one another to obtain the widest knowledge and the keenest insights. Thus we will achieve group goals and, at the same time, strengthen the individual for those situations in which he must make his decisions alone. Since discussion can be the best preparation for unified action and can contribute to the growth of each participant, we cannot afford to use the process ineptly. We cannot afford to merit the criticisms of those who say that group discussions are time-wasting producers of small results and destroyers of individuality. In order to produce worthwhile results we must understand the nature of the discussion process and also the occasions on which its use is most appropriate.

Nature of the discussion process

One way of characterizing the discussion process is to describe the attitudes and behavior its participants should demonstrate.

The members should see themselves as part of a team, to whose common purpose they voluntarily contribute their best efforts. As team members they should genuinely seek to build together the best answers they can for the issues they face. Such cooperative development demands that they hold their own ideas tentatively, trying in an open-minded way to see that all ideas—including their own—have a fair hearing. All members should listen encouragingly to each other, recognizing their responsibility to understand clearly what is meant and to help determine the relevance, truth, and significance of the ideas given the group. All members should address their contributions to each other as well as to the leader, usually offering them in the form of questions so as to invite the others to examine them carefully.

The leader of the discussion should see himself as a focuser of the best efforts of the members upon their common task, helping them to look searchingly at the new ideas before them, summarizing the understandings and agreements developed, and inviting them to explore appropriate new areas. He should intelligently apportion the available time among these areas and encourage everyone to participate. Despite this special task of focusing, the leader should feel himself a true member of the team, saying "we," "our," and "us," just as any of the other members.

Obviously, the discussion process is highly complex. If the members, however, attempt to make their efforts *voluntary, open-minded, encouraging,* and *inquiring,* and the leader attempts to *focus* these efforts on the group task, the group will be likely to develop an effective working relationship.

Assuming for the moment that a group has a suitable subject for discussion, we may ask: what ingredients go into a productive and satisfying discussion? Four ingredients are vitally necessary to effective work by members and leader: (1) the essential information; (2) straight thinking before and during the discussion; (3) attitudes conducive to cooperation and achievement; and (4) effective communication among the participants.[3]

---

3. You will find these factors given extended treatment in the following chapters: (1) Chapter 4; (2) Chapters 5-8; (3) Chapter 9; and (4) Chapter 10.

Effective discussion requires that the participants obtain the fullest available facts, and insist upon reliable sources. It asks, secondly, that the participants reason logically and in socially responsible fashion from this information, both before and during the discussion. It requires further that the participants so conduct themselves toward the ideas and the efforts of others that an atmosphere of genuine cooperation is established. And, finally, it demands that all members *speak* and *listen* in such a way as to produce efficient and pleasant interaction. These are high aims: facts are elusive and contradictory; reasoning soundly is difficult whether alone or with a group; maintaining good working relationships with others calls for much generosity of spirit and flexibility of behavior; understanding and being understood are goals perhaps seldom fully achieved. But anyone can improve in these skills and attitudes by concentrating on their development and by obtaining sufficient experience in their exercise.

Eduard C. Lindeman (3), in his eloquent list of propositions for realizing the democratic ideals propounded by T. V. Smith, declared: "Citizens of democratic societies are equipped for their role when they have acquired the skills and arts of conferring." Then he added the trenchant warning:

> Most persons believe that they know how to confer or that there is nothing important to be known except to be able to talk. Because of these easy-going assumptions, democracy is betrayed on every hand.

Clearly, it is a citizen's duty to understand the process of discussion thoroughly and to employ it skillfully in his pursuit of democratic goals, both public and private.

Occasions for discussion

Theoretically, any group of people capable of communicating with each other orally can hold a discussion on any subject. But certain occasions are more conducive to successful use of the discussion process than are others. This fact should not stop us from using the method under less auspicious conditions, but it should help us assess more correctly our likelihood of success; we will need to remember that occasions possessing certain characteristics are more likely to be productive and satisfying. The discussion method is no panacea: when it is used on wholly inappropriate occasions, it may prove cumbersome and frustrating. In such cases, however, its disappointing results must be charged not to the inadequacy of the method itself but to its indiscriminate use.

Most suitable occasions

The use of the discussion process by a small group is most likely to be successful when (1) the *task* requires the interplay of the thinking of a number of people, calling for their varied knowledge, experience, and orientation; (2) the *members* of the group possess the necessary abilities; and (3) the *time* allowed for group inter-action on the task is sufficient. Sometimes the task exists and a group and a time must be arranged, as when a mayor appoints a committee of citizens to deal with a civic emergency. Sometimes a group and a discussion time exist, but an appropriate subject must be discovered, as when a campus discussion group, interested in foreign policy, seeks a specific topic for study. The interrelationships of these three factors vary, but all are necessary in any case.

Task For what type of task is the cooperative thinking of a group most needed? It may be a task requiring synthesis of information and judgments from a wide variety of sources not available to one researcher or official, like the gathering of reports and evaluations from all parts of a flood area. It may be a task in which interpretation of the facts requires a variety of professional judgments and the solution demands a delicate adjustment of many concerns, like a decision on therapy for a retarded child. It may be a task in which the carrying out of a decision must be the difficult, even unrewarded, duty of the members acting individually, as in the planning and performing of the various steps in a cancer drive. Any of these tasks may be profitably prepared for by discussion, by a number of persons working out the problems as a team.[4]

Members For best results from group discussion, members should be sufficiently similar in overall purpose and orientation to the problem so that they will not bog down unduly in trying to agree on the terminology and basic assumptions underlying the problem or the values involved in its resolution. But, on the other hand, they should be sufficiently different in background,

4. Further information on choosing a subject for discussion is given in Chapter 3.

knowledge, experience, or training to afford each other varied insights. When members are sufficiently different to make a rich interstimulation of ideas possible, the use of the discussion process is most
likely to be effective.[5]

   Time The building of a *group thought-line*
—a continuing synthesis of the best ideas on the points so far considered, to serve as a basis for the next relevant point—is the essence
of the discussion process. But to understand others sufficiently well
to profit from their resources takes time. Walter Bagehot, writing
of political life in the England of some seventy years ago, pointed
out that advocates of swift action deplored the period as "an age
of committees."

When time is not available for an exchange and exploration of
ideas—a process which should be vigorously forward moving but
cannot always bring swift answers to problems—the occasion is not
suitable for the discussion method. We are all familiar with the
centering of political power in our President when the country is
in serious danger; an emergency situation does not allow deliberation
by citizen groups or Congressional committees. In industrial situations
the discussion time available before a decision is mandatory is known
as *real time*. If in any discussion *real time* is not available for cooperative development of ideas by the group, the process cannot be
fully effective and should not be attempted unless its partial effectiveness would still excel any alternative method.

Modifications for particular occasions

Sometimes occasions involving quite different purposes or relationships nevertheless utilize modified forms of the discussion process
with some success.

   Cooperation-enlisting discussion A discussion may be termed *cooperation enlisting* when the leader has a
plan, policy, or change which he introduces for the acceptance of
the group. In such circumstances a plan has been fully worked out
by some group or individual whose special knowledge or position
makes formulation of the plan legitimate and sensible. But since the
members of the group convened are to be involved in its implementation, their approval and cooperation are clearly necessary for its

---

5. Chapter 2 gives more information on appropriate size and composition of
a group.

success. Any student who has attended a national convention and has returned to his campus group to gain acceptance of the new organization-wide policies knows the problems the leader of a cooperation-enlisting discussion faces.

Here the leader will doubtless have an appropriate *group* and can arrange a suitable length of *time* for the discussion. But the *task* he asks of the group differs significantly from those considered most suitable. In this case there is no opportunity for the members to build strong involvement in and consequent loyalty to the plan by cooperating in its formulation. Therefore, while acquainting the group with the new plan, the leader must help the members to become sufficiently involved with it personally to be willing to carry it out.

Recommendation-weighing discussion

The use of the discussion process for weighing a recommendation made to a group is both similar to, and different from, the cooperation-enlisting form. Here again the group does not assist in the preparation of the plan, policy, or change; but it *does* decide to accept or reject the one submitted.

The recommendation is not usually introduced to the group by the leader but by some person (who may or may not be a member of the immediate group) specially qualified to present it. A traffic engineer, for example, may be asked by the mayor to recommend to the city council the best solution to rush-hour congestion. Or the superintendent may ask an architect to submit to the school board a plan for modernizing old school buildings. In such cases the person bringing the recommendation presents what he considers the best answer; consequently, he sees his task as that of clarifying the plan he recommends and urging its adoption by the group. Despite his advocacy the group must see him as a resource person and use his presentation as information from which to reason together to a decision.

Deadlock-breaking discussion

When two opposing forces set up a small group discussion to find a way out of an impasse, they certainly have a *task* on which cooperative thinking is necessary and they will not find it impossible to make adequate *time* available. But often they do not supply the group with *members* ready and willing to participate in the cooperative development of thought. In a labor-management meeting, for example, the labor representatives come to the meeting knowing that their union expects them to win the raise or the extra benefits; and, conversely, the

management representatives come knowing that they must successfully resist such demands. Indeed, the inflexibility of their positions
often makes discussion impossible without the addition of a mediator
who will attempt slowly to produce sufficient openness of mind to
effect a compromise.

This procedure resembles discussion only in its external form—
a group facing a common task at a defined time. The maintenance
of fixed positions by both forces in the negotiation violates a basic
prerequisite of discussion process. All too often the desire to retreat
as little as possible from the declared position while securing agreement replaces that necessary element of the discussion process—the
desire to seek the best answer available through the thinking of all.
Should it ever become sufficiently clear that the welfare of *both* parties
would be best served by achieving the *same* goal, the inflexibility
of their positions would be reduced and conditions for cooperation
might emerge.[6]

Training for discussion

To secure the social and individual values of discussion, effective
use of the process is clearly necessary. That is why training programs
in group discussion and leadership are set up by such firms as ESSO,
Texaco, and Bell Telephone, by Parent-Teacher Association groups
and the League of Women Voters, by insurance groups and super-
visors of aircraft construction companies. Their employees or members
often lack adequate training in joint deliberation, and these organizations seek to replace fumbling, unsatisfactory efforts with the
powerful instrument for wise action and individual growth that skilled
discussion provides. Only with its expert use will the potentialities

6. Elmo Roper reports as follows: "When the citizen delegates to the Atlantic
Convention of NATO nations met in Paris in mid-January . . . we brought
with us all the equipment of disagreement . . . . We came from different
countries, from different backgrounds, with different ideas. Some were skeptical
that the convention could accomplish anything at all; some had made up their
minds beforehand precisely what it should accomplish . . . . But we left in
agreement . . . . I suppose this unlooked-for harmony came about for a number
of reasons. I suppose it was partly because we were seated by alphabet rather
than by nation . . . . But I think it was mostly because the things that drew
us together were so much more urgent and pressing than the things that kept
us apart."—See Elmo Roper, "Toward a New Spirit for NATO," *Saturday
Review*, XLV (April 21, 1962), 15.

for social good and individual enlightenment be realized; only with such use will charges of "time wasted" and "mediocre decision" disappear.

For reasons such as these, classes and training programs throughout the country seek to assist participants in learning to use the discussion process more effectively. Two experimenters, Norman Maier and Allen Solem (4), found that groups instructed in discussion methods for only twelve hours achieved outstandingly better results than did groups of similar but uninstructed persons. The Du Pont Company (5) has held over fifty "Discussion Leading" Institutes since introducing the program in 1951 and concludes that as a result its managers are performing their functions "with greater facility in an atmosphere of participation."

Thus, as students beginning a systematic study of discussion methods, you are giving yourselves an excellent opportunity to acquire skills of major importance to your present growth and to your later competence in social, professional, and political activities.

Preliminary suggestions

Each of you is now starting a term's work in which your main purpose is to understand more clearly the nature of the discussion process and to begin to gain some skill in its use. In any given discussion—whether you are participating in the group or are merely listening to others discuss—you will be trying to increase your knowledge and insight regarding the process. And every time you have an opportunity to participate, you will need to measure your work carefully against the standards set up in your class.

Understandably, you cannot read the full textbook before you participate in the first discussion held in your class; for this reason preliminary suggestions are set out in the paragraphs that follow. Each of these suggestions will be developed in detail at appropriate places later in the book.

If you are to participate as a member:

1. Prepare carefully Investigate as many aspects of the subject as you can and spend some time organizing your thoughts on relevant divisions of the topic.

2. Offer your ideas voluntarily Speak up whenever your ideas will help the group's work, neither dominating the conversation nor holding back when you have a thought that may help.

3. Offer your ideas tentatively Do not assert your ideas dogmatically, but as thoughts for everyone to examine critically. Encourage the group to test your ideas as thoroughly as anyone else's.

4. Listen carefully Give your attention to each speaker so that you will be able to follow his statements with understanding.

If you are to act as the leader:

1. Prepare carefully Read and organize your information just as carefully as any other member; also think of something to say at the beginning that will make the members eager to cooperate in their task.

2. Help the group develop each part of the subject fully Ask questions and suggest lines of thinking that will help the members probe into whatever topic is being considered at the moment.

3. Provide transition to appropriate new parts of the subject Suggest another part of the subject for scrutiny when enough has been done about the immediate one.

4. Summarize often Before suggesting new areas for discussion, state clearly what the members have decided on the immediate topic and summarize all the important parts at the end of the discussion. Write down just enough notes to perform these services, but don't take your attention away from the group too long.

5. Develop and maintain a good attitude in the group Work energetically toward the group purpose, treating all ideas and all members as fairly as you can and showing sincere good will to all throughout.

The following is an example of a discussion, with students attempting to follow such suggestions as have just been made to you. They are engaged in a *problem-solving* discussion; comments in the left column point up some of their attempts to follow the suggestions:

Attempts to stimulate interest of group in task	**Leader** Our question today, as you know, is *How can we best provide adequate outdoor recreation areas?* This problem isn't a new one, even

though we feel it with a lot of force today. Theodore Roosevelt was interested in it for one, and Gifford Pinchot, who started the first systematic forestry work in the United States. In fact, our national forest down here on the Columbia is named for him. And remember a few years ago when Justice Douglas led that hike down across the Olympic Peninsula? He's afraid that we're going to lose our wilderness areas, and, of course, President Kennedy is concerned too. Well, recreation is a problem important to everybody, and our question today implies that our recreation areas are inadequate. Perhaps we should begin by asking ourselves what shows that they are inadequate. What *are* some of the symptoms of our problem?

Peggy Smith   Could I ask something first? Are we talking about the whole United States?

John Scala   Yes, we would just about have to, wouldn't we?

Ruth Muller   Probably so.

Phil Stewart   I wonder whether anything less would really help much, with the way Americans travel around.

Suggests transition   **Leader**   The whole United States then? OK. What can we point to that shows that the United States does have a problem of recreation areas?

Bob Bercynski   Could we clarify something else here? Just what are we including when we say recreation areas? That could cover everything from the playground in the next block to the "wetlands" in the Middle West—you've probably heard of the duck stamps they've been using. Well, I'm

Speaks tentatively   just wondering whether we want to talk about all types of recreational areas or just certain ones?

Leader   Well, we'd probably have to see what inadequacies there are in all the different types, wouldn't we? Of course, we may find that some are much worse off than others, but we'll have to look at all of them, won't we, to know where our problem really lies?

All members have now spoken once   **John**   I don't believe I know exactly what types we should list. From personal experience I know

16

that if our family has a couple of hours in late summer afternoons we go over to the city park to swim; on weekends sometimes we drive to Point Defiance State Park for the day; and for our vacation this year we're going to Glacier National Park.

Phil Sounds great! I worked at the hotel in Glacier last summer and we had a terrific time tramping around in our spare time!

Careful preparation

Peggy Mr. Clauson, the director of the Land Use and Management Program in Washington, D.C., said that they consider that there are three general classifications of outdoor recreation areas —maybe this will answer our question—user-oriented areas, resource-based areas, and intermediate areas.

John Why wouldn't they call *all* recreation areas "user-oriented," I wonder?

Peggy Well, he went on to explain that they used that term for areas, probably relatively small ones, near the users' homes, like the city parks we mentioned a minute ago. This is the most important thing about them—that they are close enough to be used a lot——

Helps group develop idea

Leader How did he explain the other two types? Let's see, what were they? Oh yes, the resource-oriented and the intermediate?

Peggy Well, the resource-oriented ones have some unusual scenic attraction or something that interests people in traveling long distances to enjoy them. I suppose they could be mountains, seashores, lake country——

Careful listening

John Many times, I suppose, they'd be national parks or national forests or something?

Several Yes. Probably.

Bob There's one left—the intermediate—would that be the one you'd go to on a day's trip or something like that?

Peggy Yes, they're the best sites available within a couple of hours of peoples' homes.

Summarizes

Leader How about our using these terms: user-oriented, for the ones near the users; intermediate, for the ones located at some interesting point that isn't very far away——

Ruth A lake, or a river, probably?

Leader Umhm. And the resource-based, for the ones we travel to because of the sights or the special pleasures they have to offer? OK with everybody?

John Sounds fine!

Several OK.

Leader Well, let's ask ourselves then, now that we're ready: how inadequate are they? By the way, which area shall we consider first?

Phil We already mentioned Justice Douglas's worry about the loss of the wilderness areas; maybe we should start with that?

Bob The resource-based areas? OK.

John Yes, let's start there. And I know a good example of the problem right down here in Oregon. It was in the Three Sisters Wilderness Area near Eugene—that's absolutely beautiful country down there—and they recently turned over about fifty thousand acres for commercial use!

Peggy Is that necessarily bad, though? I've heard that sometimes the people living near these areas have a hard time earning enough to live on when they can't use the natural resources.

Maintains good attitude in group

Leader Yes, we surely have to take into consideration these nearby communities. Do you suppose, though, we could hold off on this and concern ourselves for the moment with the recreation phase? We're talking now about preserving areas for the recreation of the public, aren't we? Shall we go on with that first? We've named one symptom of the problem—that resource-based areas are being whittled away for other purposes. I wonder—has this happened in other places besides Oregon? I mean, *is* this whittling away of the wilderness areas a pretty common thing?

On the other hand, the first discussion held in your class may be of the *enlightenment* type; if so, the situation is not changed so far as these suggestions go—try to apply them just as fully as you can. The following example shows a group in the midst of an *enlightenment* discussion on the Food and Agriculture Organization, one of the specialized agencies of the United Nations:

18

Speaks tentatively

Careful preparation

Volunteers idea

Careful preparation

Leader   Yes, one of the most stimulating efforts the FAO is making now is the Freedom from Hunger Campaign, the FFHC, as people tend to call it——

Joseph Imhoff   Isn't the FAO itself coordinating the whole thing, but individual governments, all sorts of agencies, industries too, and private individuals, even, participating too?

Mary Turner   Yes, that's an exciting thing! When the Director-General of FAO, Mr. B. R. Sen, suggested the Campaign at the FAO meeting in Rome in the fall of 1959, he emphasized that while the national committee in each country would determine that country's activities in the campaign, the campaign is, to use his words, "essentially a citizens' effort, a citizens' responsibility, a citizens' opportunity."

Joan Chillag   Yes, even though we live in America and diet to keep our weight down, we can't help but know that half the people in the world are hungry or at least poorly fed!

Paul Meier   And we can't overlook the fact that world population is increasing about fifty million people a year; in fact, the total world population will have doubled by the end of this century, doubled what we have *right now*, I mean. That's a really staggering thought!

Mary   Yes, Mr. Sen said this increase is aggravating a situation that is already "tragic" and could be "dangerous"—so he felt the Freedom from Hunger Campaign was extremely necessary——

Steve Wirtz   Somebody asked Dag Hammarskjöld why a special campaign against hunger was necessary; want to know how he answered the question?

Several   That would be good. Go ahead. Yes, have you got it there?

Steve   OK. He said: "The answer lies, I believe, in the unprecedented dangers and opportunities of our time. There is the danger of nonfulfillment of the recently awakened hopes and expectations of countless millions to see an end in their lifetime or that of their children to the age-old problems of hunger and malnutrition. There is the danger that these problems may increase in intensity and scope as a result of the vastly accelerated growth in world population. But there is also the unprecedented opportunity provided by the ability of modern science and technology to yield substantial gains in food production. And there is the opportunity of finding ways of using the great agricultural surpluses that exist side by side with widespread hunger and malnutrition."

Helps group develop idea

Leader Let's see, he listed two dangers: danger of unfulfilled hopes and of increased population——

Volunteers

Joan And two opportunities: increased production and—what was the other?

Steve Let's check—it was—*use of surpluses.*

Suggests transition

Leader It's good the picture isn't all black! But I suppose it looks darker for some countries today than for others. What about each individual country with its special problems? I should think the program would have to differ a great deal from country to country.

Paul Probably that's why each country is so much involved in the planning. Each one decides on a few key projects, I understand, and concentrates on them. Of course, not even a world-wide campaign like this could bring the answer to all of the problems in a country.

Joan One part that interests me is that the farmers and villagers are involved directly in the projects! You know, I'll never forget a picture I saw of farmers in Yugoslavia at a new irrigation project; they had helped to pipe out the underground water and they were standing together when the water began to pour out, and you should see how excited and happy they were!

Leader And the FFHC hopes to help this to happen all over the world.

Whether you participate first in a problem-solving discussion, or in one that aims at enlightenment, you will do well to prepare carefully beforehand and try to follow these suggestions in your own participation.

20

Summary

Discussion by small groups may serve two purposes: preparation for action or general enlightenment. The process requires voluntary, open-minded, encouraging, and inquiring efforts from the members and focusing efforts from the leader. To be most effective, the process demands these ingredients: the essential information, straight thinking, cooperative attitudes, and efficient communication. Discussions are most likely to be successful when the task, the members, and the time allotted are appropriate to the situation. Certain modified forms serve particular uses: cooperation-enlisting, recommendation-weighing, and deadlock-breaking. Training programs are widely used to improve use of the discussion process.

References

(1) Robert Hutchins, *Great Books* (New York: Simon & Schuster, 1954), pp. 22-23.

(2) Christopher Fry, *A Sleep of Prisoners* (New York: Oxford University Press, 1951), p. 47.

(3) T. V. Smith and Eduard C. Lindeman, *The Democratic Way of Life* (New York: The New American Library, 1951), pp. 130-132.

(4) Norman R. F. Maier and Allen R. Solem, "The Contribution of a Discussion Leader to the Quality of Group Thinking: the Effective Use of Minority Opinion," *Human Relations,* 5 (August 1952), 277-288.

(5) Letter from M. G. Peterson, Assistant Manager in the Training Division, E. I. Du Pont de Nemours & Company, Wilmington, Delaware, July 10, 1961. .

Readings and problems

1. Make tape recordings in the classroom of the discussion segments presented in this chapter, with members of the class doing the reading. Use these recordings as a basis for classroom discussion about effective use of the suggestions made in this chapter for members and leader.

2. Evaluate the efforts of the participants in the first discussion in this class. Use the rating scales that follow:

Member evaluation							
	Low						*High*
	1	*2*	*3*	*4*	*5*	*6*	*7*
Preparation							
Volunteering							
Tentativeness							
Listening							

General comments:

Leader evaluation							
	Low						*High*
	1	*2*	*3*	*4*	*5*	*6*	*7*
Preparation							
Developing							
Moving							
Summarizing							
Group attitude							

General comments:

3. Report on and evaluate in terms of the suggestions given in this chapter some classroom, community, radio, or television discussion you have listened to.

4. List ways in which training in the discussion process should be helpful to you in your future career.

5. Read the historical background of the discussion method in the United States. Examine such sources as these:

Barnlund, Dean C. and Franklyn S. Haiman, *The Dynamics of Discussion* (Boston: Houghton Mifflin Co., 1960), Chapter I.

Braden, Waldo and Earnest Brandenburg, *Oral Decision-Making* (New York: Harper & Brothers, 1955), Chapter VIII.

Ewbank, Henry L. and J. Jeffery Auer, *Discussion and Debate,* 2nd
ed. (New York: Appleton-Century-Crofts, Inc., 1951), Chapter II.

      6. Discover problems concerning the Amer-
ican people today. First, list the full-length articles published in the
most recent issues of these sources: *American Scholar, Annals of the
American Academy of Political and Social Science, Atlantic Monthly,
Bulletin of the Atomic Scientists, Congressional Digest, Current History, Foreign Affairs, Harper's, International Conciliation, Journal
of Social Issues, Progressive, Reference Shelf* (H. W. Wilson & Co.),
Reporter, U.S. Dept of State Bulletin, World Affairs. Second, as a
result of this survey make a list of five or six topics that seem to
cause the American people the most concern. Finally, answer briefly
these two questions on each topic: (1) What does the problem seem
to be? (2) To what extent do you feel that this problem—and how
the American people handle it—really affects you?

      7. Skim several pages of the *Reader's Guide
to Periodical Literature* and list subjects that you think you would
like to explore more fully and on which you would welcome the
information and opinions of others.

      8. In the sources listed below, read about
the use of the discussion method in one or more areas of democratic
life; be prepared to report your findings to the class.

Andersen, Martin P., "Discussion in Agriculture," *Quarterly Journal
of Speech,* 37 (December 1951), 463-468.

Bogardus, Emory S., *Democracy by Discussion* (Washington, D.C.:
American Council on Public Affairs, 1942).

Burton, John, ed., *Group Discussion in Educational, Social and Working Life* (London: Central Council for Health Education, n.d.).

Chamberlain, Neil W., "Group Discussion and Collective Bargaining," *Adult Education Bulletin,* 13 (February 1949), 77-84.

Chase, Stuart and Marian Tyler Chase, *Roads to Agreement* (New
York: Harper & Brothers, 1951).

Eichelberger, Clark M., "Discussion in the United Nations," *Adult
Education Bulletin,* 13 (February 1949), 88-90.

Hoffmann, Randall W. and Robert Plutchik, *Small-Group Discussion in Orientation and Teaching* (New York: G. P. Putnam's
Sons, 1959).

Jackson, Elmore, *Meeting of Minds: A Way to Peace through Mediation* (New York: McGraw-Hill Book Co., 1952).

Kriesberg, M. and H. Guetzkow, "The Use of Conferences in the Administrative Process," *Public Administration Review,* 10 (Spring 1950), 93-98.

Poston, Richard, *Small Town Renaissance* (New York: Harper & Brothers, 1950).

"Reform in the Conference Room," *Dun's Review and Modern Industry,* 69 (March 1957), 64.

Schreiber, Julius, "Discussion in the Armed Forces," *Adult Education Bulletin,* 13 (February 1949), 73-77.

Warters, Jane, *Group Guidance: Principles and Practices* (New York: McGraw-Hill Book Company, Inc., 1960).

9. Many writers have made comments that apply directly or indirectly to the characteristics and behavior of members of discussion groups. First, read the statements following and decide which of the sections—A, B, or C—would stimulate the best class discussion. Then study the eight statements of the section you select and be prepared to explain the implications of each for a discussion participant. Whenever possible, relate each to attitudes and behavior you have observed in recent discussions.

A.

1. He listens "systematically throughout the discussion" with "a healthy skepticism about . . . [his] own beliefs as well as about the beliefs of others." (1)

2. He has "an earnest desire to achieve the maximum degree of agreement consistent with integrity of belief." (1)

3. He will, even if he holds a minority view, "continue to offer unremitting assistance as the group continues its exploration of the problem." (1)

4. He seeks to "bring all ideas into the circle of discussion on an equal basis not as cases to be defended but as possible parts of the whole truth." (2)

5. He will "advocate a possibility with all the glow of reality without at the same time committing . . . [himself] to it in such a way as to embarrass modification of conviction." (2)

6. He appreciates "how the give and take of a pure discussion, which is not a debate, throws new light on old ideas, shifts emphases, corrects aberrations, and even softens emotional antagonisms." (2)

7. He "gives himself to even more thorough thinking upon the question of mutual interest and concern than he might engage in alone." (3)

8. He is not "afraid of being in the wrong"; his mistake may lead him and the group "to new and better judgments." (1)

B.

1. He realizes that "one reason that group discussion is at times dull, or that a group finds nothing to occupy its attention for more than a single discussion, is that the group members have not learned how to draw on any experience except their own, and their experience may be too limited to be very thrilling or enlightening." (3)
2. He is "as concerned about the success of the discussion as he has a right to expect the leader to be." (4)
3. He attempts "to use language which avoids the appearance of irrevocable commitment and categorical finality." (4)
4. He realizes that in a discussion group "there can be no true cooperation without a pervading sense of *equality* and *dignity*." (1)
5. He must "contribute that which distinguishes him from others, his difference." (5)
6. "Respectful listening makes argument unnecessary and rancorous debate soon yields in an atmosphere of cooperative search." (3)
7. To assure the triumph of evil, it is only necessary that good men do nothing.—*Edmund Burke*
8. Truth often suffers more by the heat of its defenders, than from the arguments of its opposers.—*William Penn*

C.

1. We rarely find that people have good sense unless they agree with us.—*La Rochefoucauld*
2. Remember that to change thy mind and to follow him that sets thee right, is to be none the less the free agent that thou wast before.—*Marcus Aurelius*
3. The deepest principle of human nature is to be appreciated.—*William James*
4. Every new opinion, at its starting, is precisely in a minority of one.—*Thomas Carlyle*
5. Opinion in good men is but knowledge in the making.—*John Milton*
6. If there be any among us who would wish to dissolve this Union or to change its republican form, let them stand undisturbed as monuments of the safety with which error of opinion may be tolerated where reason is left free to combat it.—*Thomas Jefferson*
7. A thing is not necessarily true because uttered badly, nor false because spoken magnificently.—*St. Augustine*

8. Men are most apt to believe what they least understand.—
Montaigne

(1) Russell H. Wagner and Carroll C. Arnold, *Handbook of Group Discussion* (Boston: Houghton Mifflin Company, 1950).
(2) H. S. Elliott, *Process of Group Thinking* (New York: Association Press, 1928).
(3) H. S. Elliott, *Group Discussion in Religious Education* (New York: Association Press, 1930).
(4) James H. McBurney and Kenneth G. Hance, *Discussion in Human Affairs* (New York: Harper & Brothers, 1950).
(5) Mary P. Follett, *The New State* (New York: Longmans, Green and Co., 1920).

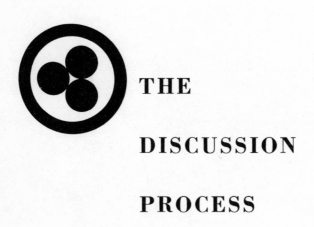

Chapter two

THE

DISCUSSION

PROCESS

In these next eleven chapters we are concerned with *group discussion*, that is, the cooperative consideration of a topic by a relatively small group of people, gathered for easy oral communication with no separate listening group present.[1] We are concerned with the process that goes on in such a conference,[2] where the members seek to achieve a common goal.

The directors of a corporation may meet to plan expansion policies for the ensuing year. A social service committee may have received reports concerning a child in a foster home and must convene to evaluate his progress there. A group of aroused citizens, living on a much-traveled street, may present instances of near injuries to their children in preparation for laying their case before the Municipal Safety Council. Or you and your friends may critically review a new play you have just seen.

In each of these situations *a number of persons* are *gathered together* and are *interacting orally toward a common goal*. In each of these situations—ranging from the somewhat formal to the distinctly less formal—the participants (if they are trying to use the discussion process to best advantage) will be hoping to build the best possible understanding of a subject or answer to a problem, through the resources at hand—the knowledge and understanding, the mental capacities and communicative abilities of all the members of the group.

Group idea-development

The building of ideas by the cooperative work of the group is the essence of the discussion process.[3] It proceeds in a sequence of sug-

1. In Chapter 13, on the other hand, we take a look at *public discussion*, the situation in which a small group discusses a question before an audience for the purpose of informing the listeners and stimulating their thinking.
2. The term *conference* is used today in several different ways. In one sense, the word *conference* is a synonym for *discussion*, as we are using that term in this textbook. In another sense, it often refers to several days of meetings of various kinds attended by delegates who are interested in the chosen subject. For example, in May 1962, top executives of defense industries and key officers of the Air Force Systems Command met for a four-day "conference" on the problem of managing the nation's resources for utmost security for the entire free world. See John F. Loosbrock, *Air Force Magazine*, June 1962, p. 9.
3. The highlights of the process were indicated briefly in Chapter 1, pages 13-14.

gestions and modifications of those suggestions by the members. One person advances the thought here, another there. Each sees the developing idea from his own vantage point, and what lies in shadow in one person's view may be in full sun in the view of another. Ideally, some member sets forth a segment of his own thought, genuinely inviting the other members of the group to ferret out its weaknesses, remedy its incompletenesses, and fortify its strengths.[4] All the others, listening, bring to bear their knowledge and experience, their critical powers and social understandings upon this embryo idea. They may question its clarity, its relevance, its accuracy, its completeness, its significance, its reasonableness. Any time a member, while listening attentively to the current speaker, believes that one of these aspects merits group concern, he raises the question to the group: he queries or illustrates or unravels carefully or tests for feasibility. And, again, all the members focus upon the point he raises, exploring its usefulness and its impact upon the line of thinking they are building together. Or the participant, agreeing in his own mind to the relevance and worth of the idea that is before the group, makes a suggestion onward from that basis. And the other members, if they also consider the former idea a sound basis, now direct their concerted power on toward this new extension of thought. Thus, the various members of the group, using their resources cooperatively and stimulating each other's thought creatively, shape the idea to their mutual satisfaction.

Over and over this sequence occurs, as one significant issue after another is approached, focused upon, used in the developing line of thought—or discarded—and the group moves on together to the next issue of importance. It is clear that this *building* process does not consist of each person contributing a preformed brick to lay up in a random construction; rather, all bring whatever materials for brick-making they possess, and together they mold the best bricks possible and erect a composite structure.

A group using the discussion process well supplies many eyes and ears to watch for flaws, weaknesses, omissions, misconstructions in

4. In an experimental study comparing cooperative and competitive groups, members of competitive discussion groups did not consider each other's ideas freely and learn from each other in the mutually productive and satisfying way characteristic of cooperative groups. See Morton Deutsch, "An Experimental Study of the Effects of Cooperation and Competition upon Group Process," *Human Relations,* 2 (No. 3, 1949), 199-231.

the ideas being considered. This group-wide watchfulness is especially valuable because the person proposing the incorrect suggestion is not likely to detect its error; one researcher (1) found that other group members discovered and rejected a mistake three times as readily as the initiator.

A brick being built into the framework of the structure will be removed when an alert eye detects a serious fault and brings it to the attention of the group; if the brick merely leans, the group will straighten it before that whole side of the edifice leans; or it may be kept in place because it had only *looked* aslant from one person's fractional viewpoint. But the group also supplies eyes and ears to be on the alert for unusual opportunities of development, for unexpected strengths which the evolving structure could utilize. Thus, an idea undergoing modification by the whole group becomes the best that the group—working cooperatively—can achieve; its final shape is produced through the combined powers of the individuals in the group.[5]

In this process each person, in making a contribution, is able to build onward from the most advanced point so far reached by the group. All that has been so far developed in the group has become his capital stock and he is thus able to push ideas forward not only from his own resources but from these new assets as well. Sometimes it is an idea clearly emerging in someone else's contribution that stimulates him; sometimes it is merely the chance word choice or accidental voice inflection or unfinished phrase of another member. This interstimulation assists in the building process by providing a rich store of ideas out of which new combinations may arise and by offering hints and half-messages that serve to trigger the creative effort which produces the new formulation. Notice how the thought darts forward, with each person using the ideas he has just heard, in the following segment of a discussion concerning world population pressures and our national aims:

> **John Vaughan**   The world's population really seems to be following an exponential curve. In some countries it now doubles every thirty-five years or so.
> **Charles Bishop**   That's about every generation!

5. Chapter 8 is devoted entirely to the process of idea-development.

No wonder Nasser said last week that the world's
exploding population was a danger equally as
serious as nuclear war.

Jane Watkins   Yes, it's so serious because it's
faster than the economic growth. In South America, for example, the population is growing by
2.3 per cent each year while the economy is up
only 1 per cent!

Paul Claussen   And this is in spite of the
billions that we've poured into the underdeveloped
countries. These funds are so desperately needed
for food for the added population that almost
nothing is left to spend for industrialization or
education.

Charles   It practically cancels out our efforts
to help them lift their living standards! Two out
of every three dollars we sent during the fifties
went for food for the extra people instead of for
any real development. President Eugene Black
of the World Bank says that soon you'll have to
be optimistic to believe that the living standards
can be held where they are now!

Leader   Population outrunning economic growth
in spite of billions poured in. The implications
of such a situation seem pretty clear, don't they,
but shall we look at them a moment?

Effective idea-building occurs when all members move alertly along
with the thought-line they are developing together.

Mary Parker Follett (2), business and professional philosopher in
England and America, wrote:

The object of a committee meeting is first of all
to create a common idea. I do not go to a committee meeting merely to give my own ideas. If
that were all, I might write my fellow-members
a letter. But neither do I go to learn other people's
ideas. If that were all, I might ask each to write
me a letter. I go to a committee meeting in order
that all together we may create a group idea, an
idea which will be better than any one of our
ideas alone, moreover which will be better than
all of our ideas added together. For this group

> idea will not be produced by any process of
> addition, but by the interpenetration of us all.

Now, of course, if the group is talking at random, doing none of this cooperative idea-building that is the essence of the discussion process, it is merely conversing. It is fulfilling the first two elements of the discussion process, (a) *a number of persons,* (b) *gathered together,* but clearly it falls short of the full meaning of the final one, (c) *interacting orally toward a common goal.* Conversation as such serves socially useful ends but should not be confused with the disciplined activity that discussion is. We can say that the *discussion process* is taking place effectively (and thereby serving the discussion purposes—*preparation for action* or *individual enlightenment and growth*) only when it involves all three elements.

A number of persons . . .

This first element of a group discussion—*a number of persons*—involves two very important questions: *How many?* and *Who shall they be?*

Size of group

How large shall the discussion group be? What number of participants will best implement the discussion process? If there are too many to allow an appropriate degree of interaction, the group purpose will suffer. If there are too few to provide ideas from a sufficiently wide array of viewpoints, again, the group purpose will suffer. Generally speaking, the ideal number is one large enough to bring a sufficient variety of ideas and small enough to function efficiently in its specified task.[6] These factors are illustrated in the graph on the following page.[7]

6. Individual capacities of those composing the group and the nature of the working unit they comprise will, of course, modify the number of persons needed to make an effective group.

7. In the three modified types of discussion groups mentioned in Chapter 1, the opportunity for seeking the optimum size is less free. For example, a man who wants to gain the cooperation of his staff must have his whole staff present (or their representatives or opinion-leaders), whether they make a group of five or twenty-five people. In the recommendation-weighing group, all must be present who will have significant voice in the decision. And in the deadlock-breaking discussion, key figures on both sides must be present. Nevertheless, when any flexibility is possible, the optimum size should be approximated.

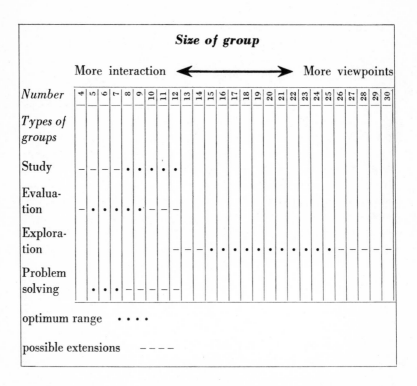

Number	4	5	6	7	8	9	10	11	12	13	14	15	16	17	18	19	20	21	22	23	24	25	26	27	28	29	30
Types of groups																											
Study	–	–	–		•	•	•	•	•																		
Evaluation	–	•	•	•	•	•	–	–	–																		
Exploration										–	–	–	•	•	•	•	•	•	•	•	•	•	•	–	–	–	–
Problem solving	•	•	•	–	–	–	–	–																			

Size of group

More interaction ⟷ More viewpoints

optimum range · · · ·

possible extensions – – – –

Enlightenment groups Whether an enlightenment discussion[8] takes the form of study, evaluation, or freewheeling exploration, the group should probably be larger than a problem-solving one. Since the outcome desired is individual development rather than group action, there is less necessity that everyone assist so fully in producing the group thought-line. Despite the fact that an individual's development will no doubt be greater if he enters the group interaction frequently, his inner and silent investment must not be completely discounted.

An optimum size for the study group would seem to be from eight to twelve. When Peace Corps volunteers back from their tours of duty meet to relate certain aspects of their experience to the national director's office, they should not be assembled in too large numbers.

8. To the best of our knowledge, Professor Gulley was the first to use the term enlightenment for discussions in which members "exchange ideas for the purpose of self-edification"; see Halbert E. Gulley, *Discussion, Conference, and Group Process* (New York: Henry Holt and Co., 1960).

The strong frustration that individuals might experience in not being able to contribute data, as well as the loss of their information to the Peace Corps office, would argue against having more than a dozen in such a group. With no more than twelve present it is probable that each would have at least several opportunities to speak.

For evaluation groups, five to nine members would seem to be appropriate. Such a group would need enough variety in experience, information, and interpretation to provide a fair view of the case being evaluated; yet the members must be few enough to agree upon a rating for the case on the relevant criteria. Sometimes, of course, the size of the evaluation group will vary from that considered optimum because of other factors. For example, a precinct committee assembling to evaluate its procedures used in the primary election campaign will be as small or as large as the committee is.

On the other hand, members of a large group who were merely exploring a topic freely would likely feel far less frustrated at the reduced opportunities for participation. If they, for example, have been highly interested by a lecture on the current American attitude toward pleasure, they may wish to sit down together and talk it over among themselves. Fifteen to twenty-five people can often take part in such a group, producing sufficiently clear lines of thinking and maintaining the high interest of all in spite of restricted opportunities for oral participation.[9]

Problem-solving groups The group that is *preparing for action* should be kept small, that is, from five to seven members. Several researchers have reasoned that five may be the optimum number, having found that members are generally less well satisfied in groups that are larger or smaller than five. For example, R. F. Bales (3) explained:

> For the particular task and time limits given to subjects in the Harvard laboratory, five seems to be the preferred number. Below that size subjects begin to complain that the group is too small and above it that the group is too large. The fact

9. At the defense industry-Air Force Systems Command conference mentioned in footnote 2, at the beginning of this chapter, the delegates participated in exploration groups, each directed to a particular area of management. Each of these seminars in which they shared their knowledge and experience was composed of twenty-six men.

that there is a distinct "saddle point" at five suggests that the notion of optimum size is meaningful, if the task, time and other circumstances are well enough specified. But the optimum size must surely vary according to conditions.

There seems to be a crucial point at seven. Below seven, for the most part, each person in the group says at least something to each other person. In groups over seven the low participators tend to stop talking to each other and center their communications on the few top men. The tendencies toward centralization of communication seem to increase rather powerfully as size increases.

In problem-solving groups—where frequent opportunities for participation, close involvement in the group-produced thought-line, sensitivity to different points of view, and dedication to group-wide agreement are essential—effective group functioning is harmed by any great increases in group size.[10]

For example, seven members are appointed to a new state advisory committee to the United States Commission on Civil Rights. Each member—attorney, chairman of the State Council of Mental Institutions, State Senator, and so on—must have an opportunity to bring his knowledge and critical thinking to bear on the issues before the group. With seven members, each person will have less opportunity to speak than if there were only five, but the governor may have wanted to ensure a wide range of opinions rather than to achieve a full consensus. If the group were truly a decision-making body, the minimum might then be exceeded for a different reason—to include all those in key positions for its implementation, like the heads of the departments involved. By cooperating in preparing the policy, these

10. To be sensitive and cooperative, the member must be alert to the presence and the attitudes of each of the others. Such awareness becomes more difficult for him with astonishing speed as members are added to the group. When he is one of five, the possible relationships to which he should be alert will number twenty; if we, however, add two members to his group, he will have forty-two relationships to which to respond. We have more than doubled the number of relationships for him by the addition of but *two* persons.

Of course, his own relationships with others would be only four in the first group and six in the second, but we cannot overlook the fact that any member needs to be aware of more than his own relations with each of the others; he must notice as well the relations among the others.

officials would be better prepared to carry it out. Either of these purposes might conceivably extend the size of a problem-solving group to ten or twelve members, despite the consequent loss of free interaction.

Composition of group

The knowledge, attitudes, and personal traits of this *number of persons* are extremely important. Obviously, ill-equipped persons cannot contribute as much to a discussion as can informed and experienced persons. The group members should possess all the information necessary to the performance of their task, plus the ability to interpret and use it. Further, knowledge and ability should be distributed quite generally through the group; where great differences in experience raise prestige barriers, group communication and cooperation are likely to suffer.

More important than the specific knowledge and attitudes of individual members in the group is the quality of the interaction they develop. Since each person's responses in a group are partially determined by his perception of the other members' reactions to him, he might show himself fair minded and purposeful with one combination of persons, but bigoted and obstructive with another. We are all aware of being our best selves in certain groups and disappointingly less in others. A group functions most effectively when its interaction creates an atmosphere of mutual respect and cooperation. Even one person, prodded into disruptive action by real or supposed hostilities, can so harm the group procedures as to water down their agreements or prevent any agreement whatsoever.

Skills in the use of the discussion process are also important in group functioning. If the members view the process as the cooperative framing of an understanding or an answer and are able to put their different abilities and knowledge to imaginative use, they are likely to work together effectively. Optimum functioning of a group is sometimes jeopardized by a member who considers that he has come to *give advice* or by one who came merely, as he says, to *listen in.*

. . . gathered together . . .

In group discussions an appropriate number of persons gather to confer. We know that men who *could* talk with a group in a multiparty telephone call will go great distances to meet the others face to face. Obviously, physical nearness is helpful in the exchange of ideas.

To begin with, facial expressions, gestures, and bodily tensions may indicate more of the person's reaction than his voice and words alone. He tends to reveal his understanding and approval or his readiness to respond or his confusion. Further, he tends to show his attitudes toward the idea being developed, the procedure and accomplishments of the group, and the values which the group is attempting to conserve. Doubtless, men meet together to obtain the use of these nonverbal cues to meaning and attitude, as well as to make more rapid use of each other's thoughts.

An added benefit in the face-to-face situation, however, derives from the physical act of coming to the central meeting place; thus the members have something in common at the outset, an investment of time and self in the meeting, and they may feel for this very reason an added responsibility to help make the session serve its purpose. The university president who at the beginning of a school year calls his most important committees to meet at a forest lodge some fifty miles from the campus is making use of this factor.

But the fact of physical nearness in the face-to-face group may be misleading. It is important to realize that each member identifies himself with a score of outside groups and that at times he may respond during the discussion more in terms of the attitudes and values of one of these groups than of those of the immediate group. We are familiar with this phenomenon at the United Nations, where all too often the interests of his national reference group outweigh for the delegate the influence of the international group. Familiar too are the labor-management groups which must exchange discussion for mediation or arbitration because the identification with opposed reference groups prevents the two parties from developing cooperative attitudes. And if you have sat on the student board of control at your university, you know how often the position you have taken was greatly influenced by the wishes and interests of the particular organization you represented there.

Reference groups are influential even where allegiance is less openly recognized. Consider Mr. Smith, who has just been elected, let us say, to the school board in his district. Mr. Smith is [1] a 35-year-old [2] man, who is [3] a husband and father, [4] a member of a prominent family, and [5] a lawyer by profession; he [6] earns $15,000 a year, [7] belongs to the Republican Party and [8] to the

Lutheran Church. Here are at least eight possible reference groups with which Mr. Smith on occasion identifies himself. When he and the other board members are discussing the role of the driver-training program in their high school, they may all be reacting as *adults* in contradistinction to the youthful drivers in the school program, or as *parents* of endangered children, or as *taxpayers* furnishing the funds. One relationship may be uppermost in their minds on a certain aspect of the problem, another on another aspect. Or, on the other hand, Mr. Smith may be reacting momentarily as a *taxpayer* while his colleagues are reacting as *parents*, and sometimes he may react from an orientation held by none other in the group, that of *lawyer*, and thus provide a unique insight.

It is clear that the members of a face-to-face group will not always have the same values or aims. Diversity of reference group loyalties helps the group to keep its discussion of any question more in line with social reality, but it also makes it harder for the members to understand each other sufficiently well. Working together on a common task, however, should bring these various forces into as productive a relationship as possible.

Place

The immediate physical surroundings of any committee meeting are important. Size and general aspect of the room; usefulness of tables, chairs, and other items of equipment; heat, light, and air; noise and interruption—any or all play a part in the group's success or failure. Aneurin Bevan of England once said that all conferences held in rooms with dull brown walls failed, but none failed in rooms with yellow walls. Major Charles Estes, former Commissioner of the United States Mediation and Conciliation Board, declared that he often registered early at a hotel where a labor-management conference was to be held to make a careful check on such details as the width of the discussion table. The leader's or planning committee's concern for these physical factors indicates the degree of respect they have for the group and its purposes; consequently, a seeming indifference to comfort or convenience may damage the self-esteem and confidence of the group members.

And, more specifically, the actual seating at the conference table or in the informal circle of chairs—who sits next to whom, across from whom, and in what relation to the leader—will often be significant in both the atmosphere and the achievement of the group. It is said that Gladstone, as prime minister of England, took pains before important Cabinet meetings to plan where each of the members would sit. Importance of seating position is suggested also in research studies, such as the one by Steinzor (4); his investigation showed that persons seated opposite each other were more likely to interact orally than those sitting immediately beside each other. Indeed, if the group has been holding a series of meetings, the seating (unless arbitrarily designated) will tend to reflect the emerging relationships.

The following conditions normally make for the best discussions: arrangements so that everyone can see everyone else,[11] more frequent contributors distributed among the less frequent ones, comfortable chairs, appropriate temperature and lighting, noise at a minimum. Groups meeting for personal enlightenment will often use more informal surroundings—a home, club lounge, or outdoor setting—than ones making decisions.

Time

The amount of time allotted to meetings affects their general success. When a problem-solving group is asked to face a task too large for the time allowed, the members will feel strong pressure to produce a quick agreement. Consequently, they will tend to examine each other's ideas less fully; they will look at fewer alternatives and be more likely to settle for a superficially good plan with some misgivings and feelings of dissatisfaction. To avoid such pressures, when the Citizens' Advisory Committee on Safety and Motor Vehicle Legislation considers proposed new laws to attempt to reduce the traffic toll in the state, it holds a day-long meeting with morning and afternoon sessions; the members find that they need these hours together to decide on their recommendations, and the noon break keeps the session from being unduly long. When members have worked vigorously together for several hours, they need rest and perhaps an opportunity to make further inquiries or think privately before resuming their work together.

11. When a group is seated around a circular or hexagonal table, or when the members sit in an informal circle of chairs without a table, seeing and hearing each speaker generally offers little problem. When a group is seated around a rectangular table, however, all must remember their continuing responsibility to so shift their chairs as to approximate a circle. But the dispersion of the members around a table must not be so wide or the circle so large that members lose the sense of being members of a cohesive unit.

If an enlightenment group has too brief a time to get its spontaneous interchange into play, the results will probably be equally unfortunate, although different. When two dozen people have come together to talk about the changing role of women in the modern world and have time only to begin, their disappointment will be great. They will tend to feel frustrated at not having been able to bring potential insights into being—the swift and exhilarating opening of mental doors will simply not have taken place.

It is important that the time allowed for the process of group interaction be appropriate to the task, and that the length of any one session be conducive to effective interaction.

. . . *interacting orally toward*
a common goal

We have defined a discussion as a number of persons, gathered together, interacting orally toward a common goal. In this interchange the members are actually responding in two ways simultaneously—to the intellectual and emotional challenges of the subject and to the intellectual and emotional challenges of the participants. And their interaction—in any effective use of the discussion process—has a group-wide aim, a goal known to and accepted by all the members.

Interaction in the group

At any given time one form of interaction may predominate over the other. You have had the experience of meeting with a new committee, not knowing what to expect of the other members; nor did they have any common ground with you. At the outset you were all responding to the stimulus of each other *as individual persons*. And it was only after everyone had become somewhat acquainted, was tentatively accepted by the others, and felt in some measure safe in being himself that you all began to cooperate on your task. When that happened, your exchange increasingly took the form of *interaction on ideas*. You knew pretty well what to expect of each other personally so that you didn't have to think much about your *interaction as persons*. Of course, if you later found someone not acting as you expected, you were suddenly alert again to the *interpersonal* aspect of discussion, and you didn't get much done on your task until you had straightened out the relationships again.

Some groups in our society meet for the sole purpose of friendly association. In the armed services, in industry, on campuses, such informal groups may also serve as outlets for accumulating frustrations and worries. In pleasant meetings or gripe sessions the topic may be relatively unimportant in comparison with the human companionship enjoyed, with the *interaction as persons*.

On the other hand, groups which meet for the primary purpose of joining efforts toward a common goal—the problem-solving or enlightenment groups with which this textbook is primarily concerned—are differently oriented. For these groups the intellectual and emotional challenges of the subject are primary. Interpersonal relations are still important, but they play a supportive role. The group should be spending its chief efforts on handling *ideas*, sparing only such attention to interpersonal relations as is necessary to keep them from becoming obstructive. When a committee of local parents meets to discuss a heated issue—what to do about the growing incidence of juvenile crimes—efforts should be focused on reaching a reasonable decision rather than on soothing ruffled feelings. Nevertheless, the group stands a better chance of making a sound decision if it sees the value of maintaining good relations among the participants and takes quick action to repair them if they have been damaged.

Whichever emphasis—on *interaction on ideas* or *interaction as persons*—better suits a group's purpose, both forms will be simultaneously and compellingly present, and trouble in either should be quickly eased to allow maximum effectiveness.

Common goal

When *a number of persons* are first *gathered together* for discussion, they are merely an assemblage of individuals, each with his own aims and expectations. This divergence of footing at the outset occurs whether or not the group has met before: if this is the group's first meeting, each member will certainly have a different concept, for he can know little of what to expect from the others; even if the group meets often, the members' different reference groups and personalities will cause them to see the purpose of the meeting somewhat differently.

Thus, it is necessary that each participant's private concept of the group goal be replaced by a group interpretation, one understood and accepted by all as the focus of their team efforts. Then the members can reinforce each other's contributions and avoid cross-purposes. Not only at the outset of the discussion, but wherever necessary within the group's collaboration, this common goal must be clarified and underlined.

Additional suggestions

In the previous chapter the preliminary suggestions for your first class discussions were focused on *interaction on ideas*. Since this chapter has emphasized the importance of the concurrent *interaction as persons*, additional suggestions will be made here for your efforts in this regard. These recommendations describe ways of indicating respect for other members and making it possible for them to cooperate effectively.

If you participate as a member:

1. Speak cooperatively to all Talk to all the members (not just the leader), inviting them by your tone of voice, glances, and gestures to consider the idea with you.

2. Listen encouragingly to all Show that you are trying to understand what each speaker really means and that you have confidence in his efforts and intentions.

If you act as the leader:

1. Encourage wide participation Keep including those who aren't talking much by your glance and your frequent attention without calling directly on them; good-humoredly restrain anyone who talks too much.

2. Keep differences from becoming contentious If members differ, try to have the whole group examine the facts behind the opposing viewpoints and show confidence that the members are all genuinely seeking the truth.

In the following example students are attempting to follow these suggestions as well as the ones for *interacting on ideas*. They are in the midst of a discussion on the problem of reducing highway accidents; comments in the left margin describe their attempts to follow these additional suggestions:

> **Leader** We've been talking about edge-marked roads as a way of reducing accidents in rural

42

Looks around inquiringly and continues talking until someone is ready to pick up the thought-line

areas. The plan sounds good to us; how well has it worked, though, where it has been tried? Do we have any direct evidence that this little extra pail—or barrel—of paint on the edge of the pavement actually has reduced accidents anywhere?

Tom Spoch   Well, yes; there's an example from Kansas. The State Highway Commission and the United States Bureau of Public Roads conducted a study together on twenty-nine pairs of road sections—384 miles of rural two-lane highways. None of the 384 miles had ever been edge-marked before. So they marked half of them and left the others, and they found a 36 per cent reduction in accidents on the edge-marked miles——

Listens appreciatively

Bill Attaya   Pretty good investment in paint!

Tom   ——with the 36 per cent being on accidents at intersections and driveways.

Leader   A real reduction! Well, then, we've seen so far that edge-marked roads are inexpensive in both installation and upkeep, and that they are particularly effective in rural areas. Let's

Consults the group

see, we mentioned a disadvantage of the plan earlier——

Mary Roberts   ——that it's a fine idea so far as it goes, but we're concerned about the accidents in the cities and on highways that are more than two-lane——

Leader   Yes, its limited scope. Now, then, what other plan for reducing highway accidents shall we consider next?

Tom   Another one is the——

Encourages one who is slower to speak up

Leader   Pardon me, Tom. What were you going to say, Sam?

Sam Blum   Well, I was going to suggest a greater use of traffic buttons to indicate lanes for motorists in cities. Concrete circles, you know, about a foot across and a couple of inches high. They're used to direct drivers into appropriate lanes. More cities ought to try them——

Speaking to all

Susan Nordstrom   I should think they'd be hazardous! What if you actually hit one of them?

Bill   Well, it would surely warn you that you were out of line——

With a laugh

Sam Out of lane, you mean?

Bill Yes, out of lane! But, really, the bump you'd get wouldn't be big enough to make you lose control of the car.

Susan I see.

Leader We've said that traffic buttons for channeling traffic would give an efficient and safe warning. Would they be expensive, do you think?

Bill Traffic engineers don't seem to think so.

Tom It's true that concrete wouldn't cost much, but what about the labor costs of constantly replacing them? For example, take some city where they'd freeze and thaw all winter. There they'd be pounded to pieces in no time—and replacing them so often *would* be expensive!

Clarifies difference

Leader We've suggested that they'd be basically inexpensive, but expensive to maintain. Let's see, would they *have* to be concrete?

Mary Well, some of the ones in Denver aren't concrete. When we were there last summer, my father got to talking with one of the garage men, and he told us they were using *steel* buttons, ones that were war surplus. And—an interesting thing —he said he thought they'd been planned for use as ballast in some of the big bombs!

Tom Quite a change! Well, freezing surely wouldn't hurt *steel* buttons, and—being surplus— they probably wouldn't be too expensive. Of course, not all cities could get them, I suppose, and I don't imagine Denver can forever.

Leader Are we saying, then, that they are an efficient and safe warning, and that—if an appropriate material is found—they'd be inexpensive?

Speaks to all to widen participation

Other advantages? Well, what about disadvantages of using them in cities?

Bill Well, I've heard that there are troubles with street cleaning—and snow removal, too, in cities that have snow—you'd have to find a way to handle these——

Much of your group's *interaction as persons* will naturally occur on the nonverbal level. You will do well, therefore, to demonstrate cooperativeness in your manner and voice, as well as in your words.

44

Summary

The discussion process requires a number of persons gathered together, interacting toward a common goal. The building of ideas by the cooperative work of the group is the essence of the process. Both size and composition of the group are important; place and time are other influential factors. The group must handle problems arising in their interaction on ideas or their interaction as persons, for difficulties on one level handicap achievement on the other. At the outset and throughout the discussion process the members must have similar concepts of the group goal.

References

(1) Marjorie E. Shaw, "A Comparison of Individuals and Small Groups in the Rational Solution of Complex Problems," *American Journal of Psychology*, 44 (July 1932), 502.

(2) Mary Parker Follett, *The New State* (New York: Longmans, Green and Co., 1920), p. 24.

(3) R. F. Bales, "In Conference," *Harvard Business Review*, 32 (March-April 1954), 48.

(4) Bernard Steinzor, "The Spatial Factor in Face-to-Face Discussion Groups," *Journal of Abnormal and Social Psychology*, 45 (July 1950), 552-555.

Readings and problems

1. Make tape recordings in the classroom of the discussion segments presented in this chapter, with members of the class doing the reading. Give special attention to fullest use of the suggestions for *interacting as persons*, trying the script several times before taping to improve in their use. Employ the making of these recordings as a basis for classroom discussion about interaction as persons.

2. Remake the tape recordings from Chapter 1, concentrating on the physical and vocal uses that will best demonstrate use of these additional suggestions. Compare the two sets of tapes to see what differences can be heard when these suggestions on *interacting as persons* are emphasized.

3. Observe carefully the speaking and listening done in some classroom, community, or television discussion.

Report the speaking behaviors that seemed to you to be conducive to cooperative thinking on the part of the other members, and the ones that did not. Report the listening behaviors that seemed to be encouraging to the speakers, and the ones that did not.

4. Evaluate a fellow student's participation in a discussion in this class. Use the appropriate rating scale below:

Member evaluation							
	Low						*High*
	1	*2*	*3*	*4*	*5*	*6*	*7*
Speaking cooperatively							
Listening encouragingly							
Improvement needed:							

Leader evaluation							
	Low						*High*
	1	*2*	*3*	*4*	*5*	*6*	*7*
Widening participation							
Handling differences							
Improvement needed:							

5. As you listen to a classroom discussion, use one of the following forms and write appropriate comments on a factor important in the discussion method. Comment on portions where the group does well and on others where they need improvement. Include the names of the persons involved so that your comments can be of benefit to them.

Discussion analysis sheet: Cooperativeness

*Round:*_____ *Group:*_____ *Meeting:*_____   *Observer:*_____
                                              *Date:*_____

1. Do members show a sincere desire to *work with* the others?

2. Do members make a genuine and sustained effort to understand clearly what others say and mean?

3. Do they try earnestly to build up the best idea of which the group is capable, not caring *whose* the original suggestion has been?

4. Are they more eager to present their own ideas than to work with the group?

Discussion analysis sheet: Group atmosphere

*Round:*_____ *Group:*_____ *Meeting:*_____   *Observer:*_____
                                              *Date:*_____

1. Is there a warm, cooperative attitude among the members (including the leader) of the group?

2. Do the members give helpful attention to the contributions of others?

3. Do all the members feel responsible for bringing each other actively into the discussion?

Discussion analysis sheet: Listening effectiveness

*Round:*_____ *Group:*_____ *Meeting:*_____   *Observer:*_____
                                              *Date:*_____

1. Do the members' comments show that they have listened actively and systematically to each other?

2. Do the members seem to be *listening to understand* rather than to be ready to go on with their own points or to refute the idea being presented?

3. Do those who speak seem concerned with whether other members are understanding their ideas?

47

Discussion analysis sheet: Sensitivity

*Round:*_____ *Group:*_____ *Meeting:*_____ *Observer:*_____
*Date:*_____

1. Are the members concerned over whether the others are feeling themselves valued members of the group?

2. Do they speak to *all* the members of the group, or only to the person who talked immediately before, or to the leader?

3. When they raise objections to an idea before the group, do they seem to be objecting to the person who suggested that idea rather than to the idea itself?

Discussion analysis sheet: Probing

*Round:*_____ *Group:*_____ *Meeting:*_____ *Observer:*_____
*Date:*_____

1. Are ideas sufficiently examined before the group passes on to other ideas? Or are they touched, abandoned, and returned to again? Or are they accepted without sufficient consideration?

2. Does the group spend too much time and effort on ideas that are either already understood or rather unimportant in the total question before them?

3. Do the members conduct part of the probing, or is it all left to the leader? or taken over by him?

Discussion analysis sheet: Penetration

*Round:*_____ *Group:*_____ *Meeting:*_____ *Observer:*_____
*Date:*_____

1. Are the members trying to get *into* the ideas to see what they really mean? Or are they satisfied with touching an idea and not truly thinking *into* and *around* it?

2. Do they recognize the same idea when it appears in different words? Do they try to get to the core of the idea *however it is expressed?*

3. Do they reach out for other ideas that should be considered along with the one they are talking about, or do they miss important ones that should be brought into the picture?

6. Think of some person outside this class
with whom it is easy for you to talk seriously and with enjoyment;
analyze what it is about this person that enables you to talk easily
with him.

7. Think of the most successful discussion
you have participated in recently. Recall the size and composition of
the group, the time and place of the meeting. How influential were
these factors in the success of the group's work?

8. Use the following paragraphs as bases for
classroom discussions. The questions following each paragraph may
serve as starting-points:

A.
One [advantage of thinking with a group] is a
great extension of the range of immediate mental
"association." In individual thought the thinker
waits (in the Problem-Attitude) till some promising idea comes into his mind and then dwells on it
till further ideas spring from it. A group of
people, however, engaged in dialectic can, like
a pack of hounds, follow up the most promising
idea that occurs to any one of them.—Graham
Wallas, *The Great Society* (New York: The Macmillan Co., 1914), pp. 245-246.

1. In what ways are "two heads better than one"?
2. Under what conditions might the members of a group fail to
   "follow up the most promising idea that occurs to any one of
   them"?

B.
But a government by discussion . . . at once breaks
down the yoke of fixed custom: the idea of the
two is inconsistent. As far as it goes, the mere
putting up of a subject to discussion, with the
object of being guided by that discussion, is a
clear admission that that subject is in no degree
settled by established rule, and that men are free
to choose in it; it is an admission too that there
is no sacred authority, no one transcendent and
divinely appointed man, whom in that matter the
community is bound to obey.—*The Works of
Walter Bagehot*, Forrest Morgan, ed. (Hartford:
The Travelers Insurance Co., 1891), Vol. IV, 546.

1. In what ways can American government be called "government by discussion"?
2. How can use of the discussion process help a person make his own individual choices?

> **C.**
>
> Since the first days of western education, men have devoted prolonged labor and the highest skill to the problem of persuasion, the rhetorician's problem of having one's own way. But this . . . can be only part of the total process. The persuasive offering of one's own thought is only the first gesture in a drama in which the other man's thought must also play a part. It is a drama in which the characters are not persons but ideas and in which victory is not the triumph of a man but the general attainment of the truth. For this we must have trained minds and a willing spirit.
> —Lyman Bryson, "Discussion in the Democratic Process," a lecture delivered as a part of the Symposium in Public Speaking, Northwestern University, 1938. Printed in James H. McBurney and Kenneth G. Hance, *Discussion in Human Affairs* (New York: Harper & Bros., 1950), p. 393.

1. Why do you suppose people thought it necessary to train themselves for persuading audiences but not for participating in discussions?
2. Why is the "other man's thought" important if you are searching for the truth?

9. Prepare to hold a class discussion on the question: *In what ways can an understanding of the creative process assist a student of the discussion method?* Consult sources on creativity such as the following:

Anderson, H. H., ed., *Creativity and Its Cultivation* (New York: Harper and Bros., 1959).

Andrews, Michael F., ed., *Aesthetic Form and Education* (Syracuse, N.Y.: Syracuse University Press, 1958).

Clark, C. H., *Brainstorming* (New York: Doubleday, 1958).

Ghiselin, B., *The Creative Process* (Los Angeles: University of California Press, 1952).

Hutchinson, E. D., *How to Think Creatively* (New York: Abingdon-Cokesbury, 1949).

Lowes, J. L., *The Road to Xanadu* (Boston: Houghton Mifflin, 1927).

Osborn, A., *Applied Imagination*, rev. ed. (New York: Charles Scribner's Sons, 1957).

Smith, P., ed., *Creativity: An Examination of the Creative Process* (New York: Hastings House, 1959).

Stein, Morris I., and Shirley J. Heinze, eds., *Creativity and the Individual: Summaries of Selected Literature in Psychology and Psychiatry* (Chicago: The Free Press of Glencoe, 1960).

Vinacke, W. E., *The Psychology of Thinking* (New York: McGraw-Hill, 1952).

Von Fange, E. K., *Professional Creativity* (Englewood Cliffs, N.J.: Prentice-Hall, 1959).

Wallas, G., *The Art of Thought* (New York: Harcourt, Brace, 1926).

Whiting, C. S., *Creative Thinking* (New York: Reinhold, 1958).

Chapter three

THE

DISCUSSION

QUESTION

You have recently enrolled for a course in group discussion, no doubt hoping that the training will assist you in your chosen profession and in your personal life. It is interesting to note how many discussable questions are brought to mind by this action of yours: *You have recently enrolled*

How does one choose a college? Who should attend college? How can we best cope with overcrowded schools? What should be the role of the junior college? etc.

for a course in group discussion,

How does academic training improve discussion skills? How could teaching machines be used in a discussion course? What kinds of groups conduct group discussion programs? etc.

no doubt hoping that the training will assist you in your chosen profession

How does one choose a future career? What counseling is available to the undecided students? What are the advantages of a liberal education for a professional man? etc.

and in your personal life.

What are the marks of an educated man? What responsibilities does every citizen have? What role should the expert play in modern life? How can the individual help shape his society? etc.

Whatever you do, you encounter dozens of interesting discussion subjects every day of your life. Some of them you probably talk about casually with other students, others you never find an opportunity to discuss with anyone—in fact, you may not even consciously think of them as possible discussion questions.

As it is with you in college, so it is with people everywhere. Sometimes a condition arises or an event occurs and a group forms to discuss it: rezoning of a residential area is suggested, and threatened property owners meet to plan their joint protests. Sometimes the group already exists when the new occasion for discussion calls them into session: the curriculum committee of a college meets when proposals for new courses are received from heads of departments. On the other hand, a group may exist for the purpose of discussion and be free to choose questions that engage their interest: *How can we learn to appreciate modern art?* or *What are the possible genetic effects of increased radioactivity?* or (using the problem-solving form of discussion for enlightenment purposes) *What form should United States aid to developing countries take?*

Wherever something is exciting in its potential or threatening in its aspect or merely unexplainable—it may provide a good discussion subject. Such encounters as the following invite discussion:

a hurt sustained by individuals or society (for example, conditions in mental hospitals);

a vague sense of unease or impending disaster (increase in international crises);

a hitch in plans, a break in expected continuity (stagnation of United States economy);

an unusual or perplexing occurrence (extreme lawlessness among youths from middle-income homes);

a demand for action (strong urging to vote for a school bond levy);

a query, unanswerable at the moment (limitations of manned space exploration);

an idea patently capable of development, an idea with a growing edge (the Peace Corps);

a hunch, an insight needing examination, a pulsing analogy (resemblances between present-day Chinese and the barbarian hordes that conquered the Roman Empire).

Many of these provocative topics come not from direct personal experience, but indirectly from hearing lectures, plays, and news commentaries or reading newspapers, magazines, and books. A student hears Mortimer Adler say that listening takes more energy than talking and raises this discussion question: *How can we improve our classroom listening?* Or he sees Sophocles' *Antigone* and asks: *How can man reconcile conflicting loyalties?* Or he hears a radio news commentator talk about filibustering in the Senate and asks: *How can we best safeguard minority rights in the Senate without impeding the will of the majority?* Or he reads in the newspaper that a newly formed community college is in search of a president, and he poses the question: *What qualities must a college president have?* Or he reads Dag Hammarskjöld's Introduction to the Annual Report of the Secretary-General on the Work of the Organization: June 16, 1960—June 15, 1961 and asks: *In what direction should the United Nations Organization develop?* Or he reads Rourke's *Secrecy and Publicity: Dilemmas of Democracy*, and asks the same question as the author: *How much should the government tell?*

Whatever event, situation, or idea engages people's deep interest or concern—the launching of a new space vehicle, an industry's dissatisfaction with its recent growth, or a new definition of national goals—it *may* provide a discussion subject. This tentativeness arises because not all subjects that seem interesting may be suitable for a particular group or a particular occasion; the subject must be carefully selected, appropriately delimited, and then suitably phrased.

Selection of subjects

Subjects for discussion are chosen in a number of ways; whatever the manner of selection, however, an appropriate subject should possess certain characteristics.

Manner of selection

Assigned subjects   When a group is a part of a large organization, it may often be requested to study troublesome issues, to recommend remedial action, or to make specific decisions. Thus the curriculum committee of a college department may be requested by the department head to recommend a new course of study for the master's degree. Or the mayor's Committee on Fair Employment Practices may be asked to investigate hiring procedures of local department stores. Or a committee may be *called into being for a particular task* and discharged at its completion, as a commission for bringing outlying communities into the water system of a city.

Or the discussion may take place in a training program or a classroom, where the director or professor may assign a particular topic to provide instruction in a specific area. For example, in a training conference for leaders in a community development program, the director may announce an initial discussion on the question: *What troubles do we frequently meet in our group discussions?* Or an instructor in the discussion classroom may assign the question: *How effective is the* Seattle Times *as a metropolitan newspaper?* In the widely known Great Books program each group discusses a prescribed sequence of readings from classic authors.

Subjects from common activity   Where the group is associated in a common activity—student government, medical research, charitable work—discussion is essential for achieving collective goals. The discussion subject arises out of some facet of this common activity: some difficulty must be ironed out, some plan of action developed, or some understanding achieved. The question must be clearly phrased so that the group approach may be systematically made. For instance, a campus group may ask itself at the beginning of its year's activity: *What are our objectives for the year?* And a discussion class group may raise a question on its own experiences: *How can a group handle an over-talkative member?*

Subjects within a general theme A study group may develop an interest in a general area and within that area select a series of related or separate topics. For example, a group interested in world population growth may plan a series of discussions organized on the basis of geographical areas, or it may select separate topics within the general theme for single meetings—such topics as means of increasing food production or factors making a high birth rate seemingly desirable in certain cultures. Such a group has considerable freedom in choosing subjects, for many topics are related to its general area of interest.

In another instance, a book club might want to determine what action it could initiate or promote for the good of the community— by way of improving the reading habits of children, of elevating the literary tastes of adults, and so forth. Or the instructor may ask his discussion students to choose subjects within the general theme of *handling disruptive members,* and in successive meetings they might elect to talk about handling the *monopolizer,* the *nontalker,* and the *tangent-goer,* who wanders off into trivial or irrelevant matters.

Freely chosen subjects And, of course, some groups meet for group discussion experience, for enlightenment, or merely for social enjoyment, and thus are free to choose subjects reflecting their current interests and purposes. After consulting the preferences of its members and checking available source materials, a campus Cosmopolitan Club may decide to discuss the effects of language upon culture or the status of women around the world or means for giving exchange students a truer picture of American life. The members of a discussion class may choose to discuss such wide-ranging questions as: *How can we increase citizen interest in public issues?* or *What is the significance of the Ecumenical Council?* or *In what ways do Bergman's films excel?*

Characteristics of good subjects

Whether the subject is assigned, arises out of group activity, is selected by the members within a general thematic framework or with complete freedom of choice, it should be (1) interesting to the members who are to discuss it, (2) worthy of their efforts, and (3) open to their investigation.

Interesting　We have said that phenomena men encounter from day to day may afford them subjects for discussion. They will find only those subjects interesting, however, which touch their particular purposes, attitudes, tastes, loyalties, or needs.

Not only will different events arouse different groups to discussion, but the *same* event experienced by *different* groups will suggest different subjects. Suppose that an exhibition of Mexican folk art is presented at a local museum; many groups attend. The members of a local Spanish class may be interested in broadening their understanding of Spanish-speaking culture. To a group of anthropologists the exhibit may provide valuable insights into the persistence of pre-Conquest religious symbols and into the influence of modern technology. The expression of political bias in Mexican art, on the other hand, might interest a group concerned with Latin-American politics. Art teachers might study the exhibit to find craft techniques applicable in their own classes, while to the staff of a travel bureau the displays might suggest effective promotional motifs.

Doubtless not all members of any group will feel an equal amount of interest in every subject; it is worth while, however, to seek one which most members of the group consider interesting. Sometimes a lack of interest stems from lack of knowledge about the subject and disappears when the issues begin to emerge and information about them is discovered.

Worth-while　For groups with a specific purpose—such as problem solving or enlightenment—topics of the greatest possible intrinsic worth are obviously preferable. A management group would likely be wiser to use its time to discuss how to solve a particular problem of production than where to place the bulletin board (unless this matter had an intimate connection with efficiency or morale). A student group on campus educational problems would likely do better to use its time discussing means of improving study habits than of eliminating seat saving in the stadium. Although probing a subject of small intrinsic importance may sometimes bring out significant underlying issues, it is clear that some questions merit examination more than others and that examining them is more worthy of the members' time and effort.

Open to investigation　If the reports are not yet published, the records not yet released by the government or the courts, the men central in the activity not yet free to reveal their information, the group interested in discussing the event might consider deferring discussion until materials are available. On the other hand, if mere speculation could serve the members' purpose, they could proceed on a frankly conditional basis. A team of air crash investigators may speculate as they travel to the scene, but their most valuable discussion will follow their direct observations; any outside group wishing to use their findings must await their publication. In most cases a group should choose a subject about which serious, methodical research can reveal the information necessary for worthwhile discussion.

Delimitation of subjects

Once the group members have settled on a subject that they are interested in, that is worthy of their time and open to their investigation, they need to determine exactly how much of the general topic they will try to cover. And after such delimitation, the subject must be appropriately phrased. Delimiting the topic is a process of narrowing the focus to a suitable segment; phrasing, on the other hand, indicates the intended approach to the area selected.

Purposes of delimitation

Suited to the discussion process Many aspects of a subject are interesting and important but not suited to the discussion process. If they are questions which can be answered by facts alone—for example, What is the enrollment of all the higher institutions of learning in the state? or What provisions are made in this state for older persons lacking Social Security benefits?—they are not usually appropriate; such questions demand recourse to sources of information rather than the cooperative interpretation of information in the light of experience and judgment of a number of people. Since the very point of discussing a subject is this integration of the experience, knowledge, and critical thinking of the members of the group, segments of the topic that make such interplay indispensable or, at least, advantageous should be selected. Anyone interested in discussing the topics suggested above must concentrate on aspects that call upon the judgment of the members: for example, *How can we best provide additional opportunities for* *college training in our state?* and *How can we take better care of older persons lacking Social Security benefits in this state?*

    Suited to the time available What would be an entirely appropriate topic for a series of two-hour meetings over a span of weeks would be a frustrating and worthless one for a single hour of discussion. For example, no group could discuss the population explosion in any worth-while way in one meeting; nor could any committee plan substantial improvements in the city's playgrounds in one session. A group seeking enlightenment only could choose to take up a segment that could be handled in one meeting, such as the success of Japan's attempts to lower its birth rate in recent years.[1] A group seeking to make a dependable decision on a complex problem cannot simply choose an interesting aspect and forego discussion of the remainder. Able to cover no more in one session than will allow full interaction among the members, yet obliged to move logically through all the problem-solving steps, this group will likely need to arrange additional meetings to complete its task; in short, the task will set the time.

  There is perhaps no greater mistake in arranging for discussion than expecting to handle too large a segment of a subject within the time available.

    Suited to the group purpose If the group's purpose is to solve a problem, the subject must include the area involved in this judgment. For instance, a group interested in bringing cultural enrichment to its campus may find that it wished to limit its discussion to the relative merits of the lecturers and entertainers whose *fees* are not prohibitive and who are *available* in the coming year. On the other hand, if the group's purpose is enlightenment, it might range more broadly over the entire field. The first group would be committed to making specific decisions, whereas the second would be seeking only increased knowledge.

Process of delimitation

  Delimitation progressively narrows the subject to a segment that is suitable to the discussion method and to the group's time and purpose.

  Because of the intricate nature of events and ideas, discussers must take care to separate central from peripheral issues. Stripping off

1. The group could, of course, take the larger subject and hold more meetings.

superfluities is important. Watch the nurseryman as he cuts the ball of earth around the roots of a sapling he is about to move, leaving the soil that is necessary for the root life, stripping off what is not necessary. Likewise, the group members must recognize what is essential for the purpose at hand and separate it from the remainder. They must recognize precisely where unity begins to be lost; unless the segment is detached at this boundary, the topic will become obscured by diverse peripheral issues. If it is cut too close to the core, however, it may wither for lack of the concepts in which it is rooted.

For example, suppose that the members of an enlightenment group are concerned with the problem of hunger around the world and that they wish to spend a two-hour discussion on some segment of the subject. They turn to the United Nations as a means of approach but realize that they must delimit the area. They think of agencies of the United Nations that are busy with the problem. They decide on the Food and Agriculture Organization as making the most direct attack upon the problem in which they are interested. And then they turn to the "Freedom from Hunger Campaign," FAO's most ambitious activity so far. Someone suggests that they study just the one example of Liberia's swamp rice project. But soon they realize that the Campaign cannot be truly represented by a single project and decide to talk about the Campaign itself with its several purposes. By a series of decisions they have settled upon a single segment that is interesting to them, appropriate to the time available, and suitable for their purpose of enlightenment.

The act of delimitation for a problem-solving group involves the same step-by-step narrowing process. Suppose that members of a community service organization are concerned about the growing unrest among teen-agers in their area. They could focus their attention on the youths already in detention or on those who are likely but as yet uncharged offenders; they prefer to consider the latter. Thinking over the problem together, they decide that they are more concerned about the lack of employment opportunities than they are about recreational outlets. And they agree to limit their study to boys only. If they now hold a series of meetings on the problem of improving employment opportunities for teen-age boys in their community, they will have a segment that is interesting to them, appropriate in terms of time, and suitable to prepare them for action.

The degree of delimitation needed will, of course, depend on the nature of the subject. When the subject is *assigned*, presumably appropriate narrowing has already been done by those making the assignment. When the subject arises out of a *common activity*, some focusing may remain to be done. When the subjects fall *within a general theme*, the choosing of that theme is only the first step of delimitation, and the other steps must be taken, either by a separate planning body (which would be, in itself, a discussion group doing a job of delimitation) or by the whole group assembled. And the group that arrives at its subjects by *free choice* must undertake the whole process of delimitation.

Sometimes the first meeting of the group is devoted to the selection, delimitation, and phrasing of its subject. Or a group may hold a preliminary planning meeting to achieve the necessary delimitation and may consider that it only begins its *discussion* thereafter. In either case, a group in the process of narrowing its subject is actually doing one of the subtlest kinds of discussion and should strive to use the best interaction of ideas and judgments of which the members are capable.

Phrasing of questions

The act of *phrasing the question* is important. When members seek words to communicate the chosen subject, they discover any remaining vagueness in the topic itself or differences in their intended approach to it. In addition, their joint search for appropriate words consolidates their understanding of the terms that they ultimately choose.

The enlightenment group mentioned earlier would probably decide to ask something like this: *How significant an attack on the world's food problem has the Freedom from Hunger Campaign made?* If some of the members had not understood that the group had decided not to include the whole scope of FAO, the search for proper phrasing would have removed this misconception.

The members of the problem-solving group would no doubt have little trouble phrasing their question: *How can we best increase employment opportunities for teen-age boys in our community?* If someone had suggested the word *provide*, they would have faced the question of whether they had really meant to secure the jobs and settle the youths in them or only to extend the number of jobs available to the boys. With the ambiguity brought to light the members might agree that the word *provide* was to mean "to make open to" instead of "to secure for" (or *vice versa*), or they could substitute a word such as *increase* as being more exact.

Starting, then, from a phrasing that all members understand similarly, they can from the outset focus their efforts more effectively upon their common task. And the phrasing they have evolved will most likely lead to good discussion if it satisfies four requirements: that it be interrogative, clear, impartial, and concise.

Interrogative

The subject should be stated in *question* form, rather than as a topic or as a resolution. In general, a topic indicates too little of the approach the group is to make. Of course, a topic can *imply* the asking of a question, as these do: effects of the European Common Market on European unity; value of participation in campus activities; improved training for the gifted child. Nevertheless, the actual intent and approach of each discussion become clearer by rephrasing the topics into their implied questions: *What are the effects of .the European Common Market on the European unity? How valuable to the college undergraduate is participation in campus activities?* and *How can we best improve the training for the gifted child?* [2]

No form other than the question indicates so clearly that the group expects to build an answer, an understanding or a decision, by cooperative efforts. Interrogative phrasing indicates that the answer is yet to be evolved, the cooperative work of the group still to be done.

Clear

The phrasing of the question should identify the topic clearly. If the members of an enlightenment group decide to examine the nature of a philosophy or the extent of a trend, the wording of their question must reveal this focus. They might ask: *What is existentialism?* or *What political changes are developing in the South?* If

2. These three types of questions are sometimes termed, in order, *fact, value,* and *policy*. In this textbook they are called *study, evaluation,* and *problem-solving* to suggest their dynamic focus; furthermore, the term *fact* is avoided in designating types of questions because discussions do not *establish* facts. No such list of categories is completely satisfactory because the distinctions are not clear cut, for all discussions are infused with value and all should start with fact. See Chapters 6 and 7 for full explanation.

they decide to examine an issue, the phrasing must point out the approach: *How badly has the United States neglected Latin America?* Or if they intend to suggest possible alternatives of action or to set standards for some activity or position, the phrasing must reveal this open-mindedness: *How can we increase college opportunities in our state?* or *What abilities should a representative of the people have?* Or, on the other hand, if the enlightenment group decides to diagnose or evaluate, it must phrase its question to indicate this approach: *How effective is student government in our university?* If the group is to make a decision in preparation for action, the question should invite selection among possible methods: *How can we best handle the dependent children in our state?* or *How can we best eliminate unethical advertising methods?*

Clarity does not demand that every word be unambiguous, although such a condition would, of course, be highly desirable. If the group is using the term *Southeast Asia,* agreement among the members as to whether India is included, and so forth, will make the term a clear and useful one. Words whose meanings are well understood in the common activity in which the members are engaged, like *reforestation* and *opinion sampling,* require only a quick check for common understanding by the group. Words whose meanings are generally clear, like *older persons,* often need to be made specific for the purposes of the discussion and should be given attention and interpretation by the group. For example, a group trying to phrase its question on improving the care of old people who have no Social Security benefits will need to agree upon a clarification:

> **Leader** Let's see, we keep using the term *older persons* here as we're trying to decide how to phrase our question. We seem to prefer these words to *aged* or *aging* or *senior citizens*——
>
> **Joseph Gross** Yes, *senior citizens* might be taken to mean elderly people of distinction, like Bernard Baruch, you know. And we don't mean that; we simply mean persons over a certain age——
>
> **Mary Beck** If we decided what that certain age is, then our term *older persons* would be fine, it seems to me.
>
> **Charles Petras** Well, when Governor Meyner addressed the White House Conference, he spoke

of people "over sixty-five"; a public health survey used the same figure, and so did a Senate Committee——

John Wilcox Yes, sixty-five seems to be the age commonly used.

Leader We seem to be saying sixty-five. Do we mean *sixty-five and over*, or *over sixty-five?* They'd have retired at the outset of that year probably, wouldn't they?

Charles Hadn't we better say *sixty-five and over?* Of course, to be really technical, a man is in his sixty-sixth year the day he's had his sixty-fifth birthday!

Looking around to get the sense of the group

Leader Sixty-five and over, then? That's what we mean when we use the term *older persons* in our question, we've decided. So our question will read: *How can we take better care of older persons lacking Social Security benefits in this state?*

In brief, a group must develop a phrasing that reflects accurately the segment of the subject it wishes to discuss and that employs terms which are understood similarly by all the members.

Impartial

The phrasing of the discussion question should not suggest an answer or indicate bias. For example, phrasing such as the following should always be avoided: What is the significance of the imposing data produced by the International Geophysical Year? The term *imposing* suggests that the significance is indeed great and in a fashion answers the question. In this phrasing—What alternatives exist to the mayor's well-conceived plan?—the bias of the group (or of whoever stated the question) is evident and would make a fair consideration of other plans less possible. Such phrasing is sometimes called "begging the question," since the question implicitly *begs* for a preconceived answer.

It is important to remind ourselves here that phrasing which reflects a bias of our culture and our times is inescapable to some extent and should not be confused with the type of bias described above. If a group asks, *How can we best protect religious freedom?* it is assuming that we all believe in the protection of religious freedom. Now such an assumption is one of the cornerstones of our form of democratic government. Therefore, we need not consider that this question violates the requirement of impartial phrasing. It would be prejudiced if the phrasing involved an assumption that we did not all hold; if such were the case (that is, if Americans did not in fact respect religious freedom), the question would have to be rephrased to take up the preliminary query of what our attitude toward religious freedom actually is.[3]

Concise

The question should be phrased as briefly as possible; numerous qualifications and elaborations tend to confuse rather than to clarify meaning. For example, consider this phrasing: What have been the structural and functional characteristics of the policies pursued by American diplomats and other leaders in the capitals of the Far East during the last decade or so? A group would find such a phrasing as the following much more usable: *What are the characteristics of recent American diplomacy in the Far East?* Parsimony is an effective principle in the phrasing of a discussion question because concise wording affords the group a common and efficient point of departure for thinking; wordiness, on the other hand, tends to blunt the concentrated attack of the group upon its subject.

Synthesis of steps

We have discussed three separate steps: (1) selection of the subject; (2) delimitation of the subject; and (3) phrasing of the question. Whether these steps are undertaken by the members of a group as the first part of their discussion or preliminary to it, or are undertaken for them by others, they are basic to successful use of the discussion process. Let us consider how these steps of delimitation and phrasing might be taken by a number of different groups who are interested in the subject of *automation*, have considered it worthy of discussion, and have reason to believe that sufficient information will be available to them.

---

3. It should be noted that this question—What is our attitude toward freedom of religion?—no longer asks for decision on policy but rather for a clarification that would underlie policy-making. When this examination has been concluded, a problem-solving question can then be formulated without being prejudicial.

Subject: automation

Delimitation	Phrasing

Problem-solving group/several meetings

1. Meaning Accurate description of electronic computers	*Should we describe our computers as electronic "brains"?*
2. Uses Teaching machines	*Should we use teaching machines in the schools in our city?*
3. Effects Providing for unskilled workers who will be displaced by automation	*What shall we do for the technologically displaced?*

Problem-solving group/single meeting

1. Meaning Origin of the term *automation*	*Whom shall we credit as the originator of the term* automation?
2. Uses Payroll automation	*Should we install a data-processing machine in our payroll department?*
3. Effects Fruitful use of increased leisure time	*Should we sponsor a Great Books program for our employees?*

Enlightenment group/several meetings

1. Meaning Automation and technological evolution	*How has automation evolved from earlier technological achievements?*
2. Uses Present and potential uses of automation	*What are the present and potential uses of automation?*
3. Effects Economic and psychological effects	*What are the economic and psychological effects of automation?*

Enlightenment group/single meeting

1. Meaning Exact definition of term	*What does the term* automation *mean?*
2. Uses Present use in the automobile industry	*How does the General Motors Corporation use automation?*
3. Effects Relationship between automation and employment figures in a specific industry	*What effect has automation had on employment in the Bell Telephone System?*

Summary

Subjects appropriate to discussion by groups are obtained in a number of ways: they are assigned or come from a common activity or fall within a general theme or are freely chosen by the members. These topics need to be (1) interesting, (2) worthy of study, and (3) open to investigation. The subjects should be delimited to suit the discussion process, the time available, and the group purpose. This delimited subject should be phrased in a clear, impartial, concise manner, and in question form.

Readings and problems

1. List several subjects you would like to discuss with some group. Phrase each of these appropriately for handling in a series of meetings or in a single meeting.

2. Select a course in which the instructor's lectures are particularly interesting to you. From the ideas presented in a week's class meetings, formulate questions for enlightenment discussions by appropriate groups.

3. Read the editorial pages of a metropolitan newspaper for several consecutive days; on the basis of the problems discussed, prepare questions that would be suitable for discussion by the following types of groups:

An enlightenment group meeting weekly, with time and inclination to read widely;

An enlightenment group holding a single meeting, interested in speculating together without making specific preparation;

A problem-solving group meeting a half dozen times, specifically interested in community improvement;

A problem-solving group holding a single meeting, intending to remedy a local problem.

4. Select a commentator whose column appears daily in a metropolitan newspaper available to you. Phrase the topic of each of the columns he writes over a given period into a clear, concise, impartial question.

5. Improve the phrasing of each of the following questions for discussion:

How can we best eliminate the crazy-quilt of overlapping jurisdictions in our local government?

The special child in the school.

What new sources of revenue can the state tap in order to acquire now the recreation areas needed for today and for the future? What about setting up a censorship board to prevent the showing of immoral films?

6. Choose a general topic of importance and of interest to you, one that you would like to discuss with a group over a series of meetings. Within this general subject prepare a number of specific questions to which the group might give attention. In attempting to narrow the general topic sufficiently, find interesting segments to consider through consulting news magazines, textbooks, journals of opinion (such as *Harper's, The Reporter, Saturday Review, Vital Speeches*), and collections of articles and speeches, such as the following: *American Issues: A Sourcebook for Speech Topics,* Edwin Black and Harry P. Kerr, eds. (New York: Harcourt, Brace and World, Inc., 1961); *Cross Currents: A Collection of Essays from Contemporary Magazines,* Harry P. Simonson, ed. (New York: Harper and Brothers, 1959); *The Speaker's Resource Book,* Carroll C. Arnold, Douglas Ehninger, and John C. Gerber, eds. (Chicago: Scott, Foresman and Company, 1961).

7. In a classroom discussion delimit and phrase one of the following general topics into appropriate segments for either an *enlightenment* or a *problem-solving* discussion of three sessions:

The Common Market	Mental health	Crime
Nuclear testing	Athletics	Mass media
Foreign aid	Overpopulation	Government
Education	Segregation	Advertising

8. Describe groups and situations to which the following questions might be appropriate for discussion:

1. How can our colleges best reconcile the demands of specialization with the needs of citizenship?

2. What should be the relationship of scientists to national policy-making?

3. Who actually governs in the United States?

4. What is the significance of the Black Muslim movement in the United States?

5. What trends are appearing in Japanese politics?

6. What does Galbraith's advice to developing countries in his *Economic Development in Perspective* mean for American foreign aid?

7. What can the United States learn from the Cuba incident of 1962?

8. How can we offer the Russian people a clearer picture of our country?

9. What is the significance of the International Decade for Hydrology?

10. What made Eleanor Roosevelt one of the most admired personalities of her time?

11. What are the effects of suburban life upon a child?

12. What use can we make of Bruno Bettelheim's *Dialogues with Mothers?*

13. What are the characteristics of the "Beat Generation"?

14. How can we improve the physical environment of our campus?

15. What's right with the United States?

Chapter four

GATHERING

INFORMATION

ON THE

QUESTION

Thomas Johnson, a widely known civic leader, was appointed to the Citizens' Advisory Committee on Metropolitan Problems. This group took up one after another the problems on which city-wide action might be advantageous—public transportation, water, sewage, parks and parkways, garbage, comprehensive planning. Whatever the issue under consideration at the moment, Mr. Johnson read everything he could get his hands on: reports from other metropolitan areas, bulletins from the United States Government, books and pamphlets by experts, a mimeographed explanation of the functions of the different units of his own city government. He met and talked with the men handling that particular problem in the outlying areas. When the Advisory Committee reconvened, he had reliable information, for he had taken pains to bolster his own knowledge and information with data and viewpoints from dependable sources.

When a Parent-Teachers Association representative starts for the national meetings with notes on interviews with every local president in her area, when a businessman leaves his office for the Civic Center Planning Committee with his head full of facts about European civic centers and recommendations from experienced directors, when a representative of the Student Union goes to the annual meeting with key figures from the year's operations clearly in mind—these prospective discussers have been taking steps to equip themselves appropriately. They have supplied themselves with the information necessary to satisfy Emerson's dictum, *Keep your feet always firm upon a fact,* and with opinions from reputable authorities. Such information is needed in a group to provide steady ground from which to construct valid lines of reasoning and to find satisfactory solutions.

Forms of accumulation

Information can be accumulated by a member of a discussion group in two ways: personal experience and purposeful research.

Personal experience

The discusser's training, experience, and individual interests are of great value. If he has been a student or even an interested observer of a subject for some time, he will have accumulated a stock of ideas and opinions upon which to draw for the discussion. The mother who belongs to one of the Family Life groups organized by the city school system comes to meetings with memories of her own childhood, knowledge of her children's experiences, information from books she has read over the years and from lectures she has attended, insights from the counselors and teachers with whom she has talked. These personal experiences provide a basis of information she can use in the discussion.

No long acquaintance with a problem, however, relieves a discusser of the necessity of familiarizing himself with the immediate situation. If the Family Life group is discussing the present counseling situation at the neighborhood school, each member should inform herself about *this*, the *immediate* situation. Any Himalayan assault team studies the present season's snows, no matter how many times the group has been on the mountain; any athletic team studies the present season's opponents through movies and scouts, no matter how many times the players have met squads trained by the opposing coach. Similarly, any discusser needs to fortify any previous knowledge he has by use of all available sources of information about the current situation.

Even if a person is to participate in the discussion of a question with which he is relatively unfamiliar, he has more resources than he perhaps realizes. Experiences and information from other fields of his knowledge may offer him useful parallels, as the researchers in scientific work have so often found; we recall, for instance, the interest of aircraft designers in the flight of the hummingbird. And, further, the discusser may well find that the immediate subject will involve issues which are quite familiar to him and which are at the heart of many an important decision—how much versus how well, immediate versus future gain, our welfare versus others' welfare, and so forth. He may never before have been concerned with a rezoning threat to a residential neighborhood, but when he begins his preparation he will find himself quickly in the midst of a familiar issue: others' welfare versus our own—in this case, free enterprise versus property owners' rights.

Your store of personal experience will be of great value to you, but this unplanned preparation should be bolstered at every possible point by thorough use of the most recent sources.[1] Situations in which

---

1. For your discussions in class you will no doubt always be expected to gather further information.

groups must talk over some trouble or make recommendation without advance preparation are rare.

Purposeful research

Reviewing what you already know to provide leads into further study and to alert you to gaps in your present knowledge, you begin your investigation. During this search you should grow increasingly aware that even with the greatest diligence you will, in most cases, be able to tap only a portion of the available sources. This recognition should make you eager to spend your time on the *best possible sources*, taking care to read from a variety of viewpoints instead of adopting as your own the first cogently expressed one you come upon. This recognition should also make you look forward to hearing information found in different sources by other members of the group. Furthermore, as you and the others proceed with your discussion together, you may well find that you need to do further research, make firsthand observations, talk to authorities, and so on. And throughout your research, both that preceding the discussion and that occurring after the sessions have begun, you must study your sources thoroughly and impartially to find what the authors or speakers actually mean instead of looking only for material to bolster some bias you already hold. In short, you must make your preparation a search for meaning and value instead of a proof of preconceived opinion.

Types of information

Two types of information are needed in thinking: facts and expert opinions.

Facts

By *facts* we mean occurrences that are verifiable. They are accounts of the objective nature of things and, as such, are useful bases for man's thinking. The daily newspaper reports that the President today signed a bill authorizing "$893,947,750 in military construction in the United States and abroad in the year beginning Monday." Such a statement is a report of *fact*. Or it may take the form of the synthesized report of many facts, that is, of *statistics*. The newspaper reports the answer to a Gallup Poll question (on the desirability of a cut in federal income taxes, even though such action meant greater governmental debt) as: "Favor—19 per cent; Oppose—72 per cent;

No opinion—9 per cent." Statistics provide a means of organizing data so as to reveal trends, relationships, patterns of occurrence.

If you are preparing on the question—*What is the significance of the International Geophysical Year?*—you will find such *facts* as these:

Two International Polar Years had preceded the IGY, one in 1882-1883 and the other in 1932-1933.

Sixty-four nations, 8000 scientists, more than 2000 stations participated.

A dozen geophysicists met informally at Silver Spring, Maryland, on April 5, 1950, and discussed ways of getting more information about the earth. Lloyd V. Berkner suggested that a time of stepped-up observation be organized similar to the polar years.

If you and your group are talking about the effectiveness of the Colombo Plan, you will doubtless find *statistics* showing, for example, what percentage of the Colombo Plan projects are road-building operations, how food intake of the workers in Nepal varied with the danger of the work being undertaken, what patterns accidents followed throughout the whole project.

Opinions

By *opinions* we mean judgments, evaluations, indications of approval or disapproval. A prominent columnist declares that "improved business psychology would help more than tax cuts"; another declares that the Russians oppose the European Common Market violently because its swift development is disproving the claims of Marx and Lenin about capitalism. Such statements are *opinions*. We must remind ourselves to avoid the common error of calling an *opinion* a "fact"; it is incorrect to say: "Every medical library should have a copy of Professor Negovskii's book; that's a fact." Instead of trying to add credibility to our opinion by declaring it a *fact*, we should present the reasons why all medical libraries should buy the book.

Expert opinions consist of conclusions drawn by persons authoritative in the field about which they are speaking. Often presenting some of the data from which they have reasoned, they set forth their interpretations from such data.

Although most of your preparations will use both fact and expert opinion, in two situations you will need to rely chiefly on authorities' opinions as your foundations for thinking: (1) when you cannot find the facts themselves because they are not available; (2) when the facts are not understandable without expert interpretation. If your question concerns freshman drop-outs, the head of the counseling service may be unable to show you the withdrawal cards, but he may tell you his judgment that the primary reason behind the drop-outs was poor study habits. If your question concerns the effects of radio-active fallout on the human organism, you may learn the amounts of Strontium-90 and Cesium-137 that are currently being deposited, but you will not know how to judge the effects of these isotopes without the interpretations of experts in medicine and biology. In other words you may have the information about the fallout materials but lack the expert understanding by which to weigh that information.

Even when facts are available and understandable to you, you often need expert opinion to assist you in interpreting them. Expert opinion is not, therefore, a court of last resort, but a necessary working partner of facts. Together they form the basis from which you build your interpretations and conclusions.

Sources of information

Where shall you turn for these necessary types of information? The answer will depend upon the accessibility of information, your knowledge of the subject, and the amount of time available to you. Acting within this framework, you will turn to these major types of sources: *observations, interviews* and *surveys,* and *written* and *oral materials.*

Observations

If, as researcher, you can give your eyes and ears to the event—either directly or indirectly—you will have first-hand information for use. If you are present as the event occurs or the situation continues, you can observe *directly:* the noon-hour congestion on the street corner, the juvenile court session, the old waterfront properties, the lost, old men on Skid Row on Saturday night. If, on the other hand, you watch a television or film documentary, you have a balcony seat at the event, and also acquire eyewitness data for your use.

If your observation is made purposely for gathering data for discussion, you must consider what conditions or changes of the object or event would be relevant and put yourself in a position to observe them. If you want to assess the listeners' reactions at a local park where soapbox orators hold forth every evening, you will have to find a vantage point from which you can *see* and *hear* what actually takes place.

What should you observe in an event? An easy answer would be: Remain open to suggestion, flexible; see what there is to be seen. But our knowledge of the traffic court's constant difficulty with the contradictory reports of different witnesses suggests that more ordered, responsible observation is needed. John Stuart Mill (1) explains the difficulty of good observation:

> . . . The observer is not he who merely sees the thing which is before his eyes, but he who sees what parts that thing is composed of. To do this well is a rare talent. One person, from inattention, or attending only in the wrong place, overlooks half of what he sees; another sets down much more than he sees, confounding it with what he imagines, or with what he infers; another takes note of the *kind* of all the circumstances, but being inexpert in estimating their degree, leaves the quantity of each vague and uncertain; another sees indeed the whole, but makes such an awkward division of it into parts, throwing things into one mass which require to be separated, and separating others which might more conveniently be considered as one, that the result is much the same, sometimes even worse, than if no analysis had been attempted at all.

We might then suggest such procedures as these: (1) Note *all* parts; *add none.* (2) Note *kind* and *quantity.* (3) Make *logical* divisions. If you concentrate solely on the people gathered around the speakers and fail to note those who are listening from park benches or assume that everyone in the surrounding neighborhood is present; if you note that some spectators jeer, some shout rebuttals, some applaud, some listen passively, but you fail to observe the proportions of each; if you count how many are teen-agers, how many are well dressed, how many are smoking, how many are women—in each of these situations you are committing one of the errors that Mill cautioned against. Remember also that you should return to the park several evenings in succession to assure yourself that your observations on the first evening were not made on an *unusual* occasion: perhaps that day was a holiday and greater crowds than usual were in the park; perhaps neither the speakers nor the listeners were typical of those who generally appear. If you observed on one evening only, you would be taking an inadequate sampling.

In any and all observations, the greatest care must be exercised in these matters of *completeness*, of *nature* and *quantity*, and of *logical division* for the reason which H. Ernest Hunt (2) explains well when he says: "These sense-messages must be clear, accurate, and definite as possible, because upon their foundation we ground the processes of thought."

And these *sense-messages* must be recorded in as accurate a fashion as possible for dependable use later in the thought process. Cards or a notebook are indispensable aids; a camera or tape recorder can sometimes assist in this important problem of keeping the data undistorted. Careful, thoughtful observation of objects or representative occurrences with immediate recording (or recording as quickly thereafter as possible)—these are the steps necessary for obtaining facts by *observation*.

Interviews and surveys

If you can arrange interviews with persons who have unusual access to data or are capable of authoritative interpretations, you may secure valuable information. If you are preparing to participate in a discussion on campus architecture, you may arrange an interview with the planning analyst; if you are going to be discussing a strike settlement problem, you may want to talk with the mediation officer of the labor department of your city; if your question concerns grass-roots politics, you may take pains to see the local campaign chairman for one of the major parties.

Your selection of experts to interview will be of primary importance, for you are preparing to use their information and conclusions as bases for your own thought. Furthermore, when you ask for facts, you hope, of course, that the expert will exercise the strictest care in giving "clear, accurate, and definite" pieces of data. When you ask for opinions, you hope that he will set forth his views with candor and explain clearly the lines of thinking from which he derives these opinions.

It is also important to plan the content of the interview and record the authority's remarks without alteration. You need to know pretty thoroughly what written sources say on your topic before you take the expert's time, particularly if he has fully published his findings or views. Further, you will need to think out pretty clearly the main questions to ask so that his statements center largely on the aspects most relevant to your study. At the interview you must listen objectively to his statements and avoid interpreting them in terms of your own expectations; also, you must be quick to follow up his remarks if they open new and profitable lines of thinking to you. And you must have notecards at hand to help you record the facts and opinions that will be valuable to you later.

Sometimes your question can be probed more effectively by the use of polls or questionnaires than by interviews with experts. If you were discussing the question—*How effective are fallout shelters?*—you might take a random sampling of opinion at several busy intersections, in theater lobbies, at supermarkets, and so on. Those polled might lack expert opinion in the matter, but their aggregate beliefs could provide useful and important material. Remember, however, that the results of polls and questionnaires can sometimes be misleading, for various reasons: inadequacy of sampling, failure to get a true cross section of opinions, psychological barriers between interviewer and those interviewed.

Written and oral materials

Written materials   By written materials we mean reports, analyses, commentaries, recommendations for action, and so on. They may be available in books, pamphlets, newspaper or magazine articles, and special publications such as yearbooks and monographs. You may, for example, write for material such as *Mankind's Children: The Story of UNICEF* by Robert L. Heilbroner (No. 279 of the Public Affairs Pamphlets) or the *UNICEF and You* brochure from the United States Committee for UNICEF; you may call at the local office of the American Association for the United Nations and discover a wealth of information.

But the *library* is the treasure house. From reports of bureaus to the newest analysis in magazine, pamphlet, or book—this repository of human knowledge is available to every researcher. You turn from the card catalog to general and specific reference books of a dozen kinds, and to special indexes and bibliographies on your particular topic.[2] You cull the recent issues of the *Readers' Guide to Periodical*

2. See Readings and Problems, pages 88-89, for a list of helpful sources.

Literature and the bulletins of the *Public Affairs Information Service* under all the appropriate headings you can think of. And, all in all, you find more to read than you can ever cover. But no preparation for any discussion is ever so good as it could be if it lacks an exhilarating search by everyone involved through the riches of the nearest library.

   Oral materials Oral sources include lectures and materials presented by tape, radio, television, and film. In fact, where such materials are available or the schedule of their public presentation known, an enlightenment group with any freedom in the selection of its subject may arrange to make use of them. And day-to-day aspects of any current problem of importance are the very essence of the broadcasts of news analysts. If you are concerned with the world power struggle, you can be alerted by a careful news commentator to the daily shifts of attention and energy of the adversaries.

  But relevant written materials are so much more abundant than oral ones, so much broader in scope and so much more at your command, that you will usually find them of greatest value. No matter how much you might wish that your favorite radio commentator would deal specifically with your discussion topic during the very weeks of your intensive research on it, you will not often be so fortunate. But you can turn to newspaper columnists or news magazines and find there thoughtful analyses on all subjects of current interest.

Combination of sources

  Often, and most effectively, the researcher will use all these types of sources—observations, interviews and surveys, written and oral materials. Aware of the freshness gained by observation, the opportunities for deeper insights offered by the interview, the wide coverage possible through survey, the immense resources of written and oral material—the researcher should choose any and all methods which offer him data and expert opinion on his particular question.

Use of sources

  But the researcher must use his sources with care. All too often an inexperienced researcher makes the mistake of believing that his own thinking should play no part during the gathering of his information, that the thinking process is to come later when he lets his own mind play upon the materials he has collected. But, of course, he has—without thinking of it—relied on his own thinking in a number of ways already: interpreting the meaning of the subject to find headings to look under, choosing the sources to investigate, deciding what sections to use in any particular source, filing some of the information for later use, and so on. To make most dependable use of his sources, he must have three qualities: initiative in finding information, skill in applying tests of credibility, and competence in recording information.

Initiative in finding information

As researcher, you must exhibit both originality and energy in your search for information. With your mind alert to possibilities of useful data in direct observations, in interviews and surveys, and especially in written and oral materials, you must utilize as many of these sources as your time will allow. You should not be contented with one or two sources only, no matter how reliable they seem to be. Even experts differ; witness the differing views you can discover on the dangers of radioactive fallout, the causes of cancer, or the best methods of education.

You should choose to spend the bulk of your time on those sources peculiarly adapted to your question. In almost every case where you have opportunity to do purposeful research, you should probably give your greatest attention to written materials; but in cases involving an immediate, specific, local occurrence you may need to spend a large share of your preparation time in observation and interviews. Whatever the topic, you should energetically pursue every lead you find so that you can make your maximum contribution to the discussion.

As observer, you search out the most propitious circumstances for obtaining the information and arrange to be present; as interviewer, you find the most appropriate persons from whom to obtain the information and arrange conferences; as user of the survey method, you send out to an appropriate sampling of people or institutions the questionnaire most likely to elicit the information; as a collector of written or oral materials, you discover and use the most reliable ones on your subject.

But the requirement of initiative is not exhausted in these preliminary steps; it plays an even more important part in the consequent gleaning of pertinent data and reliable opinion. The researcher who finds unusual but productive angles of observation shows initiative: perhaps he mingles with a crowd of harassed brokers on the floor of the Stock Exchange or he rides the police helicopter hovering above the traffic lanes. In the interview the researcher with initiative notes the phraseology and manner of the expert as well as his comments, quick to see his valuations and interests and to question him further on pertinent points: he notices that the campaign manager again and again apologizes for the present administration's handling of the lake pollution problem and he inquires about possible alternatives.

When the questionnaires are returned, the alert researcher sees relationships among the replies, patterns of information emerging. Knowing the ephemeral nature of oral materials, the pollster with initiative is prepared to jot down the unique idea, the phrase, the anecdote that bears upon his problem. In availing himself of the wealth of written materials, the enterprising researcher is shrewd in recognizing leads that he can track down in other sources: in his investigation of population problems he finds several references to Thomas Malthus and seeks further information on his theories. All these spontaneous and purposeful graspings of opportunity ask a high order of initiative from the researcher.

Skill in applying tests of credibility

In preparing your topic, you face the important task of assessing the believability of the information you uncover. Since you will be using these facts and opinions as foundations for your own thinking and offering them as reliable bases for the thinking of others, you must assure yourself as well as you can that they deserve your acceptance. You will need, then, to look attentively at two factors: the *reporting of the information* and the *information* itself. To the extent that the information survives your careful application of relevant tests, you may, with some confidence, use it as a foundation on which to "ground the processes of thought."

Tests of reporting When a researcher obtains facts from some source, he must judge the acceptability of the material by asking at least three questions concerning the person (or organization) doing the reporting: (1) *Was he capable of getting the facts?* Did he have adequate opportunity to observe the phenomenon and the ability to report it intelligently? We all recognize the unreliability of a report on social conditions in a foreign country by a person whose visit lasted only a week. (2) *How biased is the reporter?* In what direction and to what degree may the reporter be prejudiced? We all recognize the unreliability of the statements by a loyal alumnus about conditions in the old days. (3) *How consistent is his report with those of other reporters?* We all recognize the unreliability of a single bystander's report from the scene of a traffic accident.

Opinions must be checked by an additional test: (4) *Is the opinion-giver an expert in the area of which he speaks?* We all recognize a layman's unreliability in interpreting tests he knows little about, such as the Rorschach test for the analysis of personality. Only trained clinical psychologists use the Rorschach test dependably as an instrument of analysis.

Tests of information   But checking should not stop with the credibility of the reporting. Certain tests must be quickly and routinely made of the information itself. If the information is factual, the researcher must ask these questions: (1) *Are the facts clear?* That is, to what extent are they understandable? Are the terms used or the units concerned (in statistics) interpretable? (For example, if statistics reveal that 30% of the sixth-graders in your city achieved IQ scores over 100 as compared to only 2% in another town, is the meaning clear?) (2) *Are the facts up to date?* Are they recent enough to be dependable? (Would a report on a falling United States birth rate, published in 1944, be a useful source in discussing current population trends?) (3) *Are they probably true?* Do they contradict other facts he knows? Do they square with what else he knows of the situation, with what common sense tells him would be the case? (What about an article by a former government intelligence agent stating that "one out of four" Americans is a "Communist or a Communist sympathizer"?)

And if the information consists of opinion, similar tests are necessary but may be rephrased thus: (1) *Is the opinion clear?* (2) *Is it up to date?* (3) *Is it probably sound?* In applying this final test, the researcher will look carefully at the facts presented by the person expressing the opinion, assessing their probable truth and remaining aware that they have been selected with persuasion in mind and that the researcher himself must judge their sufficiency, relevance, and weight.

In summary, information and source should be subjected to the following tests:

Facts

Of person reporting
1. How capable of getting facts?
2. How biased?
3. How consistent with others' reports?

Of information
1. How clear?
2. How up to date?
3. How probably true?

Opinion

Of person reporting
1. How capable of getting facts?
2. How biased?
3. How consistent with others' opinions?
4. How well qualified to offer an expert opinion?

Of information
1. How clear?
2. How up to date?
3. How probably sound?

In the interview the *tests of reporting* must be applied to the person being consulted; and in the use of written, televised, or filmed materials they must be applied to the writer or speaker. And when the researcher himself makes the observations, he should apply the tests frankly to himself and must discount his information to the extent that he falls short.

Let us take an example. Dr. David Dressler (3), writing in *Harper's Magazine,* said: "It will take an entirely new generation of lawyers, trained in a loftier philosophy, to bring a more effective justice into our courts." This is clearly an opinion. Hence, the researcher must analyze (1) Dr. Dressler as the person reporting his opinion, and (2) the opinion as a piece of information. Let us ask the appropriate questions in regard to Dr. Dressler:

1. *How capable of getting facts?* Dr. Dressler "spent twenty years working with lawyers, judges, and young and adult criminals, in research and social-service posts in Chicago and New York. He was executive director of the New York State Division of Parole. . . ." Estimate of credibility: Clearly, *high.*

2. *How biased?* He is now "professor of sociology at Long Beach State College in California." Estimate of credibility: He would perhaps be biased in the direction of the social aspect of the law and somewhat disenchanted with the pace of trials and the diversionary tactics of certain lawyers. Such a bias, though, would not seem to impair his judgment.

3. *How consistent with others' reports?* Estimate of credibility: It would take careful reading of a number of sources before the researcher could answer this question. Even if it turned out that Dr. Dressler alone of all those examined held this precise opinion, the opinion would merit some consideration because of his experience. In such a case the researcher would know, however, that his use of this opinion must be tentative indeed.

4. *How well qualified to offer an expert opinion?* He has written "some 150 professional articles" plus two books, *Practice and Theory of Probation and Parole* and *Parole Chief*. Estimate of credibility: These publications demonstrate his long concern with the relationships between courts and criminals, and his experience with lawyers in such cases. He would seem to be well qualified.

Overall judgment: Credible reporting.

Now that we have tested Dr. Dressler as a reporter of opinion, let us ask the three appropriate questions of his statement of opinion considered as a piece of information:

1. *How clear?* Estimate of credibility: The terms "loftier philosophy" and "more effective justice" are perhaps not clear in themselves but are intelligible from the remainder of the article. (The researcher must provide definitions for such terms if he reports the opinion to the group in the discussion.) Therefore, *acceptable.*

2. *How up to date?* Estimate of credibility: How recent was the experience out of which he has formed his opinion, the researcher must ask. He does not find Dr. Dressler listed either in *Who's Who in America* or in *Who's Who in American Education,* but a look at the catalog of Long Beach State College shows him to have taken a position there in 1953. Since the opinion was published in 1961, the researcher must ask himself whether enough changes would have occurred in this eight-year span to have invalidated Dr. Dressler's observations made while working directly with the courts, and, even if so, whether he would not have maintained his interest in such matters while serving as professor of sociology. And the researcher must ask himself a further question: How long after Dr. Dressler expressed this opinion am I now using it? And, again, have enough significant changes in court practices occurred since this 1961 publication that this opinion would no longer reflect the present situation? Although aware of these conditions, the researcher would probably be justified in considering Dressler's opinion sufficiently up to date and, therefore, *acceptable.*

3. *How probably true?* Estimate of credibility: The researcher would have to know what results had been effected by efforts of social reformers, newspaper commentaries, public opinion, and so forth, to judge how pervasive the reform must be. But it does not seem out of line with human nature that only such a method could institute a change that would be thoroughgoing. Therefore, *acceptable.*

Overall judgment: *Credible information.*

Let us be clear about the use of these tests. They do not necessarily prove the information invalid, even if the item or the testifier does not satisfy them fully; rather, they raise questions, induce an attitude of wariness, and give reason for seeking further. For example, all persons have biases; thus, any person's statement must be looked at *in terms of* his bias, but not necessarily thrown out because of it. A fact may not seem consistent with what else the researcher knows about the situation but is not therefore necessarily untrue, only open to question. It does behoove the researcher, however, to depend most strongly upon materials which survive these tests with fewest doubts.

Competence in recording information

Despite his care in obtaining information from good sources and in testing it appropriately, the researcher may himself introduce error into his information if he has not developed high competency in recording data accurately.

Abstracting The researcher's first task lies in effective abstracting. As he selects the information he will record for use in the discussion, he needs to avoid such errors as overstating the fact or opinion, changing its focus or intent, omitting a relevant qualification or condition, altering the tone or implication by separation from its context. Suppose that you are discussing the problem of high automobile insurance rates and have read an article making the claim that exaggeration of whiplash injuries by dishonest doctor-lawyer teams is "one of the reasons for ever-climbing insurance rates." If you let the notes you take suggest to you later that this dishonest practice is said to be *the one cause,* you are overstating the opinion of a writer who had himself recognized a complex of causes. Suppose, on the other hand, that you are discussing the plight of agriculture in the American economy and have discovered material showing how changed the life of the farmer's wife of today is—no rough, wood-stove hands for her. If your notes suggest that she is no longer able to face the rigors of country life, you are destroying the intent of an author whose purpose was to show how an 85% rise in her standard of living since 1940 has altered her domestic habits.

Suppose that you are to participate in an enlightenment group that plans to consider in a series of meetings the broad question: *How can we best guide the physical transformation of our country?* You have read August Heckscher's *The Public Happiness* and are struck with his plea for community works that are enduring and much loved. You are introducing distortion, however, if you record in your notes his idea that calling for more public spending is easy but neglect to add his qualification that it is hard to know how best to spend public funds. And, finally, suppose that you and your group are going to talk about the invasion of personal privacy today and you have found John Ciardi (4) saying in his "A Public Answer": "Among the evidences of my liberation, I cite before all others my ability to toss mail into the wastebasket with no trace of a qualm." Although you may think that abuse of the mails is one of the facets of the invasion of privacy, you would distort Mr. Ciardi's meaning if you failed to note that this sentence appears in an article reasserting his rights as the editor of a poetry column.

Recording The researcher's second task lies in effective recording. The notes you take must indicate clearly all that you need to know about the information you have gathered. Which parts did you quote and which ones did you paraphrase or summarize? Careful use of quotation marks will give you the answer. What is the full name of the author or speaker and who, after all, is he? In what issue (and on what page) of what magazine, in what book (published when), or in what speech or discussion (given where and when), did he say this? You must be able to know precisely—*what* he said, *where* and *when* he said it, and *who* he is—in order to have dependable information for a discussion.

Synthesis of suggestions

1. Use personal experience but supplement it with purposeful research whenever possible.

2. Be energetic and imaginative in discovering as many sources of information as your time allows.

3. Select and concentrate upon the best materials from these sources.

4. Gather both facts and expert opinions.

5. Read or listen to find dependable information instead of to bolster a previously formed opinion.

6. Apply faithfully the tests of credibility of reporting and of information.

7. When experts differ, read with special care and employ the tests of credibility carefully.

8. Avoid distorting the author's meaning when you abstract. ·

9. Quote accurately and indicate quoted material carefully in your records.

10. Record fully the name of the source, the qualifications of the author, the place and the date.

Summary

The discusser supplements his personal experience, whenever possible, with purposeful research. He seeks two types of information: facts *and* expert opinions. *His major sources of information are of these kinds: observations, interviews and surveys, written and oral materials. To make dependable use of these sources, he must have initiative in finding information, skill in applying tests of credibility, and competence in recording information.*

References

(1) John Stuart Mill, *A System of Logic* (New York: Harpers, 1900), 8th ed., Book III, Chapter VII, p. 272.

(2) H. Ernest Hunt, *Constructive Thinking* (London: W. Foulsham and Co., 1954), p. 33.

(3) David Dressler, "Trial by Combat in American Courts," *Harper's Magazine,* 222 (April 1961), 36.

(4) John Ciardi, "A Public Answer," *Saturday Review,* 45 (August 4, 1962), 11.

Readings and problems

1. Hold a class discussion on a selected paragraph of a news story from a current issue of *Newsweek, Time,* or *U. S. News and World Report.* Consider each sentence to determine whether it states a *fact* or an *opinion.* You may find in some sentences that one part is fact and another opinion, and in others that a term employed in the statement of a fact in itself implies a judgment. (Remember that the purpose of the discussion is to discover the *nature* of the statements rather than to decide whether they are true or false, sound or unsound.)

      2.   Discover and characterize the particular contribution each of the following reference guides can make to the process of gathering information:

Agricultural Index
Applied Science and Technology Index
Art Index
Bibliographic Index
Biography Index
Business Periodicals Index
Cumulative Book Index
Education Index
Engineering Index
Essay and General Literature Index
Facts on File
Index to Legal Periodicals
International Index
London Times Index
Monthly Checklist of State Publications
National Geographic Index
New York Times Index
Psychological Abstracts
Public Affairs Information Service
Readers' Guide to Periodical Literature
Subject Index to Periodicals
Technical Book Review Index
U.S. Superintendent of Documents, Monthly Catalog of United States Government Publications
Vertical File Index

      3.   Locate in your library each of the following special encyclopedias and seek out its possible contributions to the gathering of information for discussions:

Columbia Dictionary of Modern European Literature, ed. H. E. Smith, 1947.
Dictionary of American Biography, ed. Allen Johnson and Dumas Malone, 1928-1958.

Encyclopedia of American History, ed. R. B. Morris, 1961.
Encyclopedia of Educational Research, ed. C. W. Harris, 1960.
Encyclopedia of the Social Sciences, eds. E. R. A. Seligman and A. Johnson, 1930-1935.
An Encyclopedia of World History, ed. W. L. Langer, 1952.
Ferm, Vergilius. *An Encyclopedia of Religion,* 1945.
Graham, Irvin. *Encyclopedia of Advertising,* 1952.
The Statesman's Year-Book, 1962-1963 (annual), ed. S. H. Steinberg.
Theimer, Walter. *An Encyclopedia of Modern World Politics,* 1950.

    4. The report of the President's Commission on National Goals, entitled *Goals for Americans* (Englewood Cliffs, New Jersey: Prentice-Hall, 1960), is "designed to encourage informed discussion by the American public." The members of the Commission were: Henry M. Wriston; Frank Pace, Jr.; Erwin D. Canham; James B. Conant; Colgate W. Darden, Jr.; Crawford H. Greenewalt; Alfred M. Gruenther; Learned Hand; Clark Kerr; James R. Killian, Jr.; George Meany.

A Investigate the training and career experience of these men; consult recent editions of biographical dictionaries such as these:
American Men of Science
Chambers's Biographical Dictionary
Current Biography
Directory of American Scholars
International Who's Who
Leaders in Education
Webster's Biographical Dictionary
Who's Who in America
Who's Who in American Education

B Consider each man on the tests of *reporting opinion* to see how satisfactory to you this make-up of a commission for crystallizing our national goals is.

C Read the report (pages 1-23) to see the statement upon which these men agreed; then consult the additional statements made by six of them, setting forth their dissent from certain explanations or implications of the report (pages 24-31). Would you have predicted these exceptions from what you have learned of the members' training and career experience?

    5. Prepare by class discussion a listing of questions that one of the members could ask were he to interview the president of an advertising agency for information on the subject:

How has increased leisure time affected the United States economy?

6. Discuss the applicability of John Stuart Mill's statement in his essay *On Liberty* to the process of gathering information for discussion:

> The greatest orator, save one, of antiquity, has left it on record that he always studied his adversary's case with as great, if not with still greater, intensity than even his own. What Cicero practised as the means of forensic success, requires to be imitated by all who study any subject in order to arrive at the truth. He who knows only his own side of the case, knows little of that. His reasons may be good, and no one may have been able to refute them. But if he is equally unable to refute the reasons on the opposite side; if he does not so much as know what they are, he has no ground for preferring either opinion. The rational position for him would be suspension of judgment, and unless he contents himself with that, he is either led by authority, or adopts, like the generality of the world, the side to which he feels most inclination.

7. List commonly held beliefs about several of the following classes of people: ministers' children, union officials, college professors, poets, astronauts, psychiatrists, spinsters, women drivers, traffic officers, jazz musicians, door-to-door salesmen. Now take a belief you have about one of these classes; think of personal experiences with *individuals* of this class. Be careful to bring in any experiences that are contrary to your belief. Does your personal experience really bear out your belief? If not, how do you explain the fact that some individuals don't fit your preconceived idea about the class? How does this realization tend to modify your belief? What does this experience suggest about attitudes necessary in gathering information?[3]

8. For each of a half dozen of the following topics, list an opinion you hold rather strongly, an opinion upon

3. Modified from a problem suggested in William G. Leary and James S. Smith, *Think Before You Write* (New York: Harcourt, Brace and Co., 1951), pp. 62-63.

which you would have to "suspend judgment" if you were to engage in objective research on the topic.

Labor unions
Government control
UNESCO
Fluoridation
Television standards
Modern art
Brainstorming
Nuclear testing
Beatniks
Working mothers
Daughters of the American Revolution
Exploration of outer space
Communist threat in the United States
Madison Avenue
Loyalty oaths
Teachers' colleges
Right to Work Laws
College fraternities
Federal aid to parochial schools
Insecticides

9. Prepare bibliography cards on the discussion question: *What makes a good newspaper?* Use the forms suggested below and on the following page:

```
(Card cat. no.)


            Author (last name first)
            Book title
            Place of pub.: Pub. co., year
```

```
(Card cat. no.)


            Author (last name first)
            "Article title"
            Magazine, Vol.: pages, date
```

10. Record on note cards information for a discussion on the question: *What is the truth about UNESCO?* Provide a brief relevant head, and use quotation marks and ellipses accurately. Use the form suggested below:

```
Publications       George N. Shuster, "The Trials and
                   Triumphs of UNESCO," Sat. Rev., XLV
                   (Feb. 24, 1962), 22

    Continued the publishing done by the League of Na-
tions International Institute of Intellectual Coopera-
tion "with an increasing measure of success . . . in
the fields of bibliography, museum direction, educa-
tional planning and statistics, the social and the
natural sciences, and art reproduction."
```

Observe these methods:

A If you prepare more than two cards from a single source, make a bibliography card. On the remaining note cards, then, abbreviate the source notation, for example: Shuster, SR, 22.

B On the back of the bibliography card (if you prepare one) or the note card, put the information about the author; in this case, you would indicate that Dr. Shuster is United States Representative to the UNESCO Executive Board.

11. Hold a class discussion on the following account of information gathering in the work of a newspaper reporter:

Mike Gorman became a municipal reporter on *The Daily Oklahoman* in 1946. When Publisher Gaylord received a complaint about conditions in the largest mental hospital in the state from an eminent bishop who had visited a patient there, he sent Gorman to do a factual article on the food, physical conditions, treatment of the patients, etc. The reporter saw the crowdedness and filth of the wards, the throwing about of food in the dining halls for psychotic women, the squalid quarters for seniles; he took twenty pages of notes, but the utter horror of it all so shattered him that writing the story seemed impossible.

So he asked to be assigned to do research on all the mental hospitals in the state. With a photographer he spent a couple of weeks doing just that, gathering an enormous stack of detailed notes.

When he had worked a full day trying in vain to get a simple outline from these crowding impressions, he asked to have time to survey the literature, for he was facing questions he couldn't answer, such as: How many doctors *should* 3000 patients have? For another two weeks he dug into all the psychiatric materials he could put his hands on, he wired the national associations for more, and spent hours talking with the city's top psychiatrist. He read mountains of material, he assembled standards, then he catalogued ten major and twenty-two important additional deficiencies in the mental institutions of Oklahoma.

The bishop had stumbled upon a problem; the newspaper had sent its reporter to gather information on the subject. And Mike Gorman had put these questions to himself in turn: What is the full picture of the situation in this institution, the depth and extent of the misery here? Then:

Is this typical of the other institutions as well? Then: How serious are these conditions so starkly revealed, that is, how far below standard are they? He began a painstaking first-hand study of the situation, turned to interviewing experts to clarify obscurities in philosophy and policy, and probed the literature to develop a scale of judgment.

In the end Mike Gorman came out with eighty pages of searing copy and thirty-five pictures; printed in *The Daily Oklahoman*, they startled the entire state into a clean-up campaign which revolutionized its system for caring for the mentally ill. Information, gathered with persistence and organized with intelligence, had furnished the initial motivation for the job.[4]

4. Summarized from Mike Gorman, "Oklahoma Attacks Its Snake Pits," *Reader's Digest*, 53 (September 1948), 139-160.

Chapter five

HANDLING

LINES OF

REASONING

In 1953 the late Lyman Bryson, lecturing at Madison, Wisconsin, on "Teaching Ourselves to be Free," said:

> We are embarked in the United States, fully now after a lot of beginnings, on the attempt to build a civilization in which as many as possible of our problems will be solved by reason. Not by authority. . . . Or by fear. Or merely by precedent. By reason. By each of us using what he has of the power to think.

As a participant in group discussion you must utilize fully your "power to think." While you gather ample facts and opinions to provide a basis for your thinking on the subject, you must carefully judge their credibility.[1] When you have assured yourself that your information is fairly complete and reliable, you are ready to *reason* from it, to organize it logically and see what inferences can reasonably be drawn. To handle this crucial part of your preparation successfully, you will need to be familiar with the principal forms of reasoning and the logical tests that apply to each. The various forms of reasoning fall under two major categories—inductive and deductive.

Forms of reasoning

Inductive reasoning

Inductive reasoning is that mode of inference in which one or more known instances of a certain class are regarded as data from which to infer a conclusion concerning other, but lesser known, members of the same class. When the data furnish the basis for a conclusion concerning many or all additional members of the class, we are said to reason by *generalization;* when a single instance serves as the datum from which we infer the character of another, a lesser known, member of the class, we reason by *analogy;* when varied pieces of information about a situation are to be accounted for, we propose a *hypothesis* that explains them as well as possible.

In all these forms of inference, a portion of relevant data remains unexamined; therefore, the inductive process cannot guarantee *certainty,* but, if it is properly used, it can assure a high degree of

1. Tests for facts and expert opinions were presented in Chapter 4, pages 82-83.

probability. The importance of the inductive method in the rise of modern science and technology is widely recognized; the accumulation of data leads to generalizations, analogies, or hypotheses, which then serve as bases for further data-gathering efforts and consequent support, rejection, or modification of the earlier inferences.

Generalization When we need to establish something about many or all members of a class, the methods we adopt are determined by practical limitations.[2] If the class is relatively small or methods of examining it are comprehensive, we may be able to examine each one of the members and hence make a factual description. For example, if we are interested in the dietary habits of an Amazonian tribe numbering fifty-three persons, we may be able to gather data on every member; or, if we are interested in the economic levels in the United States population, we may obtain full statistics from the Internal Revenue Service. In such situations we merely summarize or describe factual data about a fully examined class and do not use inference at all. We *generalize* only when we take a *part* of a class to be typical of the *whole*. A medical researcher, for example, must of necessity draw inferences about all muscular dystrophy patients by examining only some of them, since it would be physically impossible to examine all such cases.

In arriving at a sound generalization—that is, in reasoning from "some" to "more" or from "some" to "all"—the reasoner must keep these tests in mind:[3]

1. *Are the instances typical?* The instances from which the generalization is drawn should be typical of the class as a whole. If one is making a generalization about the quality of television in the United States, for example, his evidence should not be confined to programs presented by one network or on one day of the week. The supporting data should include samples from different networks, from different times of the day and week, and from different types of programs. In dealing with large classes, one should take care to see that the samples reflect whatever differences exist within the class. In general-

2. An interesting and well-illustrated explanation of what comprises a "fair sample" for an induction appears in *An Introduction to Logic and Scientific Method* by Morris R. Cohen and Ernest Nagel (New York: Harcourt, Brace and Company, 1934), pp. 279-284.

3. It is presumed that he will also check the accuracy of his data about the instances; the same presumption is made in the explanations of analogy, hypothesis, and causal relations in the pages that follow.

izing about the attitudes of Americans toward foreign aid, for instance, it would be a mistake to weigh the opinions of farmers as heavily as those of urban dwellers, since the former are a minority in the total United States population. Likewise, a generalization would be faulty if it gave disproportionate weight to the views of doctors, businessmen, ministers, or any other group not representative of the population as a whole. To ensure that his examples are typical, the reasoner must take care that they provide a *representative* sampling of the whole group.

2. *Is the number of examined instances sufficient?* Obviously, generalizations become more probable the more nearly they approach 100 per cent direct examination of the members of a class. But when practical limitations make this approach impossible, the reasoner must judge what constitutes a sufficient number of instances from which to generalize. This clearly depends upon the nature of the phenomena under investigation; the members of certain classes are more nearly uniform than are the members of others. If an experimenter observes that a glass of fresh water begins to freeze at temperature 32° F. at sea level, he may be reasonably sure that its behavior is representative of other unexamined water under the same conditions; he assumes uniformity in inorganic matter. If he examines the eating preferences of deer, he must keep in mind that the variability in organic matter is much greater. If he has offered seventy deer tomatoes and found that all refused to eat them, the probability that the seventy-first deer would also refuse is not so great as the probability that a second glass of water would freeze, for deer are subject to genetic and environmental influences which are irrelevant to the behavior of the water. Even greater variables are present in man, the most complex animal of all. Although two or three instances might suffice to establish that water freezes or tennis balls drop, they are not sufficient to establish that women are poor drivers, scientists are atheists, or Italians have musical talent. Before deciding on a sufficient amount of data from which to generalize, the reasoner must weigh any negative instances he discovers and thus assess the probable homogeneity of the class to which the data belong. Two glasses of water may be sufficient, or seventy deer, or one thousand people. The fundamental question is: *What degree of uniformity exists in this class?*

The following example from a student discussion on Latin-American politics, as of November 1962, illustrates how knowledge of sound reasoning by generalization can help to prevent fallacious conclusions:

Makes a generaliza-
tion and offers data
to support it

Robert Werner Could it be that recent events in Latin America indicate that Communism is making tremendous inroads all over the area? Look at Cuba, for instance, and British Guiana, and the frequent outbreaks of violence in Venezuela.

Points out sweeping
generalization based
on too few instances

Sherry Sagan Yes, no one can doubt that Marxist philosophy has made headway in those cases, but Latin America is a pretty large area. I mean, aren't our examples a fairly small propor- tion of the sentiments of all Latin-American countries?

Questions the
typicality of the
instances

Richard Hicks Besides, in Cuba don't we have an example of a genuine revolutionary movement —and I think no one will defend the Batista regime—being usurped by a small clique of Marxists? And isn't the same true in British Guiana? And in Venezuela, does the violence represent the sentiments of most Venezuelans or only of a small Communist clique?

Vera Smith And what about some of the other Latin-American countries? There is cer- tainly a hard-core Marxist group in Mexico, for instance, or Brazil, but can we really say that they represent the attitudes of most Mexicans or Brazilians, or are they only a sort of rallying point for a restless minority? Yes, they demonstrate, and often violently, but is this proof that Com- munism is making headway? In fact, doesn't the unanimous support by the OAS of the recent United States stand on Cuban missiles indicate a stiffening resistance to Communism?

Also questions typi-
cality of instances
and points out a
negative instance

Asks about modifying
the generalization

Leader The question, then, seems to be, How much progress is Communism making in Latin America?

Suggests a
modification

Robert Well, could we say, perhaps, that as- sertions of Communist sympathy are becoming more blatant in some parts of Latin America? And that these reflect increased Communist strength?

Suggests further
modification

Richard In the countries we named, that is, which are not necessarily typical of all Latin America?

Robert Yes, at least in Cuba, British Guiana, and Venezuela.

Analogy When we use a single known member of a class as a basis from which to draw a conclusion about a less well-known member of the same class, we reason analogically.[4] Like other forms of inductive reasoning, analogy offers only greater or less probability, not certainty. Because no two instances of a phenomenon, however similar they may be, are ever exactly alike in all respects, we cannot be entirely sure that what is true of the first will also be true of the second. For example, if one concluded, as many persons did, that John Kennedy would be defeated in 1960 as Al Smith was in 1928, he would have been reasoning from the most tenuous kind of analogy: Kennedy is a Catholic as was Smith. For while it is true that the instances were similar in this one respect, it is also true that in other and equally important respects they were highly dissimilar. Not only did the men themselves differ in personality, appearance, age, and background, but the circumstances under which they ran—the state of world and national affairs, the temper of the people, the issues of the campaigns, and so forth—were not at all the same.

Although an analogy can never yield a certain conclusion, the probability of the inference is increased as the analogy approaches the conditions specified in the following tests:

1. *Are the instances similar in significant respects?* Suppose that one were to attempt to predict the industrial potential of one community by comparing the community with another. He might find that Community A is in the Midwest, that it occupies twenty square miles, that it is built along a lake, that ten years ago it had ten thousand inhabitants, that its population was predominantly Caucasian, and that it tripled in population and industrial development in ten years. He might find that Community B today is identical with

4. Some writers on logic use the term *parallel case* rather than *analogy* when the comparison is drawn between instances of the same kind; in other words, they reserve the term *analogy* for figurative comparisons. In this textbook, however, both literal and figurative comparisons are considered analogies.

William James pointed out in the second volume of his *Principles of Psychology* (New York: Holt and Co., 1890), p. 363, that "Men, taken historically, reason by analogy long before they have learned to reason by abstract characters." We recall that the ancients found it impossible to measure the height of a pyramid until Thales measured its shadow at the very moment when he saw that a man and his shadow were equal in length. Knowing the relationship of the man and his shadow, he reasoned to a similar relationship of pyramid and shadow, and acted upon his inference.

Community A as it was ten years ago in each of these respects except the last, and so he might infer that Community B, too, will soon triple in population and industry. Yet this would be an extremely questionable inference, because the points of similarity are not clearly pertinent to the effect observed in A. The analogy would have a higher probability if he had considered factors relevant to industrial growth, such as terrain, resources, transportation, proximity to markets, and education of populace.

2. *In how many specific respects does the analogy hold?* In the example given above, suppose that the similarities between B and A as it was ten years ago are significant. The next question would be: *In how many ways* are they similar? If the two communities are similar only in terrain and educational level, the analogy is not close enough to warrant equating their potential. But if B resembles A in a dozen or more significant respects, the probability that it can reproduce A's industrial growth becomes higher. That is, when the factors which, in reciprocal effect on each other and taken together, produced the result noted in A are observed in similar confluence in B, one may with some confidence predict a similar result in B.

        Hypothesis In generalizing, the reasoner often makes only a descriptive statement about a class of things, based on his information about *some* of the members of that class: "Most narcotics addicts have personality defects"; "Many Americans are functional illiterates"; "Some Latin-American countries are dictatorships." In hypothesizing, on the other hand, he makes a statement, usually explanatory, to account for the various circumstances that he has found—that is, to suggest the probable cause of the circumstances.[5] In other words, after examining a number of particular items of information, he attempts to discover a general principle that will explain them all. For example, in preparing for a discussion on juvenile delinquency in your city, you may collect data—examples of burglary, theft, and assault; statistics on arrests; information on use of narcotics and alcohol—facts indicating that delinquency is

---

5. Beardsley clarifies the distinction between the generalization and the hypothesis in this way: "Whereas generalizations are, so to speak, 'horizontal' conclusions, hypotheses are 'vertical.' The generalization goes beyond the evidence to other things of the same kind; the hypothesis makes a leap to something of a different kind."—Monroe C. Beardsley, *Practical Logic* (New York: Prentice-Hall, Inc., 1950), p. 217.

particularly high in two areas.[6] To account for this abnormally high incidence, you might formulate several explanatory hypotheses—for example, that the youth in these two areas lack parental guidance, that they are rebelling against poverty, that they have few job opportunities, or that they are just naturally "wild." The next step would be to test these alternative hypotheses carefully and to determine which one (or which combination of them) provides the most reasonable and convincing explanation. To do this, you should ask yourself these questions:

1. *Does the hypothesis account for all the data?* A good hypothesis should provide an explanation for all, or nearly all, the information obtained. Suppose that approximately half of the students in your dormitory developed violent stomach upsets one evening. In attempting to account for this, you might consider several alternative hypotheses, such as a sudden epidemic of flu, food poisoning, or contaminated water. You would need to investigate further to determine which hypothesis accounted for the most instances. If you found that there were few occurrences of flu in other campus dormitories, that other residences used the same source of water with no ill effects, but that all of the stricken students had eaten dinner in the dining hall, food poisoning might seem the best hypothesis. The next step would be to determine what particular item on the menu was responsible by discovering which one all or most of those sick had eaten, and, conversely, which food had not been eaten by those showing no ill effects.

2. *Is the hypothesis simpler and more direct than any other explanation?* When there are alternative hypotheses, either of which might account for the phenomenon, the hypothesis which gives the simpler and more direct explanation is generally to be preferred. Suppose an archaeologist were to find, in the course of excavations in Mexico, a Toltec figure mounted on a clay horse. The design and materials of the figure are typical of many others known to date back to pre-Conquest times. Yet horses were unknown in Mexico until the

6. Larrabee characterizes such preliminary classification of findings—that is, that the delinquency is particularly high in two areas—as a form of hypothesis, specifically a *descriptive* hypothesis. But he suggests that we soon move beyond these "rudimentary groupings" of information to ask what it is that accounts for these behaviors or events; we want to know the principles or pattern behind them and thus we try to phrase an *explanatory* hypothesis. See Harold A. Larrabee, *Reliable Knowledge* (Boston: Houghton Mifflin Co., 1945), pp. 168-170.

Spanish Conquest. Hence, two hypotheses suggest themselves: that the sculpture was made after the Conquest by a Toltec descendant, who combined traditional with new forms; or that horses existed in the New World before the Spanish Conquest. Of these hypotheses, the first is to be preferred as more probable because it explains the phenomenon more directly and simply; it requires no additional explanations. The second hypothesis, on the other hand, requires additional hypotheses as to how horses came to the New World in pre-Conquest times and as to what caused them to disappear so entirely that they were unknown to the Indians when the Spanish arrived. The difficulty of establishing these additional hypotheses throws doubt upon the original hypothesis itself.

3. *Does the hypothesis contradict other well-established hypotheses?* Generally speaking, the hypothesis that accords best with previously established hypotheses is the most probable. Sometimes, of course, long accepted explanations turn out to be mistaken in the light of new knowledge, but more often new hypotheses tend to supplement, rather than contradict, already accepted ones. Thus, if one were to find that general intelligence tests given by a certain college to entering students had been notably unsuccessful in predicting college performance, he might hypothesize that intelligence cannot be accurately measured or that intelligence has no relation to academic performance. But both of these explanations contradict hypotheses established by years of experimentation. A more tenable hypothesis would be that the particular tests used by the college were poor ones or that they were improperly administered or interpreted, since useful tests can be, and often are, improperly administered.

4. *Is the hypothesis verifiable?* Since the purpose of a hypothesis is often not only to explain phenomena but to predict their future occurrence, the scientific method concerns itself with those hypotheses that are susceptible of proof. Proof may not be immediately available, but the explanation must be at least potentially verifiable by recourse to data. Thus, former beliefs that insanity was due to such things as possession by devils, evil stars, or supernatural curses have been superseded by the scientific hypothesis that human behavior is determined by a series of antecedent causes in, for example, a person's environment or physiology. The advantage of the more recent hypothesis is that it can be tested and proved or disproved, whereas the earlier could not and therefore left the reasoner exactly where he started—with mere speculation.

The following example demonstrates how sound evaluation of alternative hypotheses proves useful in discussion. The subject under consideration is the possibility of life on other planets:

Pamela Grant If there is life on other planets, since their physical conditions are probably different from ours, I suppose we must expect it to differ from ours.

William Krutch Unless all of life in the universe has a single source. Major Keyhoe, in a book called *Flying Saucers* and in several others he has written, speculates that human beings on Earth may be the descendants of space explorers who landed here 10,000 or so years ago.

Suggests a hypothesis

James Brule But what about the remains of prehistoric man that radiocarbon dating places much earlier than that? And does he claim they settled in areas as remote as Java and South Africa? Do you know about that, Bill?

Asks whether the hypothesis accounts for all known data

William He doesn't go into that. He simply suggests that intelligent life on this planet had its source on another.

Barbara Wilson What about the Darwinian theory that man evolved from lower forms of life? Hasn't that been widely accepted by modern biologists? And besides, didn't Darwin substantiate his beliefs with fossil evidence and structural resemblances?

Points out that the hypothesis contradicts a well-established theory

James Yes, if we accept Keyhoe's hypothesis, wouldn't the structural similarities between man and the higher apes—well, in fact, between man and mammals in general—depend on the most unlikely coincidence? I mean, then we have to assume that—independently in the universe—two remarkably similar forms of life arose: vertebrate, lunged, live-bearing, four-limbed, two-eyed —Doesn't it seem more logical to believe that man and mammals have these similarities because they have a common origin?

Questions the simplicity of the hypothesis

Leader In other words, we're saying that it's difficult to reconcile Keyhoe's hypothesis of the independent origin of man with man's resemblance to other living species?

James   These similarities seem to suggest that.

William   Well, although Keyhoe doesn't say so definitely, perhaps he means that the space explorers brought these other species with them; that is, maybe they all had a common origin, but not on this planet?

Pamela   Well, let's see—then we'd have to assume that these explorers engaged in a huge airlift, bringing over bovines, felines, reptiles, birds and all that, and then suddenly disappeared, leaving no trace behind. And then, too, think of how we can follow—through remains—the evolution of horses, birds, reptiles, and so forth; the explorers would have had to bring the first ones *much* more than 10,000 years ago.

Barbara   Well, might it have been longer ago? Maybe the humans were destroyed by some epidemic or a war.

James   But then, with our advanced methods of investigation, wouldn't we have found some trace of them? I mean, surely they would have built homes, left records, exploited resources, and so forth, but we've found no evidence of this.

Leader   Are we saying, then, that this is an interesting speculation—that all life in the universe has a common origin—but that no evidence supports it?

Others   Yes. It raises lots of difficulties. Doesn't seem too probable.

Again questions the simplicity of the hypothesis

Suggests that no verifying evidence exists

Causal relations   Just as we often turn to a case we think comparable to help us formulate a hypothesis about the relationships in a new set of phenomena, so we often call to mind for the same purpose generalizations about *why things happen*. Such generalizations are essential if we are to understand and control our environment; hence, we collect evidence and try to establish generalizations about cause and effect relations. If we want to decrease tooth decay (effect), we must first develop generalizations about its causes, so that we can control or eliminate the causes. If we are considering widespread use of DDT (cause), we must first collect evidence as to what effects we may expect so that we can decide whether to initiate the use of DDT.

In attempting to predict or explain cause-effect relationships, we try to discover what events or conditions are *regularly* associated. To assume that one event causes another simply because the first event precedes the second, and to assume this without testing the regularity with which the two events are associated, is faulty reasoning. Yet we often hear arguments such as these: "After he became president, the company went bankrupt, so he must be a poor manager"; "He didn't become an alcoholic until after his marriage, so his wife must have driven him to it." In each case the sole basis for asserting a causal connection is that one event preceded another. But a closer look at each statement reveals the inadequacy of such reasoning.

Suppose that we check up on the company president's previous record and find that he has a creditable record with other companies; in other words, there is evidence that his presence is not regularly associated with business losses. This should lead us to question the alleged causal relationship. Suppose we discover further that the company was in serious financial trouble before the new president took over. Clearly we must infer that causes other than the new president's policies led to the bankruptcy.

Likewise, in the case of the alcoholic and his wife, further investigation might reveal that, although he was not an alcoholic before marriage, he was regularly drinking heavily or that he regularly reacted to stress by getting drunk. We might also discover that after marriage he was subjected to financial stress or was passed over for promotion or experienced the death of a parent or was exposed to a combination of unusual pressures. Thus, to designate the wife as the sole cause or even one of several causes might be fallacious.

In testing causal reasoning, one should ask these questions:

1. *Is this effect always preceded by this cause?* If not, how often (rarely, occasionally, frequently) is the "cause" absent? How can these absences be accounted for?

2. *Are there occasions when this cause is not followed by this effect?* If so, how often does this situation occur and how can it be accounted for?

3. *Do the supposed cause and effect correspond in intensity?* That is, when the causal factor is more severe, is the effect also more severe? And when the causal factor is slight, is the effect also slight?

4. *Is the cause sufficient to produce the effect?* Or, are additional causes needed to produce the effect? A *necessary cause* is one in

whose *absence* the effect *cannot* occur. For example, today a man cannot become a distinguished astronomer if he lacks the rudiments of physical science; a nation cannot have a high standard of living if its population is largely illiterate. A *sufficient cause* is one in whose *presence* the effect *must* occur. Thus, if the assets of a country do not increase, but more money is printed, inflation must occur; if more automobiles are driven and no new roads are built, traffic congestion must increase. The danger of confusing these two types of causes is clear: a sufficient cause may involve several necessary causes. Although widespread literacy is necessary to an increased standard of living, it may not be sufficient in itself; other factors, like industrialization, stable government, capital surplus may also be essential. Similarly, although more traffic on already inadequate roads may be sufficient to produce traffic congestion, construction of new roads may not be all that is necessary to alleviate congestion: perhaps controlling such factors as the number of cars and their speed may also be necessary.

Deductive reasoning

Deductive reasoning proceeds from certain generalizations (stated or implied premises) to the particular conclusion that their acceptance makes necessary. Unlike induction, deduction gives us not probability but certainty; that is, if we accept the premises as established truths, we must necessarily accept the conclusions which the premises imply. The form in which deductive reasoning is characteristically couched is called the syllogism. The three major syllogistic types are *categorical, conditional,* and *disjunctive.*

       Categorical syllogism Every categorical syllogism proceeds from two premises—major and minor—to a conclusion. If the conclusion follows logically from the premises, the syllogism is *valid;* if not, it is *invalid.*[7] Validity, however, is not a guarantee of *truth.* A conclusion may be valid and yet untrue, depending on the truth of the premises. Consider these two examples:

All things that constitute a health hazard and have no beneficial effects should be eliminated.

7. Beardsley's book on logic gives explanations of the necessary arrangements of *major, minor,* and *middle* terms for valid syllogisms and uses Venn diagrams to illustrate how to check validity graphically. See Chapter X, "Analyzing Syllogisms" in *Practical Logic.*

Water pollution constitutes a health hazard and has no beneficial
effects.
Therefore, water pollution should be eliminated.

All things that increase unemployment should be eliminated.
Automation increases unemployment.
Therefore, automation should be eliminated.

Let us first test the *truth* of the premises. In the first argument,
we can readily admit that health hazards are undesirable and further
that they are tolerable only (as in the case of drugs, sharp objects,
and so forth) if they have some beneficial effects. But obviously if
they have *no* beneficial effects, they are not tolerable. So the major
(most comprehensive) premise is true (or, at least, highly probable,
since the inductive method does not produce certainty). We next
consider the minor premise and find it also true: although there is
considerable evidence that water pollution endangers health, there is
no evidence that it has any beneficial effects. Thus we find that the
premises in the first argument are *true.*

Now let us look at the second argument. Its major premise (All
things that increase unemployment should be eliminated) is much
simpler—but also much less acceptable. We may agree that unemployment is undesirable, but can we agree that *all* things that increase it
should be eliminated? Changes in season, for example, increase
unemployment in rural areas; efficiency increases unemployment in
previously inefficient industries. The major premise, then, since we
can find negative instances inductively, cannot be universally true.
To be accurate, we must change it to: *Some* things that increase
unemployment should be eliminated. It does not then follow that
automation should be eliminated, since we have not determined
whether it is part of the *some* or not. We can do this by qualifying
the major premise:

All things that increase unemployment and have no beneficial
effects should be eliminated.
Automation increases unemployment and has no beneficial effects.
Therefore, automation should be eliminated.

But now it becomes clear that the *minor* premise is unacceptable, and
the argument again fails to pass the test of truth.

Next we must test the *validity* of the arguments. Clearly, both examples follow the same logical form:

All A (things that . . .) is B (should be eliminated).
C (water pollution/automation) is A (thing that . . .).
Therefore, C (water pollution/automation) is B (should be eliminated).

Ignoring the terms completely and simply following the alphabetical symbols, we see that the conclusion necessarily follows from the premises: if B is true of all instances or examples of A, and C is an instance or example of A, then B is true of C. So the conclusion in both arguments is *valid*. It is now clear that the conclusion in the first argument is sound and acceptable because it is both *true* and *valid;* the conclusion in the second argument, on the other hand, is not sound because, although *valid*, one of its premises is *not true.* In fact, if a premise is faulty, there is no reason to make the second test, that of formal validity of the syllogism.

To test deductive arguments, you will have to develop skill in discovering the *implied* premises or conclusions since full syllogisms are seldom stated. For example, if someone reasons that "The workers helped plan the changes, so they will cooperate in putting them into effect," his underlying syllogism is:

All workers who help plan changes cooperate in putting them into effect. (implied major premise)
These workers helped plan the changes.
Therefore, they will cooperate in putting them into effect.

The problem now is to test the truth of the major premise. Another implied syllogism might follow this form: "All who deny the existence of God are atheists, so Darwin must have been an atheist." Here the implied minor premise—that Darwin denied the existence of God— must be stated and tested for truth.

In dealing with deductive arguments, one must be alert to the underlying syllogism, stated or implied, and he must be prepared to test both its formal logic and the truth of its premises. He must ask:
1. *Are the premises true?*
2. *Does the conclusion necessarily follow from the premises?*

If either test fails, he should reject the inference as unconvincing.[8]

   Conditional syllogism Another syllogistic form is the *if-then* form, called the conditional syllogism. Here the major premise is a hypothetical proposition (If taxes are raised, then purchasing power will decline; if the Premier is planning a trip to Japan, then he will come to the United States). Should the reasoner discover evidence that affirms the *if* part (known as the *antecedent*) of the proposition, his conclusion must accordingly affirm the *then* part (known as the *consequent*).

> If taxes are raised, then purchasing power will decline.
> Taxes will be raised.
> Therefore, purchasing power will decline.

On the other hand, should his data warrant denying the consequent, his conclusion must deny the antecedent.

> If the Premier is planning a trip to Japan, then he will come to the United States.
> He is not coming to the United States.
> Therefore, he is not planning a trip to Japan.

Actually, in these syllogisms the major premise names only *one* condition under which the effect must be expected and does not deny that there may be other conditions which would bring the same result. Thus, a minor premise that either denies the antecedent or affirms the consequent does not produce a certain conclusion.

---

8. There are many excellent books on logic which go into greater detail regarding the ideas suggested here; two in particular are extremely readable: *Thinking to Some Purpose* by L. Susan Stebbing (Harmondsworth, England: Penguin Books, 1939), and *Practical Logic* by Monroe C. Beardsley.

  Stebbing says, for example, on page 159: "People untrained in logic can detect a formal fallacy in a syllogistic argument once the argument is clearly set out. But a fallacious argument . . . may mislead all of us when stated at length in a long book, or when wrapped up with much verbiage, or when combined with appeals to our passionate interests. Some practice in detecting these fallacious modes of reasoning may enable us the more easily to notice them when we are not actively engaged in fallacy hunting."

  Beardsley presents clear explanations and a wealth of examples on both straight thinking and fallacies.

If taxes are raised, then purchasing power will decline.
Taxes will not be raised. (antecedent denied)

From these premises alone it is impossible to determine whether purchasing power will decline, increase, or remain stable, for all we are told in the premise is what will happen *if* taxes are raised. We would need additional information in order to determine how purchasing power might behave if taxes were *not* raised.

If the Premier is planning a trip to Japan, then he will come to the United States.
The Premier is coming to the United States.

No certain conclusion can be drawn here, we see easily, because other conditions might produce this same result; for example, an unexpected international crisis might bring the Premier to our shores.

Therefore, as in all forms of reasoning, you must check both validity and truth:

1. *Are the premises true?*
2. *Does the minor premise either affirm the antecedent or deny the consequent?*

                   Disjunctive syllogism   A third type of syllogism follows the *either-or* form. In this type the nature of the alternatives determines the validity of the conclusion. In the simplest form the alternatives clearly exclude each other:

Either council-mayor governments are more efficient than city-manager governments or they are less so.
Council-mayor governments are not more efficient than city-manager ones.
Therefore, they are less efficient.

This is a syllogism based on mutually exclusive terms, since one cannot be *both* more and less efficient; it thus passes the first test of validity. On the other hand, it is conceivable that an unmentioned alternative exists; that is, that these types of city government are equally efficient. Then the either-or form does not exhaust the alternatives, and denial of one does not allow a valid conclusion affirming the other. Such *incomplete* disjunctions are always invalid: "Unemployment is either unmanageable or nearly so"; "Brazil will go either Communist or Fascist"; "Birth control is either impractical or immoral." Reflection quickly reveals that it is not a matter of A or B, but of A or B or C or D or E or F, or of combinations of them.

Thus, in assessing any disjunctive syllogism, one must ask not only whether the premises are indeed true but whether the alternatives posed in the major premise allow a certain conclusion:

1. *Are the premises true?*
2. *Are the alternatives mutually exclusive?*
3. *Are the alternatives exhaustive?*

The following excerpt illustrates how a knowledge of the principles of deductive logic can be applied to discussion. The subject under consideration is the single-policy question: *Should atmospheric tests of nuclear weapons be discontinued?*

Dale McDonald   Well, many prominent scientists like Bertrand Russell, Albert Schweitzer, and the men connected with the *Bulletin of Atomic Scientists* believe that continued United States testing contributes to a growing biological threat.

Sandra Wills   But that's exactly the Communist line!

Questions the implied syllogism

John Morton   Would we have to assume that they are Communists, though? Communists aren't the *only* ones who feel this way.

Sandra   Well, no, but wouldn't a person have to be either a Communist or a Communist sympathizer to hold such a view?

Questions the disjunction

Paul Ryska   Aren't there other possibilities, though? Couldn't he be a capitalist or a humanitarian or just a concerned parent and still believe that the present level of radioactivity is getting to be dangerous?

Dale   Yes, there could certainly be other motives.

Sandra   Umhm, I suppose so.

Leader   The questions before us, then, seem to be what the tolerable limits of radioactivity are and whether they have been reached.

John   Yes, and it seems that all prominent scientists agree that the level has passed the tolerable limit. So obviously *any* further tests by either side are dangerous.

Questions major premise by citing negative instances

Dale But have they *all* agreed? Teller, for example, says that the present level is not dangerous. And Strauss, the former chairman of the AEC, agrees with him.

Modifies major premise

Paul Besides, is it as simple as that? How about saying that radioactive levels beyond those necessary to maintain our national security are undesirable? Could it be that we should take some risks to avoid greater ones?

Questions usefulness of premise

Sandra Sounds possible, but I wonder how we, as civilians, could judge how much testing is necessary to maintain our security?

Suggests modification of premise

John Could we say, at least, that any raising of radioactivity levels not justified by defense needs is undesirable?

Leader Are we saying, then, that we will define tolerable limits on the basis of our defense needs? Our next question, I suppose, is to examine what our national security actually demands.

Fallacious reasoning

As we have seen, inductive and deductive processes may be used improperly. When this is done, logical fallacies result. But in addition to these logical fallacies, we must be alert for other errors which arise out of the attempt to by-pass logical methods entirely.

Equivocation

Equivocation refers to the use of a word in a double sense. When a term shifts in meaning in the course of a line of reasoning, the result is an irrelevant conclusion. For example, someone might declare, "Communism isn't anything new historically. Look at the communistic societies found in monasteries—they're centuries old!" In the first usage he is referring to the international Communist movement, a political force that emerged in the twentieth century; but in the second he is using the word to refer to an equalitarian economic order with no political aims whatever. Any term introduced into the consideration of a topic must be used in the same sense throughout.

Appeals to emotion

Some statements are designed to persuade listeners or readers *emotionally* rather than *rationally*. Such statements typically rely heavily on emotive language and appeal to passions or prejudices. Sometimes logical arguments contain emotionally charged words, but the totally fallacious argument uses emotion as a *substitute* for reason and thus attempts to evade logical processes altogether. Such arguments often seem convincing to unsophisticated readers or listeners, but since they appeal to man's *irrational* impulses, they should be guarded against because of the dangerous, even disastrous, consequences to which they may lead. One need only recall Adolph Hitler's disquisitions on Aryan superiority to see the potential dangers.

The forms these appeals may take are as varied as the emotions involved, and a complete catalog of them would be impossible. The following, however, are among the most frequent informal fallacies:

1. Argument against the man (argumentum ad hominem) This fallacy is committed when attention is diverted from the line of reasoning to the personality of an individual advocating a particular view. This is not to be confused with a rational testing of his reliability as a source; it must be seen clearly as an attempt to impugn his motives or to focus on irrelevant characteristics: for example, "Smith's arguments for urban renewal cannot be taken seriously; he's just interested in getting more business"; "Nobody who's been divorced twice can have anything useful to say about the rehabilitation of criminals."

2. Appeal to pity (argumentum ad misericordiam) This practice is an attempt to gain support for a view by arousing sympathy or pity for its advocate. A political candidate, for example, may discuss his experiences in World War II rather than his political platform, or a company may defend its practice by asserting that its stockholders are widows, orphans, and "little people."

3. Appeal to the people (argumentum ad populum) This fallacy consists essentially of *crowd pleasing*, attempting to identify oneself (and consequently one's view) with sentiments pleasing to the majority. It generally involves echoing platitudes about helping those less fortunate, about parenthood, individual freedom of belief, or anything else sure of the listeners' favor. As long as these vague sentiments, however praiseworthy, are irrelevant to the question at issue, they have no place in rational thinking.

4. Appeal to authority (*argumentum ad verecundiam*) When someone supports his position by appealing to anything as vague as custom ("We've always done it that way") or introduces an irrelevant authority ("Roger Maris says that Nile cigarettes contain the best tobaccos"), he is relying on emotional effect rather than on reason. Such usage should not be confused with rational use of expert opinion and traditional practices based on reason.

5. Begging the question This fallacy occurs when a question is so worded that it is emotionally "loaded"; that is, the answer is already implicit in the question: "How long can our government tolerate such ruinous deficits?" "Why should we let these so-called neutrals bleed us dry?" Such statements by-pass the necessity of asking whether the current deficits are indeed harmful and whether these nations are neutral and what the advantages of giving them aid might be; furthermore, they attach an emotional charge to the favored answer.

Ideally, of course, no fallacy or other error should go undetected. But how can a discussion participant expect to recognize them all? Perhaps the best preparation is to understand clearly how they differ from logical reasoning and then maintain a general watchfulness in reading and listening. Should you detect one, you should attempt to substitute logical lines of reasoning that will be more useful to the group. In these activities nothing can help you more than a clear understanding of both inductive and deductive forms and much practice in applying tests for judging their validity and acceptability. The tests explained on these preceding pages are summarized below:

Inductive reasoning

Generalization:
1. Are the data about the examined instances accurate?
2. Is the number of these instances sufficient?
3. Are these instances typical?

Analogy:
1. Are the data about the instances accurate?
2. Are the instances similar in significant respects?
3. In how many specific respects does the analogy hold?

Hypothesis:
1. Are the data accurate?
2. Does the hypothesis account for all the data?
3. Is it simpler and more direct than any other explanation?
4. Does the hypothesis contradict other well-established hypotheses?
5. Is the hypothesis verifiable?

Causal relations:
1. Are the data about the observed cause (or effect) accurate?
2. Is this effect always preceded by this cause?
3. Are there occasions when this cause is not followed by this effect?
4. Do the supposed cause and effect correspond in intensity?
5. Is the cause sufficient to produce the effect?

Deductive reasoning

Categorical syllogism
1. Are the premises true?
2. Does the conclusion necessarily follow from the premises?

Conditional syllogism
1. Are the premises true?
2. Does the minor premise either affirm the antecedent or deny the consequent?

Disjunctive syllogism
1. Are the premises true?
2. Are the alternatives mutually exclusive?
3. Are the alternatives exhaustive?

Summary

The two major forms of reasoning are inductive and deductive. Inductive reasoning proceeds from an examination of particulars to a generalization or hypothesis; it involves use of analogy and causal relationships. Deductive reasoning proceeds from premises to a conclusion by means of a categorical, conditional, or disjunctive syllogism. Each of these forms of reasoning may be assessed by applying appropriate tests of form and substance. Violations of the tests reveal logical fallacies; other fallacies include equivocation and various appeals to emotion.

Readings and problems

1. Prepare to explain clearly and exemplify each of the following terms as used in this chapter:

inductive reasoning	disjunctive syllogism
generalization	causal relations
hypothesis	reasoning by analogy
deductive reasoning	logical fallacies
categorical syllogism	equivocation
major premise	appeals to emotion
minor premise	begging the question
conditional syllogism	conclusion
valid	antecedent
invalid	consequent

2. Select a number of recent articles on vital issues of the day by noted newspaper columnists. Prepare to participate in a classroom discussion on the forms of reasoning used in these articles.

3. Listen carefully to reasoning used in lectures, conversations, and presentations on radio and television for examples of the major forms of reasoning illustrated in this chapter.

4. Prepare for class discussion on the forms of reasoning used in the following examples. You will note that the conclusion has been italicized in each example.

1. Mary went to the travel bureau this noon. *She must be planning to take that trip to Quebec after all.*
2. All the representatives from the West are concerned with the public power issue. I haven't met the new Congressman from Oregon, but *I suppose he'll feel this same concern over the problem.*
3. Our neighbor planted a tall young apple tree in his back yard last spring. *In a few years he will likely have all the apples he wants.*
4. The club members are going camping this weekend. I know that Jim and Phil are taking sleeping bags, *so I suppose everyone is.*
5. The medieval armorers solved the problem of mobility. *Our space suit designers should take a lesson from them.*

6. The County sanitation authorities oppose the proposed licensing of mobile soft ice cream and milk shake units. The representatives of the Metropolitan Restaurant Association also oppose the suggested plan. The City Retail Grocers' Association is against the proposal too. Even the police force sees obstacles in the plan. Thus, *it seems that there is widespread opposition to the licensing suggestion.*

7. If the United States reduces its imports of lead and zinc from Mexico, Mexican miners are thrown out of work. We reduced our imports this spring. We can conclude that *Mexican miners have been thrown out of work.*

8. When death rates in a country are reduced, birth rates must go down similarly or a population explosion will occur. In our country the death rate is going down year by year, but not the birth rate; therefore, *a population explosion will occur.*

9. If a boy carries a paper route, he learns a great deal about human relations. John is carrying a paper route, so we may conclude that *he is learning much about human relations.*

10. We can hear the audience inside the hall applauding loudly and vigorously. *They must be enjoying the entertainment very much.*

11. If all the trust areas administered by a member nation of the United Nations Trusteeship Council are given their independence by vote of the General Assembly, that nation retires from the Council. Belgium's last trust territory (Ruandi-Urundi) has been given its independence by the General Assembly. Hence, *Belgium is no longer a member of the Trusteeship Council.*

12. If a modern-day miracle is to be considered news, it must be orbiting. But the "Mont Blanc Tunnel [a vehicular tunnel bored under the "almost three-mile high mountain" between France and Italy] doesn't orbit, so *it's not news.*" (Arranged from a column written by Inez Robb in the *Seattle Times*, August 27, 1962)

       5. Consider each of these examples of reasoning. List the questions that should be posed to test the validity of each one, taking care to state these questions in terms of the situation suggested by the example.

1. The state condemned a small triangle of land belonging to Myron Widdop. The point was that *the state needed this small area for a freeway access.*

(Note that reasoning from causation is being used here. What questions should be asked to test the validity of the conclusion?)

2. All small craft have been warned not to go out of the harbor in the strong winds. This boat would be considered one of the small craft. Therefore, *it has been warned.*
(It is likely that the situation itself would have supplied the minor premise of this categorical syllogism. What questions should be asked to test the validity of this conclusion?)

3. Water jets under extremely high pressure are used to rip the bark off huge logs in Western saw mills. "Finally somebody hit on the idea of borrowing the Hydraulic Barking system . . . slicing the coal off the rock in the steeply inclined seams the same as the 1700 lb. pressure water jets rip the bark off a giant log before it goes thru the headsaw." *Now the coal industry in the state may be revived, mainly through the reduction of power costs.* (From *The Argus,* 69 [August 24, 1962], 1, 5)
(What questions should be asked to test the reasoning from this analogy?)

4. In Central America the tiny state of El Salvador is attempting social reforms but having serious trouble doing so. The same is true in Guatemala and in Honduras. Thus, *the Central American countries are trying to make social progress but are finding it extremely difficult.*
(What questions should be asked to test the validity of this generalization?)

5. The bill now being considered in both houses of Congress was first introduced in either the House or the Senate. It was not introduced first in the House; therefore, *it must have originated in the Senate.*
(What questions should be asked to test the validity of this disjunctive syllogism?)

6. If the union vote meets two requirements—that "30 per cent of the membership cast ballots and that 75 per cent authorize strike action"—it means strong rejection of the contract proposal. These requirements were easily met at the recent meeting, *thus indicating strong rejection.*
(What questions should be asked to test the validity of this conditional syllogism?)

       6. Consider these patterns of valid and invalid categorical syllogisms. Prepare a syllogism to illustrate each of these forms; be ready to explain how the line of reasoning in each of your examples is valid or invalid.

1. All A is B
   C is A
   Therefore, C is B (valid)
2. All A is B
   Some C is A
   Therefore, some C is B (valid)
3. No A is B
   C is A
   Therefore, C is not B (valid)
4. (Most, some, much) A is B
   C is A
   Therefore, C is B (invalid)
5. All A is B
   C is B
   Therefore, C is A (invalid)[9]
6. Only A is B
   C is B
   Therefore, C is A (valid)[10]
7. Only A is B
   C is A
   Therefore, C is B (invalid)[11]
8. No A is B
   C is not A
   Therefore, C is B (invalid)[12]

9. This is the most frequent error in deductive logic and is usually called the fallacy of the *undistributed middle term*. The largest class is B; A and C are smaller classes that fall into B. It does not follow that A and C coincide. All arguments following this form are invalid; for example:

All Communists admire Karl Marx.
Smith admires Karl Marx.
Therefore, Smith is a Communist.

Compare this with form 1 above, where B is the largest class, all A falls into B, and C falls into A. It then necessarily follows that C coincides with B.

10. Note that this is identical with form 5 above, except that *only* replaces *all*. In effect, the major premise here means that *All B is A*.

11. The error of this reasoning can be demonstrated by this syllogism: Only women bear children; Edna is a woman; therefore, Edna bears children. Note that if *only* were changed to *all*, this would become a valid form (see form 1 above). The proper test of this form is to transpose the subject and predicate of the major premise: if *only* women bear children, this means that *all* child bearers are women; it clearly does not follow that Edna bears children, since the restated syllogism follows the invalid form of 5 above.

12. Nothing can be inferred from *two negative premises*.

7. Study the following article thoroughly as the basis for an enlightenment discussion on the question: *What can be done about the use of fallacies in contemporary public life?* Take up such considerations as these:

1. How does Mr. Harries explain each of the six devices?
2. How much can the use of these devices harm the peace and welfare of the world?
3. To what extent are these same devices being used today as in 1961 when Mr. Harries wrote his article?
4. What may be done to curtail or negate the use of these devices contrary to the public good?

122

Six Ways of Confusing Issues[13]
by Owen Harries

Anyone wishing to master the art of confusing the issues, scoring effective but unfair debating points, and persuading others to miss the point, should make a study of what is widely accepted in the West today as enlightened, liberal discussion of international politics. . . . Debating devices which are manifestly unfair and which can do nothing but mislead are accepted as normal weapons of controversy, even by, and in fact especially by, those who make the highest moral claims for their case. Such techniques are not for the most part new, but it is interesting and perhaps important to see how they are applied to the facts of contemporary international politics.

Here, then, is a short list of techniques of confusion that seem to be meeting with considerable success. The list does not claim to be comprehensive; others will be able to add their own examples.

The first technique is to confuse ends and means by insisting on treating a disagreement about means as if it were a disagreement about ends. This involves the initial tactic of appropriating some widely accepted goal to the particular means being advocated. It is seen in operation in Britain at present in controversies about disarmament. Almost invariably, except when some lunatic fringe is involved, these are controversies about means. They arise because people give different answers to questions as to the best way of securing peace. Is it better to be well armed in the hope of securing peace? Or is it better to adopt one of the innumerable schemes for disarmament? These are serious questions and there is much to be said either way. But instead of saying it, some of the participants (and usually, though by no means always, it is the ones in favor of disarmament) are certain to convert the argument about means into one about ends. Opposition to a particular means, *e.g.* unilateral disarmament, is treated as if it is opposition to the goal, *i.e.* peace—which is, in fact, held in common. Then all reason goes out through the window as phrases like "enemies of peace" and "warmongers" are bandied freely about.

Different countries provide different examples. In America this appropriation of common goals is attempted most frequently perhaps by the extreme right which tries to corner the market in anti-Communism. Anyone who does not accept its bludgeoning methods, who does not believe that sacrificing civil rights is a necessary part of an effective response to the Communist threat, who argues that complex and subtle attacks may require complex and subtle defenses, is in danger of being attacked as "soft on Communism."

13. Reprinted by special permission from *Foreign Affairs*, April 1962, pp. 443-452. Copyright by the Council on Foreign Relations, Inc. Owen Harries is in the Department of Tutorial Classes, University of Sydney, Australia.

This particular gambit stands first in my list because it not only creates confusion and misunderstanding, which is serious enough, but it also embitters and poisons public discussion to an extreme degree. It makes disagreements appear much more fundamental and irreconcilable than they really are because, in so far as it is successful, it converts intellectual differences into moral differences, into a disagreement about goals. It is one thing to tell a man that he has made an error of calculation; it is quite another thing to tell him that he is really against what he says he stands for.

The second technique is to dismiss good arguments on the grounds that they are capable of being abused, or, closely related to it, to regard the imputation of motive as a sufficient reply to such arguments. These methods are frequently encountered by someone who points out the difficulties and dangers attached to a course of action. Examples appear constantly in discussions about colonial issues. Thus some will argue that democratic self-government is not the sole alternative to colonial government, that in many cases civil war, anarchy, dictatorship or occupation by another and more oppressive foreign power may more likely result, and that in such instances there is a strong case—strong at least for those who believe in democracy—for supporting the continuation of colonial rule until such time as genuine self-government is a real possibility (simultaneously doing everything possible to hasten that time). This argument is likely to be met not with a refutation but with the reply that it is the classic excuse of the reactionary, that for him the time is never right, that he can always find reasons for perpetuating a régime which is in his own interest.

Now it is true that an argument of this sort can be abused, but it does not follow that the argument is invalid or should be abandoned. Any argument at all can be wrongly applied, and if one accepted this reasoning one would simply have to stop thinking and discussing. The conclusions that do follow are that great care must be taken in accepting such an argument, that one should be vigilant in distinguishing between proper and improper uses of it, and that everything possible should be done to expose misuses of it. These are, admittedly, more difficult and time-consuming tasks than simply shouting "Fraud!" and "Immediate Self-government!" and pretending that this constitutes an adequate reply; but then an intellectual's lot was ever a hard one.

Probably one reason why liberals cannot take such arguments seriously, but dismiss them out of hand as being the excuses of interested parties, is that, despite recent experience, they find great difficulty in considering the possibility of a change as being anything but a change for the better. Not long ago Edmund Wilson remarked that men of his generation and background find it extraordinarily difficult to divest themselves of the assumption of inevitable progress. They were brought up on it, their whole picture of the universe was constructed around it and, however much events may seem to refute it, they still cling to it. To the extent that this is so it constitutes a very great handicap for anyone trying to appraise what is possible and what is not possible in the world today.

I do not want to suggest that this form of debate is peculiar to one country or one political group; on the contrary, it is very widespread. Just as liberals often dismiss what may be a sound argument as a dishonest attempt to justify vested interests, so their arguments are in turn often dismissed, unexamined, as selfish attempts to assuage guilty consciences or as symptoms of a destructive self-hate or as a manifestation of envy. This tendency to question motives as a substitute for genuine argument, to shift attention in debate from issues to persons, may be in part a consequence of the popularization and vulgarization of psychology. Carried far enough, it rules out discussion of any kind, even of motives themselves, since it denies the possibility of a disinterested view. Faced with it, one can only keep insisting that if an argument is a good one, it is good whatever the motive of the person putting it forward. Only when an argument has been shown to be unsound can an examination of motives serve some useful purpose in discovering the cause of error. Sidney Hook once expressed this as a rule of controversy: *"Before* impugning an opponent's motives, even when they may legitimately be impugned, answer his arguments."

Another way of causing confusion and creating a distorted picture of world politics which has a considerable vogue at present is to anticipate history by a process which may be described as the projecting of presumed characteristics of the future backward into the present. This intellectual device can frequently be seen in discussions involving China. It is true that China will, *if* the pace of development achieved in the last ten years is maintained, and *if* other countries do not substantially increase their rate of growth, be one of the two or three greatest powers in the world by the end of the century. But this is no reason for proceeding as if it had already achieved this status, which is what many commentators on international affairs do, contrasting what is usually called "this new giant" or, depending on style, "this looming, menacing colossus," with the older countries of the West, to the detriment of the latter. The fact is that, in 1961, China is not in terms of power a giant at all, whatever it may become by 1991; and while the possibility of a tremendously strong China should be borne in mind in formulating long-term policy, to pretend that it already exists is to distort reality and to add to our problems unnecessarily.

China is not an isolated instance. To a lesser degree, the same process takes place in discussions about the "emergent" nations of Asia and Africa, which are credited now with the power and sense of responsibility which it is predicted they will have in the future. This accounts partly at least for the exaggeration of their importance in current international affairs.

When a country like Britain is being discussed, on the other hand, the device is used to obtain the reverse effect. Because British power has been declining in recent years, it is taken for granted that the same downward curve will inevitably continue; the collapse of British power is then projected from an imagined future into the real present; and discussion proceeds on the basis that Britain is already washed up. From assuming certain things about the future relative power of China and Britain, many commentators go on to elaborate arguments based on the thesis that the former is a much more potent factor than the latter in the world today. Indeed, one would hardly guess that the announced target of the Chinese Communists is to catch up with the British economy by 1970—a target which, even if they achieve it, will still leave them with an income per head of less than one-twelfth that of the British; and, of course, the new "giant" will still be far, far behind the United States and the Soviet Union.

. . . .

A fourth device is the use of multi-meaning words or phrases. Many of the key words in discussions about the cold war have more than one meaning. By a judicious but unacknowledged switch from one meaning to another during the course of discussion it is often possible to get people to agree with something which they would strongly oppose if they understood clearly what was going on.

The classic multi-meaning concept is, of course, "coexistence." There are at least two quite distinct meanings of coexistence. In the first place there is coexistence in the military sense, that is, acceptance by both sides of the fact of military stalemate and agreement not to go to war. Secondly, there is what Irving Howe has conveniently called "moral coexistence" which involves not merely going to war, but doing as much as possible to become more friendly with the other side, accepting the other system as politically and morally valid, not being critical of it, and relaxing military preparedness.

The two meanings are, of course, quite distinct. One can consistently accept the fact of military stalemate and still reject "moral coexistence" completely. In practice, however, they are not kept distinct, and there tends to be a sliding back and forth from one meaning to another. When a commentator sets out to persuade people to accept coexistence as something desirable he usually gives it its narrower meaning, since the case for that is easier to make. In fact, the basic argument for coexistence, summed up in the phrase "coexistence or no-existence," will support only military coexistence; the case it sets forth derives its force from fear—it is a case for not initiating war and for nothing else. But this argument having been accepted, the advocates of coexistence then proceed as if the case for "moral coexistence" had been made also. This is clear from the fact that if all that was meant was military coexistence there would be no need to get passionate about advocating it—it already exists.

"Coexistence" is not the only concept which allows its advocates to move among several meanings and to choose the best of several worlds. Other important concepts like "disengagement," "free world," and "neutralism" share the same characteristic. "Disengagement" can mean anything from the creation of a demilitarized and neutral Germany to the complete withdrawal of all armed forces behind their own national boundaries. "Free world" sometimes refers to all those countries which are not under Communist control; sometimes it is restricted to the members of various alliances; and sometimes it is restricted even further and used to refer only to the dozen or so genuine democracies. "Neutralism" can mean old-fashioned neutrality in the Swiss sense, or it can mean membership in the Afro-Asian bloc and very active interference in the affairs of the world at large.

Number five is insisting on applying irrelevant tests. An example will best explain this technique. Western democracies, in the process of defending themselves against Communism, often ally themselves with countries which are not democratic; and these alliances provide a basis for much effective criticism by those who wish to discredit the West, and are a cause of much embarrassment to those who support it. A few years ago the best example of such an alliance was that with South Korea; currently it might be that with Portugal. The effectiveness of the criticism and the strength of the embarrassment stem from treating as relevant the question: "Is the régime in Portugal one of which genuine democrats can approve?" As the answer to this question is clearly "no," the way is then open for denouncing the alliance and for accusing the West in general of hypocrisy.

The error in this manner of proceeding is that what is at issue here is not approval or disapproval of a régime but approval or disapproval of an alliance with the régime, and these are two very different matters. The character of the régime is only one factor entering into a calculation of the wisdom or morality of such an alliance. If an alliance with a non-democratic régime strengthens genuinely democratic countries (by, for example, better enabling them to withstand attack from another more powerful and aggressive and immediately menacing non-democratic régime), then a democrat both can and should support such an alliance; and no sacrifice of principle is involved. This was seen clearly during the last war when it was not felt necessary to approve or condone Communism in order to support the alliance with the Soviet Union required to defeat Hitler. . . .

Two additional points are worth making. First, to agree that Portugal, South Korea, South Viet Nam and others are not democracies is not to admit that "they are as bad as the Soviet Union." For what makes the Soviet Union "bad" in terms of international politics is not merely or even primarily its internal character but the fact that it is aggressive and expansionist. Because of its ideology *and* its power, it provides a threat to democracy and liberty throughout the world. Portugal, for example, does not. Secondly, I am concerned here not with justifying the Portuguese alliance but with showing the proper test by which to judge it. . . .

I have left until last the most widely used of the techniques under discussion, partly because it has already become notorious. This is the use of a double standard in judging the respective actions of Western countries and Communist countries. . . .

A more serious example is the way in which different attitudes are adopted toward the United Nations and its Charter on different occasions. Actions by Western governments are regularly condemned in some quarters as being "inconsistent with the United Nations Charter" or a "betrayal of our obligations under the Charter." On these occasions, political morality is equated with obedience to the Charter, and any defense of a certain action in terms of vital interests or political reality is brushed aside. But it is from the same quarters that the demand for the admission of Communist China to the United Nations comes. Now according to the Charter there is no room in the organization for a state which regards a military conflict with other states both as inevitable and desirable, as the Chinese Communist Government does. It can be argued, and it may well be true, that the United Nations would function better if China and other states not now members were admitted, that this would be politically more realistic. This is a valid line of argument; but it is not a line which can properly be taken by those who insist that the Charter stands above any consideration of interest or reality, and that consistency with it is the highest political obligation. Neither are they entitled to argue for China's admission because other states who do not fulfill the conditions laid down in the Charter are already in. This is a realistic argument and they have committed themselves to the view that realism must be subordinated to consistency with the Charter. Having committed themselves thus, the only consistent action for them is not to try to get China into the United Nations, but to try to get those countries which do not conform with the Charter out of it—however difficult that may seem.

There are various ways in which one can assess, compare or judge the two sides in the cold war. One way is to hold both of them alongside a Utopian ideal—the perfect democratic state or the perfect socialist state—and see how they measure up. Another way is to compare each with an earlier version of itself and to assess the progress it has or has not made. Now if the first of these methods is applied to one side—if, that is, Western countries are always judged by standards of perfection—while the second method is applied to the other—if the Soviet régime of today is compared with the Stalinist régime of the thirties or with Tsarist Russia—the whole process is rigged in favor of the latter. Or again, if each is judged "in terms of its own moral values" the comparison is unfair and useless (the Nazi régime would have come out well from such a test).

Another way of applying a double standard is by ignoring magnitude. Thus a single fall from grace by one side is equated with systematic evil on the other. As Professor Seton-Watson once pointed out, in the minds of some Western intellectuals a single lynching in the Southern states of America is treated as if it were the equivalent of the murder by starvation of a hundred thousand Ukrainians by the Soviet Union.

Perhaps the commonest, simplest and safest way of all of applying a double standard is merely to be silent about the sins of one side while commenting on and condemning the sins of the other. After all, what you do not say cannot be quoted against you.

Some of the worst offenders in applying a double standard are the spokesmen of the non-aligned states, who employ it not only when commenting on the cold war (see Nehru's reactions to Suez and Hungary respectively) but also when comparing their own actions with those of Western powers (see Nehru's different attitudes when the U.N. interferes in any Western colonial dispute and when it interferes in Kashmir or seeks to interfere in Goa). It might be said that this is perfectly understandable in view of the historical background of these countries; but to understand something is not to justify it, and all this amounts to saying is that there are good reasons to explain why the non-aligned nations do not have the moral superiority they claim.

Sometimes, under pressure, those who employ double standards seek to justify what they are doing by saying that of course they expect a higher standard of behavior from the West than from the Soviet Union; or that they make more of Western sins because they can hope to influence Western behavior while no such hope exists in the case of the Soviet Union. But as in most cases the whole tenor of their argument is that one side is as bad as the other, and as they frequently claim that Western democracy is a sham, it is difficult to take these justifications seriously.

It is not only left-wing critics of the West who employ double standards; they also appear regularly in the arguments of its defenders. But this latter habit, however deplorable and however much it deserves exposure, is hardly surprising, for people have always tended to give their own side the benefit in this way. We are automatically on our guard against it and make allowances for it. What is novel in the present situation is that people who insist that they are loyal to the West and what it stands for persist in operating the double standard in favor of its enemies.

The foregoing list makes no claim to being exhaustive; neither is it a balanced list, for it takes most of its examples from British political discussion, this article having been written in Britain and under the stimulus of things read and heard there. No doubt someone writing in another country would have placed the emphasis differently. However, I think the methods described are in common use in all the Western democracies. In so far as this is the case, the ability of people to see things as they are is impaired and the quality of the public debate in those democracies (and there is little public debate elsewhere) is lowered. Whether these techniques are employed consciously or unconsciously is an important question if one is concerned about the psychology of those who use them; but it is not of consequence in assessing their effect—which is to encourage muddled thinking, the assumption of irrational guilt, contempt for politics and politicians, and the perpetuation of illusions about how international politics really work. If, as we are often told, the battle is for men's minds, these fraudulent techniques amount collectively to a formidable fifth column.

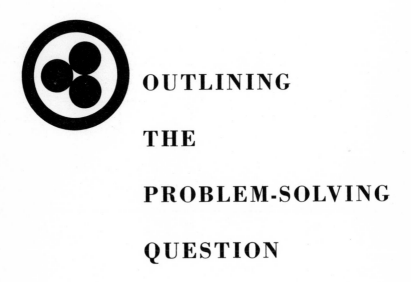

Chapter six

OUTLINING

THE

PROBLEM-SOLVING

QUESTION

Before taking part in a problem-solving discussion, you should prepare an outline setting forth your understanding of the question and your relevant data. There are occasions, of course, when committees are called together with no opportunity for such preparation. But when preparation is possible, you will benefit greatly by thinking out the question before your group holds its discussion, to develop sound reasoning based on your experience and your research findings.

You need to *think through the subject* before you face the complications of *thinking with other discussers*—complications introduced by differing information and interpretations of that information, by the emotional pressures of group cooperation, and by the difficulties of communication. No matter how complete your research and how careful your individual reasoning, you are not likely to discover *all the facts* nor will you have seen *all the connections* and *implications*.[1] Realizing that the viewpoint you develop will be somewhat limited in both scope and interpretation, you should look upon your preliminary thinking as tentative and should anticipate the development that the group—including yourself—will be able to make when all of you move cooperatively through these same lines of inquiry.

Viewing the approaching discussion, then, as your opportunity to rethink the subject with the resources of the other members of the group added, you will prepare as carefully as possible for effective participation. Having enlarged your own information and understanding by the most careful research possible, you now give attention to the outlining of your ideas. Such organization not only will help you clarify your ideas but also will provide you with a ready source of ideas to which you may wish to refer during the actual discussion.

In a problem-solving question the reasoner must move from his realization of the existence of the problem to the selection of a plan for its solution and a method for putting the plan into operation. There are various ways of preparing an outline for a problem-solving discussion, but one of the most useful is based upon John Dewey's analysis of the way we deal with problems. The five steps recommended here are as follows:

Step I   Description of the problem

----

1. Actually, if the question *could* be fully explored or satisfactorily solved by one researcher alone, it would not in most cases be considered a suitable discussion subject.

Step II   Analysis of the problem
Step III Proposal of plans for solution
Step IV   Selection of the best plan
Step V   Selection of the method of putting the best plan into
          operation.[2]

If your group is going to discuss the question *How can we best improve occupational opportunities in the community for persons over 60 years of age?* you will need to move from a realization of the present limitations of such opportunities to the best possible plan for their expansion and a way of getting this plan into action. Such an extensive movement of thought involves a closely knit series of steps, each one requiring specific intellectual tasks as you prepare the outline and, of course, again as you move through these same steps with the other members in the discussion itself.

Step I: Description of the problem

This first step in problem solving, the description of the problem, involves seeing what the problem actually is—its nature and size. One of the most frequent errors in problem solving is attempting to find solutions for a problem which is not fully understood. This descriptive step—plus Step II, Analysis—assures full understanding of the problem before its solution is undertaken in the steps that follow. The elements of this first step are:

A. Clarification of problem terms
B. Specification of symptoms
C. Appraisal of size of problem
   1. Extent and seriousness
   2. Implications for future
   3. Assessment of present programs, if any exist
D. Summation: nature and urgency of problem

---

2. Dewey names five fairly distinct phases: "(*i*) a felt difficulty; (*ii*) its location and definition; (*iii*) suggestion of possible solution; (*iv*) development by reasoning of the bearings of the suggestion; (*v*) further observation and experiment leading to its acceptance or rejection . . . ." See John Dewey, *How We Think*, (Boston: D. C. Heath & Co., 1910), p. 72.

It should be noted that in the sequence recommended above we have omitted Dewey's first suggestion; that has been handled in Chapter 3, which considers selection of the question. Dewey asserted that the first two steps were frequently merged. We have added a final planning step.

Clarification of problem terms

If the members of the discussion group have chosen and phrased the question together, doubtless there is common understanding as to the meaning of the terms.[3] In preparing for the subsequent discussions, you will need only to recall the agreed upon definitions and use them as guides. If the question concerns *older persons*, for instance, and the group defined this term as "65 or over," you will use this definition. But if you are one of a group to which a question has been assigned, you must yourself—while doing the preparatory research and individual thinking—decide as reasonably as you can what the terms in the question mean or what they rightly ought to mean; then you will be prepared to help the group determine precise definitions for all the problem terms.

A member preparing to participate in a somewhat lengthy series of discussions on the question *How can we best improve United States-Latin American relations?* began his outline like this:

I. Description of the problem

    A. Clarification of problem terms

        1. The term "Latin America" refers to the 20 countries in the Western hemisphere south of the Rio Grande, namely: Argentina, Bolivia, Brazil, Chile, Colombia, Costa Rica, Cuba, Dominican Republic, Ecuador, El Salvador, Guatemala, Haiti, Honduras, Mexico, Nicaragua, Panama, Paraguay, Peru, Uruguay, and Venezuela.

Specification of symptoms

In preparation for problem solving you must assure yourself that the problem does indeed exist and should try to discover of what it consists, that is, what the symptoms, or "hurts," are. In studying the United States-Latin American relations question, the member decided that the wide news coverage accorded it—reports on television and radio, in newspapers and magazines—and the initiation of an extensive new aid program indicated that a problem did indeed exist.

But he was further concerned with the ways in which the problem manifested itself, the hurts it produced. He asked himself as he prepared his outline: What really is the *nature* of this problem of United States-Latin American relations? That is, what evidence is there that our relations are not what we would desire them to be?

3. See Chapter 3, pp. 61-65.

And his research and thinking provided information, including such items as these: widespread charges of "Yanqui imperialism" and "business exploitation"; repeated demonstrations against U.S. embassies; stoning of Vice-President Nixon in Caracas, Venezuela, in 1958. These, and as many other evidences of the problem as he could uncover, he organized and listed in his outline.

Under each symptom (or manifestation, or evidence, or hurt) he set down as many details as possible of its occurrence, plus information as to its extent and severity, its increase or decrease. At this point he tried to avoid any concern with *why* specifically these hurts were occurring; such considerations involve causes and background factors, a separate intellectual task which should be given rigorous examination in Step II. It is better to concentrate first on getting a clear picture of how the problem manifests itself.[4]

The student's specification of symptoms for the United States-Latin American relations question began like this:

B. Specification of symptoms
   1. Refusal of L.A. governments to join U.S. in imposing sanctions on Cuba in 1960
      a. Brazil and Argentina were ready to concur but did not as U.S. intervention took clearer form.
         (Arthur Whitaker, "Yankeephobia: The United States and Latin America," *Current History*, January 1962. Mr. Whitaker is Professor of Latin American History at the Univ. of Pa.; he has lectured at the Univ. of San Marcos and the Nat. Institute of Colombia; wrote *The United States and Argentina* and *The Western Hemisphere Idea: Its Rise and Decline.*)[5]
   2. Demonstrations of anti-American feeling, attributed to Communists and student agitators[6]

4. Sometimes the line between symptoms and causes is so thin that the researcher will need great sensitivity and judgment to distinguish between them. This matter will be clearer after you have studied the explanation of Step II.
5. There are other acceptable ways of introducing the source of your information, including: (1) put a superscript after the information and a numbered list of your sources at the close of your outline; (2) put the author, magazine, date and identification of author in the left margin.
6. Sometimes the details—the conditions surrounding the occurrences—are causative (Step II) but assist in specifying the nature of the problem and so should be listed here nevertheless.

a. Bomb damages U.S. embassy, Caracas, Venezuela (*New York Times*, Jan. 23, 1962)
b. Embassy attacked and 4 diplomatic cars burned, Santo Domingo (*New York Times*, March 9, 1962)

Appraisal of size of problem

The researcher—and later the group—should also try to determine (1) the extent and seriousness of the problem and whether it is increasing or decreasing; (2) its implications for the future if nothing further is done to handle it more satisfactorily; and (3) the evaluation of present programs, if there are any, to solve the problem.

Although details you have presented about a particular symptom in the preceding section of your outline may appropriately have included data about its extent and seriousness, you should now take a look at how large the *overall* problem is. Only through such appraisal do we have any idea of how extensive the efforts we suggest in Step III should be. For example, the student working on the problem of United States-Latin American relations needed to decide: Do we make an all-out effort to eliminate this problem of poor United States-Latin American relations? Or does its total effect not justify wholesale exertions, risks, and expenditures? The severity of a problem can be judged by how wide the gap is between the present bad conditions and the desired conditions considered possible, between *what is* and *what might and ought to be*. Not only should you discover how far below the desired standard present conditions really are but whether their harmful effects are increasing or decreasing, for both the urgency with which we take action and the characteristics of what we do may well be influenced thereby.

Furthermore, to grasp the true size of a problem, you should try in your reasoning, using expert opinion and historical analogy, to calculate its implications for the future. You should try to think out the undesirable results that can be expected, the likely long-range consequences to individuals and society that will later have to be reckoned with—or endured—if nothing effective is done about the problem *now*. This shadow on the future must be assessed as a very real part of today's problem.

Solutions have already been attempted to most problems you will deal with. That programs now in effect are not handling their task fully or effectively is clear from the very existence of troubling symptoms. These present programs may be *partial* ones, used at various locations or on specific segments of the problem, or more comprehensive ones that are striking at the whole problem but without a sufficient degree of success. Only after you have evaluated the effectiveness of the current major programs, will you be able to estimate sensibly how much actually remains to be done.[7]

An outline of the United States-Latin American relations problem might have the appraisal of the problem organized as follows:

C. Appraisal of size of problem
    1. Extent and seriousness
        a. Distrust of the U.S. is all pervading.
            (1) "The distrust is so deep, widespread and of such long standing that it must be reckoned with in nearly every inter-American problem confronting the U.S. today."

                (William Benton, "The Voice of Latin America," feature article in *1961 Britannica Book of the Year*. Mr. Benton is former Senator from Conn. and former Asst. Sec. of State; special consultant to Nelson Rockefeller after he became coordinator of inter-American affairs; U.S. delegate to 8 international conferences. He here reports a 12-nation tour of 2 months' duration in 1960.)

        Etc.
        b. Economies of L.A. and U.S. are closely interwoven.
            (1) L.A. as a whole provides $\frac{1}{4}$ of our imports and receives almost $\frac{1}{5}$ of our exports.
            (2) U.S. has about 10 billion invested in other American republics; $\frac{4}{5}$ of this is private investment.
            (3) U.S. depends on L.A. for strategic raw materials and foodstuffs: copper, tin, iron, zinc, petroleum; coffee, sugar, bananas, etc.

                (Robert J. Alexander, "Trade Policies in Latin America," *Current History*, August 1962. Mr. Alexander is Professor of Economics at Rutgers

---

7. If you discover programs that are working out fairly well and that seem to need only amplification or support to solve the problem with an acceptable degree of success, you should keep them in mind for use when you take up possible plans of solution in Step III.

Univ. He has traveled widely in L.A., has worked for the Office of Inter-American Affairs and for the Board of Economic Warfare; he has published *Communism in Latin America, The Peron Era*, and numerous articles.)

Etc.

c. Severity revealed by contrasts
   (1) We have destroyed the favorable attitude of our good neighbor policy of the 1930's.
       (a) "Today they still feel that we then treated them as partners in the Americas, that we then accorded them the dignity of equals, that we listened, that we carefully avoided positioning them as 'beggars at the table of the rich man.' "

          One Latin American leader explained that the difference is that *then* we thought of them as trusted and worth-while friends.

       (Benton)

   Etc.

2. Implications for future
   a. Peace in our hemisphere will be destroyed.
      (1) "As things are now going, the greatest upheaval in history is brewing in Latin America. In 5, 10 or 15 years, unless the United States acts, you'll see country after country explode. The Cuban upheaval will seem mild in comparison."

         (Eduardo Santos, former president of Colombia and world-renowned publisher of *El Tiempo* of Bogota. Reported by Benton.)

   b. Communist take-over in L.A. may follow and threaten us in our own hemisphere.[8]
   Etc.

3. Assessment of present programs
   a. U.S. private investment in L.A.

---

8. You should consider your outline a representation of your best thinking during the preparation period. Of course, you will not always be able to provide strong support—facts or expert opinions—for all your ideas, but put them in anyway.

(1) Totals $8,800,000,000—four times U.S. govt. loans; net profit does not exceed 2 per cent of total investment.
(2) L.A. attitudes toward this investment are those of resistance and suspicion; for such reasons as:
    (a) Lack of local participating capital
    (b) Belief that U.S. is exploiting L.A.
    (c) Belief that U.S. govt. policies are tuned to strengthen position of U.S. corporations in L.A.
    (d) Distrust transferred from L.A. investors to U.S. investors
    (Benton)
    Etc.
(3) Probable that private investment is making larger contributions to L.A. economy than is realized, and more by some firms than others. Suspicious attitudes will need understanding and change before full contributions can be made.
    Etc.

Summation: nature and urgency of problem

Your examination of the symptoms and size of the problem will prepare you to make a brief, clear statement of the nature of the problem. Further, it will give you some notion of how quickly a solution must be found. Another factor affecting the urgency of the situation is the prospect of imminent change. Thus, if you found that changes in the situation are impending, changes that would markedly extend its present harmful effects or render any solving of the problem in the future significantly more difficult, you would rate the urgency high.

To assess urgency was the most important part of General Eisenhower's decision on the eve of the Allied invasion of Europe in World War II. Bad weather had held up the assembled fleet for twenty-four hours. Only a slight and temporary improvement in weather was predicted for the following day, then worsening weather indefinitely. If he, as Supreme Commander, ordered another delay, the fleet might ultimately (and with no assurance of improved weather) face an alerted enemy. His handling of this crisis must be credited to his accurate assessment of the factor of urgency.

The summation for Step I might be outlined as follows:
D. Summation: nature and urgency of problem
  1. Nature: impatient and suspicious attitudes of L.A. toward U.S., and susceptibility to revolution and Communist influence
  2. Urgency: very great
    a. Important matters at stake for U.S. and world
    b. Threat to L.A. exports by the U.S.-backed European Common Market intensifies urgency
      (1) In 1960 about 30 per cent of all L.A. exports were to Western Europe
      (2) Inclusion of African states as ECM associates may shut off L.A. exports to ECM countries of important products—coffee, cocoa, lead, zinc, sugar, wheat, etc.

        (Walter J. Sedwitz, "A Common Market for Latin America?" *Current History*, July 1962. Mr. Sedwitz is Director of Dept. of Economic Affairs of the Pan American Union; he served as economist with U.N. and with U.S. Dept. of Commerce, and as advisor to several L.A. banks. Was director of L.A. studies at the Council of Foreign Relations.)

Step II: Analysis of the problem

There is no more important nor more interesting step in the problem-solving process than the analysis of the problem, none which demands more scrupulous attention to the data you have gathered. The elements of Step II are:
A. Discovery of causes
B. Establishment of criteria for plans of solution
  1. Restatement of *urgency* of attack
  2. Choice of *direction* of attack
  3. Recognition of *boundaries* of attack

Discovering the causes

As a researcher—and then later as a cooperating member of the group—you will need to search out all the major causes of the problem under consideration. It isn't enough to find *some* of the major causes; in your preparation, come as close as you can to finding *all the causes* of any significance so that you will have as substantial a basis as you can for reasoning onward from this point. To search out causes, you should do a number of things: read analyses from authoritative sources; gather from your reading suggestions of why these symptoms have come about; do additional thinking yourself as to what the causes probably are. Through all these interweaving activities you should compile a list in which you explain as fully as possible—before you have the advantage of thinking the problem through with the other members of the group—what has caused the problem.

On the United States-Latin American question the list might begin something like this:

II. Analysis of the problem
　A. Causes
　　1. U.S. past support of dictators
　　　a. Pres. of U.S. presented medals to two of the worst dictators of the post-World War II period, Odria of Peru and Jimenez of Venezuela.
　　　b. U.S. was "partially responsible" for Trujillo's 30 years of dictatorship in the Dominican Republic.
　　　　(Robert J. Alexander, "New Directions: The United States and Latin America," *Current History*, Feb. 1962)
　　　Etc.
　　2. Thoughtless neglect of U.S.-L.A. relations
　　　a. Main govt. attention centered elsewhere; attention to L.A. only in crises
　　　　(1) "Only when some crisis arose—when Peron figuratively thumbed his nose at this country, when President Arbenz threatened to establish a Communist regime in Guatemala, when the Vice President of the United States was spat upon in Caracas, or when Fidel Castro virtually declared war on this country—did the authors of U.S. foreign policy pay any attention to Latin American affairs."
　　　　(Robert J. Alexander, Feb. 1962)
　　　Etc.

b. Vacillation between global and regional responsibilities
  (1) Acted on hemispheric terms in intervening in Cuban affairs in April 1961, but then has treated Latin America like rest of world for economic aid.
    (Arthur P. Whitaker, *Current History*, Jan. 1962)
  Etc.
3. Persistent Communist anti-U.S. propaganda
  a. Success observable mostly among the intellectual classes
    (1) Salvador de Madariaga, "Peoples and Politics," *Saturday Review*, March 25, 1961, declared it "a serious threat to our civilization." (The author is a distinguished Spanish diplomat and author.)
  Etc.
4. Disparity in U.S.-L.A. standards of living
  Etc.

Establishing criteria for plans of solution

When you have listed all the important causes of the problem that you can discover, you are ready to turn to the establishment of criteria for the plans for solution. Probably the first thing you should do is to remind yourself of the need for a solution—how large and pressing is the problem?

Next, you should make a tentative decision as to the *direction* in which the problem should be attacked. Usually it is best to select one of the *causes*, the one whose elimination or substantial reduction promises the greatest decrease in the most hurtful symptoms. A cause which is important but is past and cannot be remedied (such as United States support of past dictators) is, of course, not usable. In some situations the symptoms are so intolerable or the opportunities for their correction diminishing so rapidly that the attack must be launched directly on them instead of upon some more basic factor from which they stem. If your house is burning, you try to smother the blaze and rescue what possessions you can; only later do you try to find out the cause of the disaster. For efficient handling of most problems, however, it is important to decide by careful analysis of the relationships between the causes and the symptoms they produce *which cause* is most truly the *key cause;* this decision on a direction of attack is made with the express purpose of finding an effective method (Steps III and IV) of striking at the problem.[9]

But *boundaries* within which the attack upon the cause may be launched successfully and wisely should not be overlooked. The reasoner must realize that no matter how important the solving of a particular problem may seem to be, remedial action must not jeopardize other values too much. He must ask himself what customs, laws, beliefs, standards, institutions must be preserved while making this attack on the immediate problem. *Boundaries* are expressed negatively to indicate limitation and as matters of degree to suggest counterweighing of values. For example, plans for improving the

9. You may say: But I have found *three* major causes and won't I need to strike at all three to solve the whole problem? Let us suppose that you are correct, that you *would* have to strike at all three to solve the problem completely. Even so, each one of the causes operates somewhat separately in producing the symptoms and is therefore primarily responsible for certain ones. You should trace these lines of responsibility as clearly as you can, decide which of your three sets of "hurts" (produced by the three causes you have described as basic) is really most serious, and choose the cause most responsible for them as the *direction* of your attack.

If you think it important to eliminate a larger share of the problem than your attack upon this one cause will eliminate, you can choose between two methods: (1) After you have worked with the first cause, take each of the other two causes in turn as your direction, look at alternative plans (Step III) and select the most effective (Step IV); then with a plan chosen for striking at each of the causes, organize these three separate plans into a strong "program of action." When the President, in his State of the Union Address, proposes a number of plans for striking at unemployment from different directions, it goes without saying that each one has been selected from all possible alternatives to meet a particular segment of the problem and that care has been taken to coordinate the various plans so that they will work together efficiently. (2) Select from all possible alternatives the best plan for striking at this one cause (Steps III and IV), and put it into effect (planned in Step V). When the operation of this plan has brought whatever reduction of the symptoms it can, then reassess the situation (Steps I and II), select the now most important cause and proceed as before. You must decide on the basis of your findings in Steps I and II whether the problem with which you are dealing would be better handled by a broadside (method one) or by a series of blows with reassessments of the problem in between (method two).

The basic nature of the problem-solving process, however, can be most clearly seen by following through Steps III, IV and V on one cause only; hence, it is likely that your classroom discussions will be limited to this approach. Furthermore, many questions can be well handled by striking strongly at a single cause.

quality of television programming must not violate too much the rights of sponsors to choose the programs they pay for, must not permit too much control by any group subject to political pressures, must not concentrate too much on the tastes of a small number of viewers.

By discovering the urgency of attack, the best direction of attack, and the boundaries within which attack is feasible, you provide yourself with criteria against which you can measure alternative proposals for remedial action.

Criteria might be indicated as follows in the outline on United States-Latin American relations:

    B. Criteria for plans for solution

        1. Urgency: very great; the action must be swift and capable of seeming consistent to the Latin Americans.

        2. Direction: The plans for solution must strike at the thoughtless neglect of U.S.-L.A. relations, because

            a. Thoughtless neglect is closely tied to the widespread distrust of the U.S. by Latin Americans.

            b. Thoughtless neglect keeps our very real present contributions to L.A. welfare from being recognized.

        Etc.

        3. Boundaries:

            a. We must not harm the L.A. countries' self-esteem too much.

            b. We must not endanger too much the financial stability of the U.S.

            c. We must not handicap our world leadership in other underdeveloped areas outside the hemisphere too much.

        Etc.

Step III: Proposal of plans for solution of the problem

In Steps I and II you try to see what the problem really is—its symptoms, size, and causes—and then you decide tentatively on criteria by which you will measure alternative ways of handling the problem.[10] In Step III you need to take a good look at a variety of

---

10. It may be useful to think of Steps I and II as "problem" steps and Steps III, IV and V as "solution" steps.

ways of attempting to solve the problem. The elements of Step III are:
   A. One possible plan: _____
      1. Nature
      2. Strengths
      3. Weaknesses
   B. Another possible plan: _____
      Etc.

Where does a researcher look for plans which might be effective in solving the problem? Some of his best sources are: (1) Proposals now under public discussion or suggestions frequently made for such problems; (2) Plans now in use elsewhere that may suit or be adapted to this situation; (3) Present programs which may be modified to meet the problem more satisfactorily than they are now doing; (4) General suggestions found or heard during his research which may now be developed into specific plans to fit the immediate problem; (5) His own ideas or hunches.

When you have assembled a list of plans which propose to solve the problem in somewhat different ways, you will need to work with each one separately in preparing your outline. Under each plan you will need to set down three things: (1) an explanation of the plan with sufficient details of its operation to make assessment of its potential success possible; (2) a list of the expected strengths of the plan in meeting the criteria established in Step II; (3) a list of its weaknesses in terms of the same criteria.

On the United States-Latin American question, Step III might look something like this:

III. Proposed plans for solution
   A. One possible plan: establishment of regional universities (suggested by Albion Patterson, director of U.S. technical cooperation with Argentina)
      1. Nature
         a. Each univ. would attempt to develop distinction in one or more major fields, such as science, technology, or management.
         b. This plan would be a major project under Point Four.
         Etc.
      2. Strengths
         a. The beginning could be made at once since Point Four is already operating in Latin America.
         b. The resulting improved education of L.A.'s future

leaders would help to provide the stability which must underlie a fair view of United States-Latin American relations.

  c. Point Four funds have financed the very successful university-to-university relationship between the Catholic University of Santiago, Chile, and the Univ. of Chicago; there are 14 other such contracts in operation.

  d. Its cost would be worth while.

    (1) "I am persuaded that no single area of action open to the United States and its philanthropists in L.A. is more promising per dollar than the effort to lift the level of its higher education."

      (Senator Benton, *1961 Britannica Book of the Year*)

  Etc.

3. Weaknesses

  a. The results would not actually be felt for some years, during which time the bad feeling would continue.

  b. The relationship between a university education and attitudes toward the U.S. would not be widely recognized, nor widely spread.

  Etc.

B. Another possible plan: an expanded United States Information Agency program

1. Nature

  a. Reintegrated into the state department and headed by an undersecretary of state

  b. Increased budget, improved personnel in L.A. staffs

  c. Broadcasts in Spanish and Portuguese much stepped up in both quantity and quality

2. Strengths

  a. Would have wide immediate effect because it could be established quickly and would encounter no language barriers

  b. Would counteract Communist propaganda by providing factual information from U.S. viewpoint about Communism and about the U.S. cultural tradition

    (1) Suggested by Crisólogo Larralde, leader of People's Radical party in Buenos Aires, 1960

  c. Would give the state department the counsel of USIA

officers and would, conversely, afford these officers better guidance on state department policies

Etc.

3. Weaknesses
   a. Can't make inroads against the already-established Communist propaganda machine
      (1) Communists have been spending as much in L.A. alone as U.S. all around the globe
      (2) Countering their charges with words is rather ineffectual

Etc.

C. Another possible plan: launching a wide program to eradicate hoof-and-mouth disease among the beef cattle in L.A.
1. Nature
   a. Push the disease-free area wider by compulsory vaccination and other methods
   b. Financed through the Inter-American Development Bank

Etc.

Step IV: Selection of the best plan

The selection of the best plan is parallel in importance in the "solution" steps to the selection of the direction of attack in the "problem" steps. Your outline up to this point has been a careful, step-by-step investigation intended to prepare you to distinguish the best plan from among those proposed. Here, then, you pit the first plan in your list against the second, the one that you decide is the better of these two against the third, and so on, until you have found which plan (in your tentative and temporary judgment) will strike best at the problem with the speed you think necessary and with appropriate heed for the boundaries. The elements of Step IV are:

A. Comparison with alternative plans
1. Plan A compares with Plan B as follows:
2. Plan A (or B) compares with Plan C as follows:
   Etc.

B. Comparison with untouched symptoms

When you pit one of the plans against another, you need to do as thorough a job of examination as you can, comparing one plan's estimated potential with the other's, claim by claim, weakness by weakness. You will then select as the best the plan that passes the comparative tests most successfully. And, in the end, if you can improve the selected plan by addition of some virtue from one of the other plans, it is this modified plan which you consider your best plan.

Once you have chosen what seems to you to be the best plan, you should focus again upon the problem, giving special attention to the symptoms which result from causes *other than* the one at which your plan is striking.[11] Mindful of those hurts which will likely continue no matter how effectively the chosen plan operates upon the part of the problem for which it was designed, you take a renewed look at this best plan—its high potential but also its requirements of time/materials/personnel and its uncertainties in operation and effect. You weigh these factors—this best plan on the one side and these hurts which the plan will *not* cover on the other—and ask yourself frankly: *Is it worth it?*

Doubtless, in many cases, you can answer Yes, because your chosen plan will eliminate a significant share of the problem; you are ready then to move on to Step V and the task of planning to put your solution into operation. If you decide, however, that your plan—good though it is—makes too small an attack upon the problem as a whole, you should probably at this point take another cause, consider alternative plans for removing it, select the most promising, combine this with your earlier solution into a useful program, and plan to put that program into effect.

An outline of Step IV on the United States-Latin American question might take a form such as this:

IV. Selection of the best plan
    A. Comparison with alternative plans
        1. The "establishment of regional universities" compares with the "expanded USIA" plan as follows:
            a. Although the regional universities would train much-needed personnel and, as models, serve to upgrade the whole of higher education in L.A., the U.S. involvement with the institutions might be widely overlooked; on the other hand, the direct approach of the USIA

11. If you have a problem with *only one major cause*, you will not have to worry about hurts that your plan will not be at least attempting to handle; presumably this best plan will handle them all more or less successfully. It is when you are facing a more complex problem with several somewhat varied major causes that your attack upon one cause will not necessarily eliminate the interwoven effects of them all.

       programs would keep the U.S. involvement continually before L.A., an important factor in light of the persistent Communist anti-American propaganda.

    b. Although initiated at once, the results obtained by the universities' plan would be so long range as to have little effect except publicity upon the present situation, and the Latin Americans have previously lost faith in slow U.S. performance after promises; on the other hand, the effect of the stepped-up USIA program (admittedly less technically educational although widely and intensely practical) would be immediate.

  2. The "expanded USIA" plan compares with the "eradication of hoof-and-mouth disease" plan as follows:
   Etc.

Conclusion: the "expanded USIA" plan is better.

B. Comparison with untouched symptoms

  1. Although the "expanded USIA" plan will not affect directly the disparity in living standards between U.S. and L.A., its potentialities for re-establishing our past neighborly relationships seem great enough to warrant its adoption.

Etc.

Conclusion: the expanded USIA is worth while.

Step V: Selection of the method of putting the best plan into operation

You have reason to suppose that your plan can be put into operation effectively because you concerned yourself with reasonable goals (Steps I and II) and observed appropriate boundaries in making your choice of the plan (Steps III and IV). Nevertheless, it is useful to bring any remaining obstacles to the *installation* of the plan into clear view at this point and decide how to meet them. The elements of Step V are:

  A. Obstacles to be faced

  B. Possible methods of handling obstacles

  C. Best method of handling obstacles

You must ask yourself what groups or agencies will be hostile to the plan or will actively resist it or will simply be uncooperative in the task of getting the plan under way. You are not considering as obstacles the mere tasks that must be undertaken to start the plan but only *factors which would make the doing of these tasks unnaturally hard.* When you have found these obstacles, you will need to think of several alternative methods of handling them and select the seemingly most effective method.

Your outline of Step V will likely be relatively short. Step V of the United States-Latin American relations question might be outlined as follows:

V. Selection of the method of putting the best plan into operation
  A. Obstacles
    1. Congressional opposition to giving the program more status and more funds
    2. Indifference of the general public in the U.S.
    Etc.
  B. Methods of handling obstacles
    1. Wide publicity campaign by mass media
    2. Letters to Congressmen
    3. Nation-wide organization of small discussion groups
    Etc.
  C. Best method: a wide publicity campaign would reach both Congressmen and the general public.

You have now moved through the complete line of thinking—from your first task of seeing the problem accurately to the choice of a wise solution and a workable method of putting it into operation.

Single-policy question

Sometimes your group may be asked to consider a single-policy question, one that asks: *Shall we adopt the XY proposal?* Here a specific plan of solution is suggested and your decision is either acceptance or rejection.

In handling a single-policy question, you should clarify the steps of thinking by-passed in the phrasing of the question. Otherwise, this type of question strongly invites biased thinking. It is very likely that an inexperienced reasoner would—because of his own preconceptions or because of the first materials he read or the first persons he interviewed—place himself for or against the proposal at once and then do his research and preliminary organization to support this view. Such an approach would give him but a partial understanding of the subject, whereas his true task involves the measuring of the proposal against the problem it purports to solve rather than the finding of support for a particular point of view.

Thus, it would be desirable if (in the preparation stage and in the discussion itself) the question were broadened at once into a full-scale problem-solving one. Not *Shall we adopt fluoridation in our city?* but *How can we best preserve our children's teeth?* Often, however, neither time nor the motivation of the group makes this procedure possible or feasible in any complete sense. But minimum preparation must surely include: (1) a quick look at the problem, that is, a rough estimate of Steps I and II; and (2) an equally quick look at the alternatives to this proposal, that is, Step III. This rapid survey will certainly not be the tightly developed line of thinking of a full problem-solving treatment, but it will heighten the group's awareness of these considerations in general and to that extent broaden the study of this single-policy question. If the reasoner is interested in the *direct* worth of the plan being discussed (its estimated effectiveness in solving the problem) as well as its *relative* worth (in comparison with alternatives), he will thus have a more valid basis for making a decision.

Your outline of a single-policy question would attempt to handle such questions as these:

I. What is the problem the proposed plan is designed to handle?
II. How well will the proposed plan remedy the problem?
    A. In costs (men, money, equipment, time), sacrifices, and risks?
    B. In probable effects on the problem?
III. What alternatives to the proposed plan are there?
IV. Do the probable results of the proposed plan outweigh the probable results of each of the alternative plans?

If, for example, you and your group were to discuss the question *Shall we adopt the expanded United States Information Agency Plan?* you would be wise to study not only the proposed plan but to prepare as thoroughly as you could on the whole problem of United States-Latin American relations and on other plans which might be adopted instead of the USIA plan. Only then could you make an informed decision for or against the proposal.

Summary

Outlining a problem-solving discussion question involves the organization of lines of thinking and supporting information through five interlocking steps: (1) Description of the problem; (2) Analysis of the problem; (3) Proposal of plans for solution; (4) Selection of the best plan; (5) Selection of the method of putting the best plan into operation. Preparing for discussion of a single-policy question should include consideration of the general problem with which the proposed policy is to deal and of alternatives to the proposed policy.

Readings and problems

1. Define these terms as they are used in this chapter: symptoms, implications, direction, boundaries.

2. Prepare to join in class discussion on these questions about outlining the problem-solving question:

1. If you know that a problem *exists*, why do you need to search out *of what* the problem *consists*, that is, what the symptoms are?
2. If you find that a problem is increasing, how does that influence your line of thinking? If it is decreasing?
3. How does an appraisal of present programs help to determine the size of the problem?
4. In what ways is choosing the key cause the most important part of the problem steps?
5. Why are boundaries important? Why should they be stated in the negative and as matters of degree?
6. Why is it better to suggest alternate solutions for one cause at a time rather than for several?
7. What is the relation between the criteria of Step II and the strengths and weaknesses of the plans in Step III?
8. After deciding which is the *best* plan, why is it useful to look back at the symptoms again?
9. Why should you consider the obstacles to be faced in putting the plan into operation?
10. Why should you bring in the often omitted steps in the discussion of a single-policy question?

3. Listen to a classroom discussion on the problem steps of some contemporary question. Outline the symptoms and causes developed by the group.

   4. Listen to a group discussing alternative proposals for a problem (Step III); make note of the nature, strengths, and weaknesses of each plan as the members develop them.

   5. Review the forms of reasoning explained in Chapter 5. Prepare to participate in classroom discussion on examples of the different forms you can discover in the segments of the United States-Latin American question outline presented in this chapter.

   6. Complete the United States-Latin American question outline from this chapter in preparation for a series of classroom discussions on the subject. Follow the framework provided in this chapter:

   I. Description of problem
      A. Clarification of terms
      B. Symptoms
      C. Size
         1. Extent and seriousness
         2. Implications
         3. Present programs
      D. Summation: nature and urgency
  II. Analysis of problem
      A. Causes
      B. Criteria for plans
         1. Urgency
         2. Direction
         3. Boundaries
 III. Possible plans
      A. One possible plan: _____
         1. Nature
         2. Strengths
         3. Weaknesses
      B. Another possible plan: _____
      Etc.
  IV. Selection of best plan
      A. Comparison with others
      B. Comparison with untouched symptoms
   V. Putting plan into operation
      A. Obstacles
      B. Methods of handling obstacles
      C. Best method

Chapter seven

ORGANIZING

FOR AN

ENLIGHTENMENT

DISCUSSION

Discussion groups often assemble for the purpose of enlightenment. The participants gather in single sessions or for series of meetings, seeking to increase their understanding and insight by the mutual exchange of ideas.[1] Engineers meet to discuss trends in their field, artists to discuss exhibits of paintings, other groups to view and discuss documentary films of significance. Scientists, teachers, ministers, businessmen, political leaders—all meet to consider questions within their own particular areas of interest or to participate as individuals in general groups that seek enlightenment on stimulating topics. Throughout these varied activities runs one common purpose, that of increasing the participants' knowledge and understanding of the subject considered.

These enlightenment discussions usually take one of three principal forms: study, evaluation, or exploration. The forms are similar in their goal—that of general enlightenment—but different in their patterns of approach. Anyone seeking to improve the quality of his participation in the discussion process should give attention to the patterns of organization useful for these three forms.

Study discussion

Preparing for participation in study groups involves the gathering and organizing of relevant information as a basis for increased understanding of the selected subject. Questions suitable for such groups ask for more than the routine gathering of facts lying easily at hand; indeed, if the research of a single individual could actually supply all the relevant information and interpretation, there would usually be no reason for holding a discussion upon the topic. Excepted are those occasions when individuals lack time or motivation to obtain and study data available to each of them; then, holding discussions on questions of importance to pool the results of their admittedly inadequate individual efforts would be amply justified. For example, group members might find it convenient and rewarding to pool their information on the Southeast Asia Treaty Organization (commonly referred to as SEATO) and then to draw an inference together as to its actual significance for the area and the world. Each participant

1. Thomas Jefferson wrote in a letter to Du Pont de Nemours, April 24, 1816: "Enlighten the people generally, and tyranny and oppressions of body and mind will vanish like evil spirits at the dawn of day."

would do well to organize his findings under such headings as the following:

I. What conditions of aggression and insurrection developed in Southeast Asia after World War II?
   In South Korea
   In the Philippines
   In Malaya
   In Indochina
II. What was the origin of SEATO?
   When? Where? By whom?
   Pacific Charter
   Southeast Asia Collective Defense Treaty
   Purposes
III. What is its organization?
   Headquarters
   Council of Foreign Ministers
   Council Representatives
   Military Advisers
   Expert Committees: Committee of Security Experts; Committee on Information, Cultural, Education, and Labor Activities; Committee on Economic Experts
   Ad Hoc Committees
IV. What are its activities and accomplishments? Its setbacks and failures?
   In countering Communist subversion
   In increasing military effectiveness
   In promoting progress—economic, educational, medical
V. What, then, is the significance of SEATO?
   To Southeast Asia
   To the United States
   To the United Nations

In general, however, only those questions should be chosen for group study whose effective handling demands the interplay of varying interpretations and the stimulation which comes from mutual exchange of views. Enlightenment groups may wish to study a problem simply to understand its nature and extent more clearly; they will then undertake systematic description of the problem, the same step a problem-solving group uses to begin its decision-making process. To inform themselves, these participants may want to examine some problem of society that interests or involves them—youthful crime, alcoholism, violence on television programs, fraudulent advertising. They may wish, on the other hand, to examine a concept, a movement, or a trend, and thus choose to study existentialism, the Montessori system of education, automation, or the Alliance for Progress. They may want to move into the realm of speculation, analyzing the likely nature of future events—the colleges of tomorrow, the possibility of further inflation, the probable results of the Radio Free Europe program.

In preparing for a study discussion, you will need to make an appropriate outline of the facts and inferences you are ready to offer. If you are preparing to participate in describing a problem, you may use the framework employed for this preliminary step by a problem-solving group:[2]

A. Clarification of problem terms
B. Specification of symptoms
C. Appraisal of size of problem
   1. Extent and seriousness
   2. Implications for future
   3. Assessment of present programs, if any exist
D. Summation: nature and urgency of problem

If you are studying not a problem but a concept or trend, you will be asking yourself: What *is* this concept? this trend? What are its component parts and organization? the characteristics which distinguish it? the origin and history of development? And your outline should use as its main headings topics central to these questions. If you are speculating, for example, on the colleges of tomorrow, you may employ relevant headings such as: (1) student body; (2) faculty; (3) curriculum; (4) physical plant; (5) financing; (6) scholastic standards.

---

2. It may be that the enlightenment group will wish to go beyond the description of the problem; it may in fact wish to undertake the full problem-solving sequence, not with the intention of taking action but with the goal of increased knowledge and understanding. If so, the group can use the outline form explained in Chapter 6.

Sometimes a *Study Guide* will be prepared for the discussion group by a parent organization (such as the League of Women Voters) or by the chairman or by the group itself in preliminary session. Although such guides vary in form and completeness, they present a usable organization of topics to suggest areas of consideration.[3] If the group member receives a copy of the Study Guide before the time of the discussion, he can include the suggested topics in his research and preliminary thinking and set down useful data at relevant points. Sometimes, on the other hand, the Study Guide is handed to the group at the time of the meeting. Although such a procedure offers no guidance during preparation, it can provide the members with a framework for thinking at the time of the actual discussion.

The value of study discussions is apparent—each individual finds his factual knowledge amplified, his interpretations widened or modified, his understanding more complete and profound.

Evaluative discussion

As individuals concerned with our own development and as citizens concerned with shaping the society which does so much to shape us, we make constant evaluations.[4] Enlightenment discussions lend themselves very well to evaluation of programs, organizations, and proposals of all sorts because, as Charles Nixon (1) explains, "the reason of one man will be aided, supported, and checked by the reason of several."

Unlike problem-solving discussions in which a program, policy, or method is weighed against its alternatives, evaluative discussions focus on one item alone and measure it in terms of relevant criteria. Such assessment reveals its points of strength and weakness but not its superiority or inferiority to alternatives. Members of evaluative

3. The outline suggested above on the SEATO question would serve as an effective Study Guide.

4. "Democracy is at bottom an agreement to hold civilized discussion of issues that count, and those that cherish it must find and cultivate the techniques of reason." Clinton Rossiter, "The Democratic Process," in *Goals for Americans,* report of the President's Commission on National Goals, administered by the American Assembly, Columbia University (Englewood Cliffs, N.J.: Prentice-Hall, 1960), p. 72.

discussion groups address themselves to questions like these: *How great was Hemingway's influence? How well do military schools educate? How powerful is the Organization of American States? How effective is our city park system?*

You may organize your thinking and data for such a discussion simply by listing pros and cons, advantages and disadvantages, strengths and weaknesses of the organization, proposal, program, person.[5] For instance, you might appraise the practice of filibustering in the United States Senate by searching out its advantages and disadvantages, presenting all evidence and reasoning possible under each claim, as a problem-solving group does on each plan in Step III.[6] Or you may wish to measure the program (or proposal, person, product) against standards appropriate for any program of such a type. You may measure your city police force against criteria suitable to law enforcement agencies, the typical Indian diet against nutritional criteria established by the World Health Organization, the quality of a play against criteria appropriate to dramatic presentations.

Sometimes you and the other participants will find a set of criteria suitable for your purpose already prepared. For example, if you were planning to evaluate your city newspaper, you might be interested in using the standards for a good newspaper drafted by a committee of six veteran editors for the Associated Press Managing Editors Association (2). Or, if you wished to judge the accomplishments of some public official, you might turn to John F. Kennedy's speech of January 9, 1961, to a joint session of the Massachusetts legislature. He designated four qualities on which he expected history to judge him or any officeholder (3):

> Of those to whom much is given, much is required. And when at some future date the high court of history sits in judgment on each one of us—recording whether in our brief span of service we fulfilled our responsibilities to the state—our success or failure, in whatever office we may hold, will be measured by the answers to four questions:

5. The evaluation question differs from the single-policy question, explained in Chapter 6, by aiming only at careful judgment, not at recommendation for action. Further steps involving comparison with alternative programs would have to precede any choice of action.
6. See Chapter 6.

First, were we truly men of courage—with the courage to stand up to one's enemies—and the courage to stand up, when necessary, to one's own associates—the courage to resist public pressure as well as private greed?

Secondly, were we truly men of judgment—with perceptive judgment of the future as well as the past—of our own mistakes as well as the mistakes of others—with enough wisdom to know what we did not know, and enough candor to admit it?

Third, were we truly men of integrity—men who never ran out on either the principles in which they believed or the people who believed in them—men whom neither financial gain nor political ambition could ever divert from the fulfillment of our sacred trust?

Finally, were we truly men of dedication—with an honor mortgaged to no single individual or group, and compromised by no private obligation or aim, but devoted solely to serving the public good and the national interest?

In this set of criteria some explanation of the meaning of each standard is presented; nevertheless, anyone preparing to use these standards in the assessment of the accomplishments and general effectiveness of some particular officeholder would need to give careful attention to the exact meaning and scope of criterion before using it as a basis for judgment.

If no such set of criteria is available or seems suitable as a basis for judging the material under consideration, each participant will need to prepare a list of his own.[7] In doing so, he should try to avoid overlapping among the standards and to include all items that are relevant. Further, if he considers certain standards more important than others, he should indicate this difference on his list so that

---

7. Often an evaluative group finds it worth while to hold a preliminary meeting to build the list of criteria together and then to assess the case (person, program, product) by these standards at the subsequent meeting. In such an arrangement each participant prepares the best list he can for the preliminary meeting but uses the set established by the group for the ensuing evaluation.

the judgments on these particular items will be given appropriately more weight in the total evaluation.[8]

Whether the participant is to use an agreed upon set of criteria or his own, his preparation for evaluative discussion is the same. Deciding upon a suitable rating scale,[9] he applies each criterion in turn. He studies the program carefully for information indicating how well it fulfills the demands of that criterion; reasoning from these facts, he decides on the program's degree of excellence on this criterion and assigns a tentative rating. Suppose you and your group planned to judge the record of the governor of your state on the criteria for officeholders suggested by Kennedy; each of you should organize your outline for the discussion in such a fashion as that illustrated below:

I. *An officeholder should be a man of courage.*

    A. Examples of governor in situations requiring courage

Note the turn to evidence without taking a point of view.

        1. Governor A resisted the warning of his advisers that his concern with the right-to-work proposal would lose him votes in the next election.

            The _____ Gazette, June 18, 19___

Source must be given. Sufficient detail must be given; examples must be typical.

        2. Governor A exposed the pressures brought to bear on him by the real estate lobby and gave specific reasons for maintaining his previous point of view.

8. When Professor Russell Fitzgibbon was preparing to conduct polls on the degree of democratic progress made in the Latin American countries, he developed a list of 15 criteria for democracy (see Readings and Problems, question 4, p. 171) and gave each criterion what he considered its appropriate weighting. For example, he gave the criterion "Free elections—honestly counted votes" twice as much weight as most of the others and "Reasonable freedom of political life from the impact of ecclesiastical controls" half as much. The specialists on Latin America who judged each country by the criteria on his list used a 5-point scale (from excellent to insignificant) to indicate their measurement of that country on each criterion. Adjustments were then made in their ratings to give the more or less important criteria their appropriate weight in the total judgment. Although the specialists in this example acted individually in arriving at their judgments, they used the evaluative pattern recommended above for a group. See William S. Stokes, *Latin American Politics* (New York: Thomas Y. Crowell, 1959), pp. 511-514.

9. Simple linear scales (as from 1 to 7, perhaps with 1 as low and 7 as high), or linear scales with word descriptions (as 7 *excellent,* 6 *very good,* 5 *good,* 4 *fair,* etc.), or words only—these are all possible rating scales for such use.

Dissimilar examples should be noted.

> The _____ Times, July 6, 19__
>
> 3. In the face of clear-cut evidence of foreign trespassing on the state's fishing grounds, Governor A hesitated to take a stand.
>
> The _____ News, June 30, 19__
>
> *Etc.*
>
> B. Reasoning from the examples
>   1. The first two examples are typical of his reaction to improper pressures brought to bear upon him for positions already taken. Such pressures seem unable to sway him, no matter how strong they are.

Inferences from these examples should be carefully drawn out.

>   2. His hesitation to take a stand against the trespassers does not seem characteristic of his unusual approach to new threats to public welfare, but it cannot be overlooked. One should call to mind the vigor of his efforts to negotiate fairer rules for use of the fishing grounds earlier this year. No other example of such delayed responsiveness to public problems could be found.
>
>   *Etc.*

General assessment should precede assignment of a rating.

> C. Overall judgment: in general, highly courageous.
>
> **Rating:** 1 2 3 4 5 ⑥ 7

Each of the other criteria would be handled similarly, and then a composite judgment computed. Since Kennedy did not indicate that any one quality was more important than another, no adjustment for the weight of individual criteria will need to be made.

Two cautions are important in making such evaluations: (1) avoid using only examples that sustain a previously taken point of view; and (2) avoid creating an *artificial* balance between favorable and less favorable examples because of a desire to be "fair." Open-minded examination of the official's handling of a number of significant problems demanding courage must underlie any sound judgment of him on this trait. Richard E. Neustadt (4), has suggested some of the problems that he thinks will serve as bases for judgments of Kennedy's use of Presidential power:

When, therefore, a few years from now, students come to appraise Mr. Kennedy's approach to Presidential power, his relative success in speeding his transition tasks ought to be a factor in his favor. But his performance up to now, however judged, will count far less than the performances ahead. One already begins to see the situations and events which will supply evidence for judgment on his style of operating and decision-making. One thinks of the unfolding of the Berlin situation. One thinks of the new trading and political relationships required after Britain joins the common market (if she does). One thinks of the re-emergence of inflation as a problem here at home (a recession was inherited, but inflation, if it comes, will be the new Administration's own). One thinks of the tempo of demands for integration. One thinks ahead to the infighting at the session of Congress, and to the conduct—and consequences—of next year's Congressional elections. On the administrative side one thinks of the dilemmas clustering around the status, organization, and operation of the Department of State. From Kennedy's response to challenges like these —posed by problems which transcend transition and outlast it—students should have evidence enough to begin their appraisals of this President . . . as a user of the power of his office.

Examination of relevant information, careful reasoning, then judgment—these are the steps you should take on each criterion as you prepare to participate in evaluative discussion.

Exploratory discussion

By exploratory discussion we mean the use by all the participants of designated material intended to open provocative lines of thinking. Such a "common body of material" may be *oral*—a lecture, discussion, interview, conference, or drama (direct or indirect through radio, film, or television); or *written*—a magazine article, book, published report, editorial, or essay. Each participant, instead of making his own selection of sources of information (as in all forms of discussion explained up to this point), listens to or reads the specified material as the basis for the group's exchange of ideas. It is highly desirable, of course, for him to use additional sources to amplify his knowledge on any points suggested by this material.

If the basic material is oral, the prospective discusser needs to be alert for ideas that capture his interest and make him wish to pursue them with others. Perhaps some famous man speaks at your college and your group decides to use his lecture as the basis for an exploratory discussion. For example, Sir Julian Huxley talked about "The Humanist Revolution" at the University of Washington in the spring of 1962. The audience heard him say such things as these:[10] "We need a fulfillment society, not a welfare state"; "People need a sense of significance; people want their ideas and feelings in touch with something transcending the immediate"; "If a person manages to develop into a highly realized person, he is assisting the cosmic process; this is his unique contribution to the whole process"; "The exploration of this inner world [of the mind] is more important than of outer space, but what is being done is only a fraction of what is being done in other fields"; "To think out a science of human possibilities we need a chair, and a faculty!" Brief notes on the lecturer's ideas will preserve them for the listener with something of their original flavor; and if he can arrange to make a tape recording of the talk, it, of course, will provide the listener with ample opportunity for selecting the speaker's seminal ideas.

When you have completed the primary task of understanding the ideas, you should go further. You should think of provocative questions suggested by each of these springboard ideas so that you can help open lines of inquiry for the group. With Huxley's reference to the "highly realized person" for a springboard, you might think of (and perhaps jot down) such questions as these: *What is a highly realized person? How does such a person differ from others? How does one go about becoming one? In what ways is our society not conducive to the development of such persons?* In the actual discussion, it may turn out that your first question will generate enough momentum to carry the group into further excursions. Nevertheless, you should prepare succeeding questions in case they are needed to help probe the idea profitably.

10. These excerpts are quoted from Huxley's lecture at the University of Washington, Seattle, Washington, April 24, 1962.

If the common body of material is a written source, you should read it thoroughly several times and prepare by going through the following steps: (1) outline the material so that you have a detailed knowledge of its content and organization; (2) underline or list ideas that have a "creative, growing edge," that is, ones which seem to lead the mind outward into further speculation; and (3) set down, in the margins or in your notes, a sequence of developmental questions that lead from these springboard points, each one reaching farther out along the line of development than the former.

The most stimulating questions avoid asking for *yes* or *no* answers that throttle rather than promote thinking; they ask rather, such questions as *To what extent? Under what conditions?* Presenting or requesting needed facts, they lead on by raising relevant lines of inquiry. In exploratory discussion the emphasis is upon opening new intellectual horizons, moving outward freely and spontaneously from one suggestion, speculation, or viewpoint to another.

Suppose that you and your group were to use Woodrow Wilson's Address to Congress (5), declaring war, April 2, 1917, as your common body of material; after carefully studying the speech for the President's intended meaning and outlining it to fix its structure in your mind, you might indicate springboards and suggest questions as shown in the following preparation on the closing paragraph:

It is a distressing and oppressive duty, Gentlemen of the Congress, which I have performed in thus addressing you. There are, it may be, many months of fiery trial and sacrifice ahead of us. It is a fearful thing to lead this great peaceful people into war, into the most terrible and disastrous of all wars, civilization itself seeming to be in the balance. But the right is more precious than peace, and we shall fight for the things which we have always carried nearest our hearts—for democracy, for the right of those who submit to authority to have a voice in their own governments, for the rights and liberties of small nations, for a

Are we asking too much of our presidents? What could we do to reduce the demands of the office?

How will we know what is "right"? Why is the "right" more precious than "peace"? What obligations has the president in helping the country decide?

From what does "authority" derive? In what sense do the governed have a "right" to a

universal dominion of right by such concert of free peoples as shall bring peace and safety to all nations and make the world itself at last free. To such a task we can dedicate our lives and our fortunes, everything that we are and everything that we have, with the pride of those who know that the day has come when America is privileged to spend her blood and her might for the principles that gave her birth and the peace which she has treasured. God helping her, she can do no other.

"voice"? How should they exercise their "voice"?

Why do we Americans often find it hard to explain the principles for which we stand? How necessary is it that we be able to do so? How can we increase our ability?

Notice the use of springboard ideas and developmental questions in the following portion of an exploratory discussion on Wilson's address. The discussion leader does not happen to speak during this segment, for the members proceed animatedly on their own initiative.

Takes a springboard idea; raises a question

Starts consideration

Note the turn from speculation to fact

John Day That phrase of Wilson's, "a distressing and oppressive duty, Gentlemen of the Congress," leads right into the duties American Presidents are called upon to take. What about the duties we expect of them? Could we be asking too much of them, more than any individual could possibly handle well, no matter how dedicated and able and energetic he was?

Pete Galsworthy Even at the start of our country there was too much for a President to do—didn't Washington complain, in that first year —1789—that he simply didn't have time to read and reply to all the dispatches that came flooding in to him from every direction?

Mary Stone And the President's duties have mushroomed since that time, with the growth of the country and our position in the world. Today we ask him to carry out the laws we have and lead the way in making new ones, to formulate our foreign policy, to act as Commander in Chief, and to act as our national symbol—that is, to represent us all before the world—and these are all heavy responsibilities.

Note the specific illustrations

Bob Scharnikov   Even in a time of national emergency we keep him busy with small duties— he presses the button that opens our fairs and starts our new hydroelectric dams; he pitches out the baseball in the first game of the season; he plays host to every celebrity who comes to our shores——

Note the comparison

Claire Dudek   And I suppose it's important that he, as President, does show his interest and support of all these things. It's interesting to think, though, that in Britain it's Queen Elizabeth who does these things, and the prime minister and the cabinet are left free to handle the important affairs of the country.

Perceives that the group has assured itself of the overburdening of the President; raises a further question

John   I wonder whether something could be done to reduce the demands of the Presidency? We've added bureaus and boards and advisers by the hundreds, and the President is still overwhelmed!

Glenn Hawkins   Well, we won't accomplish very much unless we're willing to make a pretty substantial change. Herman Finer of the University of Chicago has suggested a cabinet of eleven Vice-Presidents to assume executive responsibility with the President. These men—all twelve of them, including the President—would be elected by the country from members past or present of the House of Representatives or the Senate and would serve four years. They would sit frequently with the House and participate in Congressional business——

Gloria Benich   I suppose there are a lot of other aspects to the plan that you haven't mentioned, but there's one element in what you said that really intrigues me. If membership in Congress were the only road to the Presidency, think how much better the work of Congress would be! Men would have to demonstrate their ability on the floor of the legislature in order to be considered for a cabinet position.

Recognizes the need for exact information

Cal Hendricks   Would the Vice-Presidents be responsible equally with the President in Mr. Finer's plan? Do you know, John?

John No, as I understand it—and we'd probably better study the ramifications of the plan if we're really interested in it—the President would have the advantage of extended discussion with those men elected to serve with him, but the final decision would be his.

Claire It just occurs to me—do I have it right? —that under this plan the defeated presidential candidate wouldn't disappear from public life but would stay in Congress and lead the opposition!

John Yes, that would be true if Finer's suggestion—that any defeated candidate for the cabinet who didn't have a Congressional seat at the time be given one—were adopted.

Recognizes the need for a new springboard, and introduces one quickly enough that no loss of group spirit or momentum occurs

Bob Surely are some ideas there to think about. Think we're ready to move on? I was interested in Wilson's description of us as a "great peaceful people"—in what ways do you suppose we would really be called "peaceful"? At the time Wilson spoke, of course, we'd never really fought a world war, but it seems to me we'd been in armed conflicts frequently: The War of 1812, the Spanish-American War, and so forth. So, how "peaceful" are we?

Had a member not raised the new issue at this time the leader could have suggested taking a new idea; he would have made no summary because of the obstruction that would have offered to the free flow of group thought

Dennis Schramm Well, I do think it would be fair to say that we stay out of wars as long as we can—we keep trying to negotiate. That's as a nation—what about as individuals? I sometimes wonder whether we aren't almost too slow as individuals to leave our peaceful state of mind and take issue against abuses around us——

Berta Clayborne Remember that instance Norman Cousins told a couple of years ago in

Saturday Review—how he was standing in a train station in the Eastern United States somewhere— that a woman ran in with a man pursuing her and she screamed for help, but servicemen and by- standers here and there all over the room paid absolutely no attention? When we get to the point where we won't jeopardize our own peaceful state to help in the obvious distress of someone else, isn't that going entirely too far?

Despite the freedom of the participants in exploratory discussions to pursue any idea that interests them as far as they wish, then abandon it and choose another, they are yet responsible for using appropriate facts and for taking relevant assumptions and goals of their society into account. It is likely that more of the needed information will be available, that more provocative lines of inquiry will be suggested if the members have whetted their interest in the interchange by responding vigorously to the material during their preparation.

Summary

Enlightenment discussions take three principal forms: study, evalu- ation, and exploration. Preparation for a study group involves organ- ization of relevant information into an outline appropriate to the topic; Study Guides are often provided to suggest relevant subtopics for consideration. Preparation for evaluative discussion consists of listing pros and cons of the program, policy, or person, being discussed, or of measuring the program against suitable criteria. Preparation for exploratory discussion requires becoming familiar with a common body of material, choosing springboard ideas from it, and developing a series of provocative questions from these ideas.

References

(1) Charles R. Nixon, "Vital Issues in Free Speech," *Ethics,* 62 (January 1952), 103.

(2) John H. Colburn, "What Makes a Good Newspaper?" *Saturday Review,* 45 (June 9, 1962), 50-52.

(3) "A New President Aspires," *Newsweek,* 57 (January 23, 1961), 15.

(4) Richard E. Neustadt, "On Appraising the Presidency; Truman, Eisenhower, Kennedy," *Graduate Faculties Newsletter,* Columbia University, November 1961.

(5) Ashley H. Thorndike (ed.), *Modern Eloquence (World War,* Vol. XII), (New York: P. F. Collier & Son, 1936), pp. 205-214.

Readings and problems

1. Listen to enlightenment discussions heard in the classroom, public lecture hall, or on the air, with the purpose of classifying them as study, evaluative, or exploratory.

2. Prepare to participate in a classroom discussion of the study type on the question: *What is the significance of the International Geophysical Year?* Copy the following Study Guide and enter appropriate information you discover in your research:

I. What is meant by the IGY?

Main purpose

Held when

Number of countries participating

II. What was the origin of the IGY?

Earlier programs of international scientific cooperation

Preparation for IGY

Origin of idea

International Council of Scientific Unions (ICSU)

Special Committee for IGY (CSAGI); meetings; recommendation of rocket and satellite programs

National Committees in each country

III. What was the organization of the IGY?

Observation stations

World calendar

World Days

"Alerts"

World Meteorological Intervals

World Communication Network

Extent and financing of national programs (general arrangements for)

Logistic support from military organizations of major countries

Exchange of data

World Data Centers
Discussion of political problems
IV. What were some of the major findings of the cooperating scientific disciplines?
Upper atmosphere
  1. Geomagnetism
  2. Aurora and airglow
  3. Ionosphere physics
  4. Solar activity
  5. Cosmic rays
  6. Rockets and satellites
Earth's heat and water system
  1. Meteorology
     Antarctica
  2. Glaciology
  3. Oceanography
Earth's structure and interior
  1. Seismology
  2. Gravity
  3. Latitudes and longitudes
V. What are some of the major results of the IGY?
Standardization of instruments
Educational influence
Political significance
Post-IGY activities
VI. What, then, is the significance of the IGY?

3. Prepare a Study Guide for a study discussion on the European Common Market or on the significance of one of the United Nations Specialized Agencies, such as the Food and Agriculture Organization, the World Health Organization, or UNESCO.

4. Prepare to participate in a classroom discussion of the evaluative type on the question: *How democratic a country is Mexico (or Costa Rica or Guatemala or Argentina,* etc.)? Use the criteria suggested by Professor Fitzgibbon for the polls referred to on page 161 (the numbers following each of the items represent relative *weight* to be given each in final evaluation):
  1. An educational level sufficient to give the political processes some substance and vitality. 1
  2. A fairly adequate standard of living. 1

3. A sense of internal unity and national cohesion. 1
4. Belief by the people in their individual political dignity and maturity. 1
5. Absence of foreign domination. 1
6. Freedom of the press, speech, assembly, radio, and so forth. 1½
7. Free elections—honestly counted votes. 2
8. Freedom of party organization; genuine and effective party opposition in the legislature; legislative scrutiny of the executive branch. 1½
9. An independent judiciary—respect for its decisions. 1
10. Public awareness of the collection and expenditure of governmental funds. 1
11. Intelligent attitude toward social legislation—the vitality of such legislation. 1
12. Civilian supremacy over the military. 1½
13. Reasonable freedom of political life from the impact of ecclesiastical controls. ½
14. Attitude toward and development of technical and scientific governmental administration. 1
15. Intelligent and sympathetic administration of whatever local self-government prevails. 1

    5. Prepare to participate in an evaluative discussion on the question: *How effective is the* _____ *as a metropolitan newspaper?* Use a well-known paper from your area for this discussion. Set up criteria for metropolitan newspapers in general in the first meeting of your group; then study numerous issues of the selected newspaper and make the evaluation in the second meeting of your group.

    6. Prepare to participate in a classroom discussion of exploratory type on the following paragraph from the article "A Frenchman Appraises U.S. Schools," by André Maurois, whom the *Saturday Review* describes as "a European scholar, novelist, and member of the Académie Française who was educated in France but has had long familiarity with the American people and their schools" (*Saturday Review*, 44, April 15, 1961, 54-55, 74):

> Most French educators would say that current affairs are out of place at school. My own master, the philosopher Alain, used to say, "Education should be resolutely in arrears." He meant that

the task of school and university is to transmit to
the young generation the culture patiently accumulated by centuries. If in school one does not
study Homer and Plato, Shakespeare and Molière,
Dickens and Tolstoy, there is a good chance he
will never read them at all. If one neglects history
in favor of current affairs, first he will never know
history, and second he will not understand current
affairs. The part of schools is not to expedite
current affairs but to initiate students in timeless
affairs.

At the close of the exploratory discussion, participate in class evaluation of this discussion on these criteria:
1. Worth and soundness of ideas expressed
2. Spirit and spread of participation among members
3. Degree of interest aroused for subsequent individual exploration

       7. Bring to class a listing of current articles
and chapters in books that you think would serve well as common
bodies of material for exploratory discussions by the members of
your class.

       8. Prepare to participate in exploratory dis-
cussion on one of the following articles or on some other challenging
article assigned by your instructor. Move through these three steps
on this common body of material: (1) Make a one-page outline of
the structure of the article; (2) Find at least six springboard
sentences; (3) Prepare at least three developmental questions for
each springboard.

Vannevar Bush, "Automation's Awkward Age," *Saturday Review,*
    45 (August 11, 1962), 10-11, 47.

Loren Eiseley, "The Long Loneliness; Man and the Porpoise: Two
    Solitary Destinies," *The American Scholar,* 30 (Winter 1960-
    1961), 57-64.

Clarence Faust, "Rising Enrollments and Effective Use of Faculty
    Resources," *The Key Reporter,* 22 (April 1957), 1-5.

Jerome D. Frank, "Are You a Guilty Parent?" *Harper's Magazine,*
    214 (April 1957), 56-59.

Robert L. Heilbroner, "The Revolution of Economic Development,"
    The American Scholar, 31 (Autumn 1962), 541-549.

Randall Jarrell, "The Appalling Taste of the Age," *The Saturday
    Evening Post,* 231 (July 26, 1958), 18-19 ff.

John A. Kouwenhoven, "What's American about America?" *Harper's Magazine*, 213 (July 1956), 25-33.

Russell Lynes, "Time on Our Hands," *Harper's Magazine*, 217 (July 1958), 34-39.

Joseph Margolis, "Juvenile Delinquents: The Latter-Day Knights," *The American Scholar*, 29 (Spring 1960), 211-218.

Martin Mayer, "The Trouble with Textbooks," *Harper's Magazine*, 225 (July 1962), 65-71.

Francis E. Rourke, "How Much Should the Government Tell?" *Saturday Review*, 44 (May 13, 1961), 17-19, 31.

Barbara Ward, "A Direction for the West," *Saturday Review*, 45 (January 27, 1962), 10-12, 59.

David Yellin, "I'm Married to a Working Mother," *Harper's Magazine*, 213 (July 1956), 34-37.

Chapter eight

DEALING

WITH IDEAS

IN THE

GROUP

With preliminary research completed and tentative judgments formed, the participant is ready to join in a group discussion of the subject. If the situation has allowed no such opportunity for specific preparation, he draws as well as he can upon his general knowledge and understanding of the subject in order to participate helpfully in the discussion. Now he and the others will move through the necessary steps together, developing ideas cooperatively.

Cooperative idea-development

How may the thinking of an individual in a discussion group differ from his thinking when alone? If the group in which he is participating is using the discussion process effectively,[1] he will have a greater store of ideas from which to choose—others' contributions and new extensions of his own through group stimulation; and he will also profit from the group's help in finding and correcting flaws in his own reasoning. By the same token his participation creates the same opportunities for other group members.

Opportunities in cooperative idea-development

Addition of others' ideas The contribution of other members will provide ideas to supplement those of each individual participant; their information from experience and research, their differing interests and points of view will add to his resources for further thinking. As Arthur Twining Hadley (1) said to his Yale students:

> The man who looks at events from one point only sees them flat. The man who looks at them from several standpoints sees them solid. He gets their depth as well as their surface.

Despite the attempts an individual may have made to see events from more than one point of view, there is no question that hearing the interpretations of others will greatly extend his understanding.

Profound differences in point of view were found extremely valuable in the fifteen months of work on United States industrial rela-

1. Problems of attitudes are considered in Chapter 9, problems of communication in Chapter 10, and of motivation in Chapters 11 and 12.

tions by the Labor Study Group initiated and supported by the Committee for Economic Development (a national organization of leading businessmen and educators). Nine prominent men, headed by University of California president Clark Kerr,[2] analyzed the influence of collective bargaining on the American economy. Chairman Kerr (2) described the differences of viewpoint which appeared in the committee discussions as follows:

> One axis of argument was between freedom of action as against result. Some people felt a·little more strongly that we should preserve freedom of action regardless of result. Others said that at this stage in American history it is result that should be foremost. Thus we were confronted with the age-old question of the relative values of the means and the ends that are sought.
>
> Another axis of discussion was the question of how much attention should be paid to the rights of the individual, how much to the stability and survival of the group, how much to the interests of society at large. Such considerations touch on one's whole philosophy regarding society itself.

Out of these lengthy committee deliberations, however, came a set of policy proposals that are significant for their courageous dedication to the public interest. Basic to such discussions is the increased stock of ideas available to the individual through the contributions of his colleagues.

Stimulation of one's own ideas Working with the group will tend to stimulate the individual's use of his own experience and knowledge; additional areas of his experience may become unexpectedly relevant. A hunch which he had thrust aside,

2. Members of the Study Group making the report on collective bargaining were Clark Kerr (chairman), formerly a labor mediator of wide experience on the West Coast; Douglass V. Brown, professor of industrial management, Massachusetts Institute of Technology; David L. Cole, practicing attorney and arbitrator, Paterson, N.J.; John T. Dunlop, professor of economics, Harvard; William Y. Elliott, professor of government, Harvard; Albert Rees, professor of economics, University of Chicago; Robert M. Solow, professor of economics, Massachusetts Institute of Technology; Philip Taft, professor of economics, Brown University; George W. Taylor, professor of labor relations, Wharton School of Finance and Commerce, University of Pennsylvania.

an example which he had by-passed in his preparatory thinking may gain value and appropriateness as the group thought-line makes them relevant.

If you are participating in a discussion on national leadership, for instance, the group may focus thought momentarily on the decline of citizen responsibility, an aspect that had not occurred to you in your preparation. But you suddenly think of a report in the newspaper on the action of local "Societies for Individual Responsibility" in your area. Your spontaneous account of the principles and achievements of these SIR groups becomes a clear and relevant contribution to the discussion and can assist the group in checking its reasoning up to that point.[3]

We have all experienced the heightening of our powers when we participate in an effective discussion group.[4] Any of us has information, suggestions that can lead to stimulating lines of thinking, and insights that are not available to us when thinking alone but that present themselves when our thought is stirred and enriched by participating in the cooperative activity.

Improvement of one's own ideas Often others are able to see flaws in our ideas better than we ourselves can. Frequently we proceed on slim but vivid evidence, especially if the experience is our own; we are overimpressed by the testimony of an expert we admire; we point our reasoning toward the achievement of certain goals and overlook probable results to other relevant ones. But others, looking at these thought-movements with different eyes, can see their weaknesses and suggest improvements. Thus, the errors that creep into the thinking of a person working alone can often be detected and straightened out by this cooperative effort of his colleagues.

Furthermore, each individual in the group can incorporate into his own thinking the best explanations and the most perceptive com-

---

3. A brief report of the first six months' activity of these groups is given in the article entitled, "SIR: A Study in Citizen Initiative," by Mary Kersey Harvey, in *Saturday Review*, 45 (June 2, 1962), 14-15.

4. When Ferenc Merei and his research assistants tried a careful experiment with nursery-school children, he reported that "Our experiment refutes the prejudice . . . that the group, through an evening effect, lowers the level of the individual. We observed exactly the opposite: the strength of the group strengthens its members." In "Group Leadership and Institutionalization," *Human Relations*, 2 (No. 1, 1949), 35.

ments made by other members. In this respect a well-functioning discussion group resembles an effective search party in a heavily wooded area. Each searcher covers a different territory, but a shout from one collects them all at that point where the clue has been discovered, and all—no matter what their previous individual labors have been—start off anew from this discovery. Graham Wallas (3), in a frequently quoted comparison, declared that "a group of people ... engaged in dialectic can, like a pack of hounds, follow up the most promising idea which occurs to any one of them." This opportunity to select the best idea from among alternatives upgrades an individual's thinking in a group.[5]

Forms of cooperative idea-development

These are among the forms of contributions that make up the idea-development process (4):

Initiation—the earliest mention in the discussion of an inference or a piece of information.

Restatement—repetition in identical or similar terms.

Clarification—development of the idea at hand by elaboration, example, analogy, or explanation.

Substantiation—proof on an issue before the group.

Extension—carrying an idea beyond its previous logical limits.

Simple request or response to request—remark to set a point straight in order to facilitate group understanding.

Pro and con modification—major or minor revision of an idea before the group.

Stated acceptance or rejection—declaration of approval or disapproval of an idea before the group.

Synthesis—combining the best ideas discovered or produced.

Summary—restatement of major points previously established.

The following excerpts from a classroom discussion show different forms of contributions that occur in a group's attempt to establish a set of standards; each participant came to the discussion with a

---

5. Marjorie Shaw conducted a study of groups and individuals meeting a task in which each separate step had to be correctly taken before the right answer was obtained; she found that other members were three times as likely to detect errors in a mistaken idea as the person who had originally contributed the idea. See "A Comparison of Individuals and Small Groups in the Rational Solution of Complex Problems," *American Journal of Psychology*, 44 (July 1932), 491-504.

tentative list of criteria and was ready to participate in the cooperative idea-development:

> **Tracy Hoffman (leader)** We are concerned today with the question, *How effective is the* Seattle Times *as a metropolitan newspaper?* and our first aim is to suggest appropriate criteria by which to judge any metropolitan newspaper. (*Initiation of information*) You have all, I am sure, heard of the recent Ravenna cave-in. (*Initiation of inference*) This was an excellent opportunity for people to take a poll to see how quickly news like this travels and through what channels. (*Extension of inference*) And a poll was taken, and it was found that, oh, in something like 24 hours or 48 hours after this cave-in, 96.8 per cent of the people questioned knew about it. (*Extension of information*) Eighteen per cent of the people contacted knew from conversation, 18 per cent also knew from television, 24 per cent knew from radio, and an amazing high of 36 per cent of these people contacted knew about this recent event through the newspaper. (*Extension of information*) Despite the popularity of radio and television, the newspaper still seemed to afford this information to a greater percentage of people. (*Synthesis of inference*) The important job we have, then, is to suggest criteria by which to gauge a metropolitan newspaper's effectiveness. (*Restatement of information*) So let's get right into it, if we may. What is one—let us consider one— criterion for a metropolitan newspaper? (*Request for initiation of inference*)
>
> **Joan Morris** It should bring to the people an accurate and unbiased account of the news, I think. (*Initiation of inference*) That would be about the first thing that you would put down. I feel that this is of prime importance. (*Extension of inference*)
>
> **Bill Jacobs** You're concerned here with just the news section, then, aren't you? Not the editorials and feature sections. (*Request for clarification of information*)

Joan   No, just the news report. (*Clarification of information*)

Bill   Um-hm. (*Acceptance of inference*)

Leader   Could you explain it a little bit further for us? What exactly do you mean by unbiased? (*Request for clarification of inference*)

Joan   Well, the main reason you read a newspaper is to find out about news. (*Substantiation of inference*) And I think that we deserve to find truthful news instead of news cluttered with the reporter's or publisher's opinions. (*Clarification of inference*)

Betty Janisek   In other words, they should just report the facts—— (*Clarification of inference*)

Joan   That's right. (*Acceptance of inference*)

Betty   ——and allow the readers to form their own opinions. (*Extension of inference*)

Joan   Or if they are going to add opinions, they should move the article to the editorial page. (*Pro modification of inference*)

Betty   Um-hm. (*Acceptance of inference*)

Leader   Could we make a statement then? That is, I feel, a good criterion (*Acceptance of inference*); can we make a statement that we can use— just kind of bring this together now? Can some of us do this? (*Request for synthesis of inference*)

Sandra Rupert   Before we do that (*Acceptance of inference*), I would just like to say that I think it would be important to include things like timeliness and clearness and conciseness in reporting the news, not just objectivity. (*Pro modification of inference*)

Shirley Richards   Did you say conciseness? (*Request for information*)

Sandra   Yes. (*Response to request for information*) I'm including all these different things in reporting the news. It should be timely, clear, and economically stated—that's what I mean by concise. (*Restatement of inference*)

Leader   So far, then, we have that a metropolitan newspaper should give the public accurate, unbiased and timely news coverage. (*Summary of information*)

From this point the group moved on to the formulation of a second criterion, then a third, and so forth. Having completed this criteria-building phase, the group members moved through an evaluational phase in order to answer their basic question about the effectiveness of the one particular newspaper.[6]

You have seen that the onward flow of contributions is not a steady one. In effective discussion, the forward surge of ideas—the *idea-composition*—is accompanied and underlaid by another process, that of *idea-correction*: careful examination of ideas to ensure their soundness and appropriateness is as important as vigorous production of ideas. Thus, the conclusions drawn cooperatively moment by moment—from evidence supplied by the members, from opinions of experts upon whom they rely, and from motivation provided by the values toward which they strive—are subjected to rigorous testing so that errors which would lead the group further and further from the truth can be corrected.

But the two activities of producing and testing ideas are not rigidly separated in the discussion process, as they are in the method of creating ideas labeled "brainstorming."[7] In discussion the two activities take place concurrently, as the focus of the participants alternates from one to the other.

Idea-composition

In the cooperative development of ideas a thought comes before the group like a piece of modeling clay, tentatively shaped for group consideration by one member; in the hands of the group it is changed, added to, reshaped as the members move collectively toward their goal. This piecemeal task is accomplished by suggestions from the entire group, each member contributing his best insights into the matter at hand. Attempts to determine which participant is con-

6. See Chapter 7 for an explanation of appropriate preparation for *evaluative* discussion.

7. In the brainstorming procedure members of a small group give rapid-fire, spontaneous suggestions for handling a specific, limited problem, with no critical judgment of any suggestion permitted. Later the list thus produced is carefully studied for ideas which might actually be fruitful; if 5 or 6 per cent are deemed worth while, the session is considered a success. Originated by Alex Osborn, the method is much used in industry and government, with valuable results claimed.

tributing most are fruitless and irrelevant.[8] The group-produced line of thinking is the important thing; one member carries the thought-line onward until another takes over its development momentarily and then another. The members are pursuing a line of thinking together; each helps wherever he can.

Two kinds of contributions assist in *idea-composition,* those that concern the subject of the discussion itself and those that concern matters of the group procedure. Contributions relating to the actual discussion question are termed *substantive* contributions; in the excerpts given above, Tracy's comments about the reporting of the Ravenna cave-in are substantive contributions. Those relating to mechanics—methods of accomplishing the mutual task, matters of participation or use of time, and so forth—are termed *procedural;* Tracy's first comment and two final ones in his opening statement are procedural contributions. Undoubtedly, substantive contributions will far outnumber procedural ones in any successful discussion, since the sole purpose of the latter is to assure optimum flow of substantive contributions.

Idea-correction

Where the discussion process is being used well, the members check all contributions for relevance, clarity, soundness, and significance.

Relevance

With each idea suggested for the group thought-line members must guard against irrelevance, for if the contribution is not relevant, its incorporation may lead the members off on a tangent. Suppose in the student discussion on metropolitan newspapers Joan (or one of the others) had remarked, after Betty's suggestion that newspapers should "allow the readers to form their own opinions": "Yes, the

8. R. S. Woodworth has explained cooperative action, using the illustration of two boys carrying a log together: "By acting together upon the same object, the individuals composing the group coordinate their behavior, and the total behavior consequently possesses a unity analogous to that of a group of muscles in a coordinated movement. Similarly, when a group of people are working together upon a problem, the contributions of the several individuals toward the solution may be impossible to disentangle; at any rate, the behavior of the group has a coordinated unity due to the common object of thought upon which their individual efforts are directed."—From "Review of Allport's Social Psychology," *Journal of Abnormal and Social Psychology,* 20 (April 1925), 105.

Seattle Times really does this pretty well." This remark, no matter how true, is irrelevant at this moment, for the group is attempting at this point to establish criteria by which *any* metropolitan newspaper could be judged. If this premature assessment of the *Seattle Times* had turned the group aside from its immediate task, irrelevance would have been the cause.

Clarity

Sometimes the group needs to test for clarity before the question of relevance can be settled. Suppose that after Betty's suggestion someone had commented: "But maybe they can't." The members would have needed to discover what the person meant before they could have judged whether the remark was relevant. If the speaker meant that perhaps readers of metropolitan papers lack the ability to form their own opinions, he would have been raising an objection to the criterion being formulated by the group; whether or not his comment was well reasoned, it would have been relevant. If, on the other hand, he had meant that reporters on the *Seattle Times* were pressured by the publisher into injecting bias into news reports, then clarification would have revealed the irrelevance of the remark at this stage of the discussion. Often, of course, ideas that have passed the test of relevance will still need clarification.

Soundness

Often, when relevance and clarity have been established, the idea is acceptable to the group as an obviously sound inference or piece of information without further examination. But sometimes it must be subjected to the further test of soundness.

Much of this testing goes on silently in the minds of the members. If every idea contributed in the group were tested orally without reference to its importance or its surface believability, the whole process of idea-development would be seriously crippled, never achieving its true momentum and vitality. But on all baffling and crucial points, the combined efforts of the group follow the reach forward with a test of the point—the same sequence as that of the skilled climber making his way up a steep rock face. His choice of the ledge is guided by a general notion that it will test out, but his consequent use of the ledge is determined by how well it did in truth test out. And it is thus with the group: it reaches with information and inference toward new segments of the thought-line, but on important and questionable segments tests aloud the sturdiness of the new segment before trusting it as the basis for the next reach forward.

In maintaining this inner alertness that subjects all ideas to logical standards and in performing the oral testing of important segments, the members first identify the rational process as: (1) facts-to-conclusion; (2) expert opinion-to-conclusion; or (3) premise-to-conclusion. Then they apply appropriate tests and suggest any necessary corrections.

If the movement is facts-to-conclusion, the tests are these: *Are the facts true?* and *Is the reasoning from them sound?* [9] If the movement is expert opinion-to-conclusion, these questions are asked: *How authoritative is the expert? How sound is his reasoning?* If it is premise-to-conclusion, these are the questions: *Is this premise one we accept?* and *Does the conclusion follow from it logically?*

Examples of these thought-movements occur in the preceding excerpts:

1. Joan's reasoning "Well, the main reason you read a newspaper is to find out about news" is an implied facts-to-conclusion movement. No facts are actually presented, but she asserts this as a general truth. If the assertion had rung untrue to any member, he would have initiated a probing into its acceptability as a generalization from which one could reason.

2. Suppose that Sandra, in suggesting the inclusion of the three additional factors, had quoted her journalism professor as to their desirability. Despite the fact that he would probably have passed the *expertness* test, the opinion itself would have been examined rather than incorporated without question into the group's thought.

3. Joan's statement, "And I think that we deserve to find truthful news instead of news cluttered with the reporter's or publisher's opinions" is part of a premise-to-conclusion movement; it asserts a *value* which is to provide a basis for the conclusion with which she had started her comments to the group. If others had not considered *deserving truthful news* one of the values of our democratic society, or had thought newspaper reports unrelated to this value, they would have brought these questions to the attention of the group and the decision on the soundness of the reasoning would have been made cooperatively by the members.

9. For a review of the tests of evidence and reasoning, see Chapters 4 and 5.

Thus, it is clear that many ideas are so obviously acceptable that they require no oral testing, whereas the implications of others must be orally stated and explored before they can be judged. Further excerpts would show also that the elements of a thought-movement need not proceed in a straight line nor be presented by the same person. If any idea does not survive the candid application of these tests by the members, it is then abandoned, modified, or replaced.

Significance

Granted that an idea is clear, relevant, and sound—is it being used with appropriate weighting? Here the discussion participant asks himself: *Is this idea being given too little importance? Or too much?* In order to answer his query, he looks at the idea's relationship to the larger framework of the total discussion. It is probably Sandra's inward application of this test that prompts her to ask the inclusion of *timeliness, clearness,* and *conciseness* along with *objectivity* in the presentation of news.

Idea-composition and idea-correction

For the segment of a discussion on unemployment given below, comments at the left point out the members' attempts at idea-correction:

George Ruby (leader)   To summarize what we've been saying so far: we've seen that the rate of unemployment in our country remains high, with hardship for millions of our work force and their families, that this causes a severe drain on public funds and gives the Communist agitators a ready talking point wherever they are spreading their propaganda. Now we're ready to suggest the causes of our problem of unemployment; we've defined it as severe and likely to increase, and Bernard Nossiter of the *Washington Post* has described it as "one of the most paradoxical and obstinate of our times." Well, how shall we start? What factor shall we look at first as a possible cause of this problem?

*Asserts premise;
members should ask
selves whether they
subscribe to it*

Bill Voorhees I suppose we could point at the weakened demand for goods or at the immobility of our work force or the fact that most of the workers have just one skill and are thus prey to "hard-core" unemployment, but I think we ought to take the most important one first, and that's surely automation——

Questions premise

Leader Let's hold up a minute! You named several things we'll want to consider—reduced demand, lack of mobility, lack of needed skills, "hard-core" unemployment, automation—we'll want to take them one by one, and, you know, we don't *have* to take the "most important" first——

*Also questions
premise*

Pete Green That's a good thing, because we don't really know which is most important, do we, at this point?

Denies premise

Jim Johnson In fact, there are two studies that say it's *not* automation—let's see, Robert Solow from the staff of Walter Heller, Chairman of the Council of Economic Advisers, and, what's the other? Oh yes, the Knowles and Kalachek study for the Joint Economic Commission for Congress—both of these point out that unemployment has not shown any unusual increase where there has been the most automation——

*Holds back from
substituting an
authoritative statement
for group thinking*

Pete Well, let's back off from that and do some looking at it ourselves.

Leader Yes. Well, where shall we start—with automation, since we've already been talking about it?

John Bao Yes, why not? And then go back to the others.

*Presents
facts-to-conclusion
contribution*

Allan Worth Well, I'm wondering whether automation really is a cause of unemployment after all. Look what it did in the automobile industry; certainly it killed jobs like harness-making and carriage-building, but it added a hundred jobs for every one it knocked out. Actually, automation created employment!

Pete True *in the long run*, for sure. But what happened to those particular harness-makers and

Begins to test the reasoning that is under consideration all through this segment
Note the shift from unemployment in a general sense to unemployment in a specific sense; speaker recognizes shift and so no fallacy of equivocation occurs

carriage-builders? Do we know that they—those very men—actually found jobs in the automobile industry? Or, in fact, anywhere? And, unless they did, wouldn't we have to say that automation did in fact cause their unemployment?

Bill It surely did! Just like the Industrial Revolution in England, when the cotton mills did so much harm——

Jim You know, though, Vannevar Bush—he's the Honorary Chairman of the Massachusetts Institute of Technology—spoke about that; let's see, here's what he said in the *Saturday Review* for August 11, 1962: "It took a twentieth-century English philosopher, Alfred North Whitehead, to

(Note that Whitehead was testing similar reasoning by suggesting that the alleged cause was not a sufficient cause)

point out that most of the terrible sufferings which accompanied the Industrial Revolution were in fact unnecessary and were not caused by the steam engine or the power loom; they were instead the consequences of a giant step achieved in technical innovation with no corresponding step at all in social, political, or economic innovation." Isn't Whitehead just saying that it's bad when these technological advances—which are bound to come and we really wouldn't want it otherwise—aren't accompanied by—or synchronized with—other changes?

Leader We might say, "Unsynchronized automation," then?

Requests clarification

Allan Wait a minute; I'm not sure I get it——

Jim Well, it's just that if other changes were made at the same time, the bad effects wouldn't occur; it's when the rest of the total situation doesn't change that technological change hurts——

Allan OK, then, let's suggest what some of these changes should be.

Leader notes irrelevancy; may have stifled needed clarification of present matter, however

Leader   Could we hold our suggestions for remedies until a little later? We're trying to determine whether automation——

Returns to test earlier reasoning

John   Excuse me, could we go back just a minute? Aren't we confusing displacement with unemployment? Those carriage-makers were displaced, for sure, but can we actually count them as unemployed? Displacement doesn't *have* to mean unemployment, does it?

Whenever you participate in any sort of discussion—to plan the solution of a problem facing you and your colleagues, or to study, evaluate, or explore something to expand your knowledge and understanding—you are engaged in developing a thought-line with others. You will be of most assistance in making this development both forward moving and sound if you keep in mind the following suggestions:

1. Strive for *clarity, relevance, soundness,* and appropriate weighting of *significance* in your own contributions, and hope that, to the extent that you fall short, another participant will notice the error and start some remedial action.

2. Should someone's contribution not be clear to you, ask for explanation or state what you think is meant and inquire whether you have it right.

3. Assist in checking the relevancy of any idea which seems remote from the matter under consideration.

4. Whenever the group is developing a link in its thought-line that seems unsound to you, help the group to apply appropriate tests. Note quickly whether the movement is facts-to-conclusion, expert opinion-to-conclusion, or premise-to-conclusion and begin appropriate inquiries: (a) If the questionable link involves facts-to-conclusion, help the group to look at the lines of reasoning involved and the evidence on which they are based; (b) If the questionable link is expert opinion-to-conclusion, help the group to test the expertness of the opinion as well as its probable acceptability in terms of logic; (c) If the questionable link is premise-to-conclusion, help the group to look at the premise asserted and the conclusion it is said to lead to.

Increasing your ability to assist responsibly in *idea-composition* and *idea-correction* is of great importance in developing skill as a discussion participant.

Summary

Cooperative idea-development enriches the individual participant through addition of others' ideas, stimulation of his own ideas, and correction of his reasoning. It takes many forms: initiation, restatement, clarification, substantiation, extension, simple request or response to request, pro and con modification, stated acceptance or rejection, synthesis, and summary. Cooperative idea-development has two phases—idea-composition and idea-correction. *Contributions in composing the thought-line may be* substantive *or* procedural. *Idea-correction is the process of detecting and remedying errors in relevance, clarity, soundness, and significance.*

References

(1) A. T. Hadley, *The Moral Basis of Democracy* (New Haven: Yale University Press, 1919), p. 135.

(2) Clark Kerr, "Collective Bargaining in Crisis?" *Saturday Review*, 45 (January 13, 1962), 20-21.

(3) Graham Wallas, *The Great Society* (New York: The Macmillan Co., 1914), p. 246.

(4) These categories and the excerpt from a class discussion immediately following are paraphrased from the article entitled "Categories for Analysis of Idea Development in Discussion Groups," by Laura Crowell and Thomas M. Scheidel in *The Journal of Social Psychology*, 54 (June 1961), 155-168.

Readings and problems

1. Bring to class examples from your own experience where the comments of someone else in a conversation or discussion (a) recalled to your mind a piece of information you would not have otherwise thought of contributing; (b) helped you find a flaw in a line of reasoning you were suggesting to the group.

2. Classify each of the thought units indicated in the excerpt from the metropolitan newspaper discussion on pages 000-000 as *substantive* or *procedural*. Is the proportion between substantive and procedural comments appropriate?

3. Read about the brainstorming process in current periodicals as well as in these three books:

Charles H. Clark, *Brainstorming* (Garden City, N.Y.: Doubleday and Co., 1958).

Creativity, Paul Smith, ed. (New York: Hastings House, 1959).

Alex Osborn, *Applied Imagination*, rev. ed. (New York: Charles Scribner's Sons, 1957).

Conduct a brainstorming session on a specific classroom or campus problem, such as test-taking procedures or campus parking arrangements or facilities in the student union building. Discuss afterward the results you found in being free from critical judgment during the creative period. What implications does this finding have for your use of the discussion method?

4. Give attention to *idea-development* in conversations and discussions you hear in campus or community gatherings or over radio or television. Prepare to report examples of difficulties which arose from lack of *clarity* or *relevance* in the contributions of the participants.

5. Substitute a metropolitan newspaper from your area for the *Seattle Times* in the question: *How effective is the Seattle Times as a metropolitan newspaper?* Continue the discussion begun in this chapter, stopping several times to apply pointedly the tests of *soundness* to a thought-movement you are considering. At the close of your work in setting up the list of criteria, give attention to the relative *significance* of these criteria and assign a proper weighting to each.

6. Study the following excerpt from a discussion on the radio program *The University of Chicago Roundtable* with participants Herman Finer, professor of political science, University of Chicago; T. V. Smith, Maxwell Professor of Citizenship and Philosophy, Syracuse University; and John W. Taylor, executive director, Chicago Educational Television Association.[10]

A Separate the contributions into thought units and characterize each as one of the ten types of idea-development:

10. From "When Gown Talks to Town," *University of Chicago Roundtable*, No. 896, June 12, 1955. Reprinted by permission of the Office of Radio and Television, The University of Chicago.

Initiation	Simple request or response to request
Restatement	Pro and con modification
Clarification	Stated acceptance or rejection
Substantiation	Synthesis
Extension	Summary

B Characterize each thought unit as substantive or procedural.

C Find the elements (or supply them if they are implied rather than stated) of a half-dozen thought-movements in the excerpt. Describe each one as facts-to-conclusion, expert opinion-to-conclusion, or premise-to-conclusion.

D Apply appropriate tests of soundness to each of these selected thought-movements.

(The panel, with Mr. Smith as moderator, is in the midst of public discussion of the enlightenment type on the question of communication between professors and the public. The "gap" is the lack of such communication that often exists.)

1 **Mr. Smith** Now, you are telling us, Finer, about specific experi-
2 ences you have had in bridging this gap. Will you go on and tell
3 us a little more about it?
4 **Mr. Finer** I found, to begin with, that, for people who are intelli-
5 gent and want to be more intelligent, we can serve them by telling
6 them what the press does not, and perhaps cannot, do; behind every
7 fact that is precipitated into a newspaper column there is a whole
8 world of history and philosophy and social knowledge. The news-
9 paper is ephemeral; it cannot present that world. But the academic
10 man can; he knows current affairs but just does not want to talk
11 about current affairs alone but wants to talk about all the vast back-
12 ground that precipitates current affairs.
13 **Mr. Smith** I do not understand you to be dispraising the press——
14 **Mr. Finer** No; not at all.
15 **Mr. Smith** ——but rather praising the genius of this other
16 medium.
17 **Mr. Finer** Yes. It can support it; it can explain. It can put it
18 into perspective, so that the press becomes more important with that
19 which enables us to understand what the press is trying to say. That
20 is one thing that I found very strongly marked.
21 **Mr. Smith** Have you the impression that most people are ear-
22 minded rather than eye-minded and that therefore the radio appeals
23 more or less to the average person?
24 **Mr. Finer** I do not know about that. I would think it would vary.
25 The press has the one great advantage that it is visual, and we can

26 keep it with us and look over the words once again that we think
27 we may have forgotten or misunderstood. But there is something,
28 also, in the spoken word which depends, I think, partly upon the
29 personality of the speaker, which has a kind of cleavage power into
30 the mind of the listener.
31 **Mr. Smith** But when the two conspire to a common end for the
32 eye and for the ear, we have a magnificent chance to bridge this gap.
33 **Mr. Taylor** That is just what I was going to say. It seems to
34 me we cannot really say that people are ear-minded or eye-minded
35 but that they are obviously both, unless, of course, they do not have
36 their sight or hearing.
37 **Mr. Smith** Are you generalizing from your experience on the
38 *Round Table* on radio or the television experience you have had,
39 Finer?
40 **Mr. Finer** I take both of them, because we get our responses
41 from both. Another thing that is very important is this: Our life is
42 spent in a democratic community. It is important for us to under-
43 stand our statesmen; but if we hear a statesman speak on radio, he
44 is a practicing statesman, with a desire for longevity in the political
45 field. He has a great difficulty. He cannot say all that he would like to
46 say because what he says is a commitment. It can be "proved in
47 court," as it were, against him. But the independent, the academic,
48 who understands him and the issues that he has been playing with,
49 can come in to the public who wants to know about these things,
50 and thereby he can supplement; he can do what the politician, on
51 pain of death or suicide, practically cannot do.
52 **Mr. Smith** Taylor, did you notice that word "longevity" of the
53 politician?
54 **Mr. Taylor** I certainly did.
55 **Mr. Smith** We could put this in much simpler language: his
56 desire to be re-elected.
57 **Mr. Finer** Yes, his horizon is the next election. The academic
58 man's horizon, I am not going to say is eternity; that is too long.
59 But it is somewhere between the next election and eternity.
60 **Mr. Smith** Some say that the statesman is only the dead politi-
61 cian; but you are making a distinction between them while they are
62 still alive, aren't you?
63 **Mr. Finer** That is right. This is no denigration; I love them.
64 I was just thinking that the average person tends to be in the field
65 of society (with his modern, enormous, mammoth societies) rather
66 like the position that William James once assigned to those newly
67 arrived in the world: "There is a big booming, buzzing world in
68 front of them." And I think that can be focused and sharpened by
69 all the people.

70   **Mr. Smith**   You not only love them, Finer; you live off them,
71   don't you? Finer is a political scientist. He would not have a job
72   except for the work of the politician.
73   **Mr. Taylor**   It seems to me you were in Congress, weren't you,
74   Smith? You ought to know something about this, too.
75   **Mr. Smith**   I heartily agree with what Finer is saying, except I
76   think he perhaps overplays the amount the politician has in mind
77   that he is not willing to talk about in the interest of longevity.
78   **Mr. Finer**   Then I thought there was one other thing. There is
79   always something a teacher (in whatever field) must have if he is
80   worth being listened to—and one should not misuse a medium which
81   is a God-given one. He must be someone who has something unique
82   to offer. And I ask myself, "What do I mean by unique?" It can
83   be one of two things. He has either been a great scholar in that
84   he has excavated human experience and put something on the table
85   for us; and/or he has an interpretation, a way of looking at things,
86   and valuations on what is known, what has just been discovered,
87   and what has long been known. If he is unique in this respect,
88   very different from others, then he has a great contribution to
89   make. . . .

Chapter nine

MAINTAINING

EFFECTIVE

ATTITUDES

IN THE GROUP

In the preceding chapters we have considered the intellectual posture which members should adopt before and during the discussion. But emotional attitudes are also important. This chapter concerns three attitudes which members should maintain in order to achieve effective group interaction: (1) an open-minded attitude toward ideas; (2) a supportive attitude toward participants; and (3) a sense of personal responsibility.

Open-mindedness toward ideas

One primary requisite for good discussion is *open-mindedness* toward the ideas of others as well as your own. John Dewey (1) pointed out that open-mindedness is

> . . . very different from empty-mindedness. While it is hospitality to new themes, facts, ideas, questions, it is not this kind of hospitality that would be indicated by hanging out a sign: "Come right in; there is nobody at home." It includes an active desire to listen to more sides than one; to give heed to facts from whatever source they come; to give full attention to alternative possibilities; to recognize the possibility of error even in the beliefs that are dearest to us.

Considering others' ideas fairly

Open-mindedness means the "active desire" to give any idea fair consideration, to understand it fully and examine it without bias. It means willingness to grapple with a new idea[1] and to cooperate in finding as nearly as possible where truth really lies.

---

1. The difficulties in accepting a new viewpoint are explained by Walter Bagehot, a prominent political writer of nineteenth-century England: "One of the greatest pains to human nature is the pain of a new idea: it is . . . so 'upsetting'; it makes you think that after all your favorite notions may be wrong, your firmest beliefs ill-founded; it is certain that till now there was no place allotted in your mind to the new and startling inhabitant, and now that it has conquered an entrance you do not at once see which of your old ideas it will or will not turn out, with which of them it can be reconciled, and with which it is at essential unity."—*The Works of Walter Bagehot*, Forrest Morgan, ed. (Hartford, Connecticut: The Travelers Insurance Co., 1891), Vol. IV, *Physics and Politics*, Chapter V, "The Age of Discussion," pp. 547-548.

Sometimes, however, a member gives fair consideration only to ideas that hold an immediate appeal for him; he fails to pursue vigorously ideas that do not catch his imagination and interest at once. For instance, in a discussion on *improving the rehabilitation of prisoners,* he may fail to give fair consideration to a proposal for changing the parole system. His neglect may arise from lack of interest in a measure that comes so late in the process of rehabilitation; or he may believe public apathy would ruin the plan's chances of success; or he may simply fear "letting prisoners out too soon." In such cases he lacks an "active desire" to consider a suggestion not immediately attractive to him, not sufficiently developed, seemingly hard to handle, or somewhat disturbing. Or he may neglect the parole suggestion because it was contributed by someone who has been reticent in volunteering ideas or who phrased the suggestion poorly. By rejecting the idea for its lack of immediate appeal or its contributor's lack of influence, he has failed in open-mindedness. *Open-mindedness means fairness of consideration, not uncritical rejection.*

Nor, on the other hand, must the member accept too quickly a new, unexamined idea. The novelty of the idea may be attractive or the need to make quick progress in the group task or merely the desire to be considered a cooperative member—but these are not good reasons for accepting an idea without considering it fairly. Nor is the fact that the idea has been vigorously championed by the most articulate or the most experienced or the most affable member of the group a good reason for acceptance.[2] Whoever accepts an idea without careful consideration because of such external reasons as these has failed in open-mindedness. *Open-mindedness means fairness of consideration, not uncritical adoption.*

Recognizing possibility of error in one's own beliefs

Being open-minded not only requires the group member to give fair consideration to the ideas of others; it asks him to be objective

2. Researchers at a summer workshop found that discussion group members reported themselves not only as agreeing more with statements made by persons they liked but as perceiving their own statements being agreed with more by such persons. See M. W. Horowitz, J. Lyons, and H. V. Perlmutter, "Induction of Forces in Discussion Groups," *Human Relations,* 4 (No. 1, 1951), pp. 57-76.

about his own, to admit to himself that he may be wrong.[3] Benjamin
Franklin's plea for the adoption of the Constitution reveals his willingness to doubt his own beliefs (2):

> Mr. President, I confess that there are several
> parts of this Constitution which I do not at present
> approve, but I am not sure I shall never approve
> them: For having lived long, I have experienced
> many instances of being obliged by better infor-
> mation or fuller consideration, to change opinions
> even on important subjects, which I once thought
> right, but found to be otherwise. It is therefore
> that the older I grow, the more apt I am to doubt
> my own judgment, and to pay more respect to
> the judgment of others. . . .
> In these sentiments, Sir, I agree to this Consti-
> tution with all its faults, if they are such . . . I
> doubt too whether any other Convention we can
> obtain may be able to make a better Constitution.
> For when you assemble a number of men to have
> the advantage of their joint wisdom, you inevi-
> tably assemble with those men, all their preju-
> dices, their passions, their errors of opinion, their

3. Judge Learned Hand said that "the spirit of liberty is the spirit which is
not too sure that it is right." "I submit," Judge Hand said, "that it is only by
trial and error, by insistent scrutiny and by readiness to re-examine presently
accredited conclusions that we have risen . . . from our brutish ancestors; and I
believe that in our loyalty to these habits lies our only chance not merely of
progress but even of survival." Quoted in *The New York Times*, April 11,
1959, p. 12.

At hearings by a subcommittee of the Senate Committee on Labor and
Public Welfare, June 28, 1951, Judge Hand was characterizing Oliver Cromwell
as a man who did not use abstract principles for every occasion but rather
sought compromises, treating each incident by itself; Judge Hand said: "Let
me give you, as an instance, one utterance of his which has always hung in
my mind. It was just before the Battle of Dunbar; he beat the Scots in the
end, as you know, after a very tough fight; but he wrote them before the battle,
trying to get them to accept a reasonable composition. These were his words:
'I beseech ye . . . think that ye may be mistaken.' I should like to have that
written over the portals of every church, every school, and every courthouse,
and, may I say, of every legislative body in the United States. I should like to
have every court begin, 'I beseech ye . . . think that we may be mistaken.'"
In *The Spirit of Liberty: Papers and Addresses of Learned Hand*, collected by
Irving Dilliard (New York: Alfred A. Knopf, 1952), p. 229.

> local interests, and their selfish views. From such
> an Assembly can a perfect production be expected?
> . . . Thus I consent, Sir, to this Constitution be-
> cause I expect no better, and because I am not
> sure, that it is not the best. . . .
>
> On the whole, Sir, I cannot help expressing a
> wish that every member of the Convention who
> may still have objections to it, would with me, on
> this occasion doubt a little of his own infallibility
> —and to make manifest our unanimity, put his
> name to this instrument.

Indeed, a person who is dogmatically committed to his own ideas
cannot truly have an attitude of open-mindedness toward the ideas
of others. If he presents his conclusions on a matter as if they were
final and views their modification or rejection as a personal attack
requiring self-defense, he lacks in objectivity and open-mindedness.

Preparatory to the formation of the United Nations Atomic Energy
Commission in 1946, a United States State Department Committee
appointed a Board of Consultants to suggest a formulation of policy
to assist the American representative. David Lilienthal of the Tennes-
see Valley Authority and four other prominent men[4] became the
Board of Consultants and met almost daily over a period of two
months to study and prepare their report. Men of diverse backgrounds
and high individuality—two businessmen, one chemist, one physicist,
one government administrator—they were alike in their distrust of
committee techniques. Wisely, then, these men spent their first meeting hours discussing the most common causes of committee failure.
Norman Cousins and Thomas K. Finletter (3), analyzing the group's
final report, reported one consultant as saying:

> It seemed to be fairly well agreed that most
> committees break down because many members
> come to their job with fully formed conclusions,
> having almost property rights in their own ideas,
> and spend all their time proposing and exhorting

4. Chester I. Barnard, President of New Jersey Bell Telephone Co.; Dr. J.
Robert Oppenheimer, of the California Institute of Technology and the University of California; Dr. Charles Allen Thomas, Vice-President and Technical
Director, Monsanto Chemical Co.; Harry A. Winne, Vice-President in charge
of Engineering Policies, General Electric Co.

rather than listening and considering. It was inevitable that the old system would make for a
clash of personalities even more than for a clash
of ideas.

Our first joint decision, then, was to liberate
all our discussions from idea-possessiveness. No
point would be argued down; we agreed that we
would attack the problem inductively, working
from the ground up, assembling all facts pertinent
to the problem as a basis for conclusions, implied
or implicit. We agreed that all questions coming
up were to be considered as being brought up by
the group as a whole rather than by any single
member. If a member had an objection to any
one point, it was to be regarded as something that
troubled the group as a whole. . . .

At first, it was hard to do this. Every now and
then the discussions would break down just because one of us found it difficult to get used to
the science of joint thinking and would lapse into
the role of prosecutor or defendant. But little by
little, the preconceived ideas dropped out; the
clash of conflicting personalities became less and
less apparent.

Out of the group objectivity thus created came a remarkable report
that has been extremely valuable as a guide for private and public
discussion. And the advice for conquering idea-possessiveness is
extremely worth while for all persons interested in manifesting attitudes conducive to successful discussion.

Instead of militantly defending his idea, the member should explain
it further so that the others can examine it fairly; he should join
with the others in seeking out whatever weaknesses it may have and
suggesting appropriate changes. In fact, although he may not be
able to spot the weaknesses in his own idea, he is particularly well
fitted to help in its modification and he should not deprive the
group of his assistance through oversensitivity, petulance, or mis-
construction of others' motives. Indeed, the member's attitude toward
ideas must be one of true open-mindedness; he should show a genuine
desire to search for truth and an ability to respect it wherever it
arises in the interaction of the group. He should conduct himself
in the spirit which Montaigne recommended in his *Essays:*

When a man differs from me, he raises my attention, not my anger; I advance toward my opponent and profit from his instruction. The cause of truth ought to be the common cause of both of us.

The truly open-minded member views modification of the idea which he has presented as a valid part of the group's progress toward its goal and adds his best efforts as a fully cooperating member.

An honest skepticism toward his own infallibility, however, should not impel a member to abandon his idea quickly at the first sign of criticism. He should not withdraw with an abrupt loss of confidence in the idea or a feeling of being rebuffed by the group; he should not seek to get out of the spotlight of group attention as quickly as he can. If his ideas were the result of careful research and thinking, they have some value that deserves the consideration of the group. He should resist any tendency to abandon his ideas too quickly: perhaps the group needs further explanation or needs to focus on the ideas longer to perceive their actual worth.

Thus, a member must neither be overly defensive of his own ideas nor abandon them too quickly; staying between these extremes is one of the most important aspects of open-mindedness.

Supportiveness toward members

No matter how open-minded the attitude of the members is toward ideas, the group can be severely handicapped in its cooperative interaction if the members do not maintain mutually supportive attitudes. An attitude that enables others to do their best work includes *acceptance* and *expectation*.

An accepting attitude by one member toward another means a welcoming of the other into full-fledged partnership in the work of the group. Acceptance of the person does not mean uncritically accepting his ideas—these must be judged on their own merits. It means, rather, demonstrating good will toward the individual, inviting him to participate in an atmosphere of general and generous receptiveness. It means recognizing his worth and appreciating the loyalties he feels to other groups and other causes.[5]

5. At times a member's reference groups can be part of his strengths; at other times they can constitute blocks which must be understood, respected, and handled effectively by the other members of the group. See Chapter 2, pp. 000-000, for an explanation of reference groups.

This extension of sincere friendliness must not be transitory. Unless an accepting attitude is constantly shown, it will be seen as a reward for a particular behavior or opinion, and those who value the supportive relationship most highly will be likely to alter their contributions in order to bring the acceptance back again. The consequent distortion of the thought-line is obvious. Acceptance is not an attitude to be turned on and off; it should be steady and dependable; otherwise it produces more problems than it solves.

And this accepting attitude must be shown toward *all* members impartially. If it is extended to certain members only, their participation and influence in the group may eventually come to dominate the discussion and shut the others out. Likewise, if acceptance is shown to all in the group but one, such pointed exclusion is likely to stop his contributions or arouse belligerence. Obviously, limitations of acceptance—through favoritism or thoughtless neglect—inhibit the effectiveness of the whole group; acceptance must be impartially extended to all members.

The second component of an effective attitude toward others is that of expectation. The member shows as he speaks and as he listens that he expects others' efforts to be whole-hearted and their motivations sincere. He shows that he regards them as responsible members of a cooperative team.[6] Extending his confidence to all implies that, despite any differing status among members in the group, he regards *all* members as valuable partners in the group's work and solicits and appreciates *all* their efforts. The effect of an attitude of *expecting the best* becomes clear when contrasted with an attitude of *expecting the worst*. You have noticed members with negative attitudes reacting with barely suppressed groans to some talkative, overforceful, or somewhat boring individual.[7] But notice how much more effective is the attitude of the member who sincerely values all contributions and solicits the group's attention to them. By acknowledging the potential worth of all ideas, he supports and encourages the participation of all group members.

6. In one investigation, for instance, the researchers found that those discussions in which the members lost themselves in the work of the group to the extent that they later found it hard to remember *who* had said *what* were highly satisfying to the participants. See Leon Festinger, A. Pepitone, and Theodore M. Newcomb, "Some Consequences of De-Individuation in a Group," *Journal of Abnormal and Social Psychology*, 47 (April 1952), pp. 382-389.

7. See Chapter 12 for suggestions for handling disruptive members.

Personal responsibility

Within a discussion group of which he is a part, each individual has personal responsibility to act at the highest level of integrity and creativity that is possible for him. He is personally responsible for (1) volunteering information and ideas on the subject and suggesting procedures for handling it; (2) resisting pressures to conformity; (3) rebuilding group interaction and atmosphere when necessary; (4) combating injustice, ignorance, and blundering; and (5) exposing misuse of group methods.

Volunteering

The member should recognize his continuing responsibility to put his thoughts (substantive and procedural) before the group without being urged or requested to do so. This does not violate his right to remain silent or to choose the time and manner of his contribution; yet he must recognize his constant responsibility to help provide the material on which the group efforts converge.

He must volunteer when something he knows or surmises may help the group effort—not only the products of his research and preliminary thinking, valuable groundwork though they are, but also the additional thoughts springing up in his mind from the suggestions of others. He should not be hesitant in expressing his thoughts: catching the attention of others, also engaged in formulating new suggestions, he should begin to put his nascent ideas into words.

Thus, volunteering means a willingness to try an idea out with the group even before you are completely sure of it yourself. If you feel that you must always be *right* in your ideas, you will hold back and thus deprive the group of many suggestions, worthy ones among useless ones. You must dare to present thoughts without having had opportunity to frame them completely or test them adequately.[8] Other

8. Ernest Dichter explained: "Creativity can be engendered and developed if we train ourselves not to be afraid of our own thoughts. Utter honesty and understanding of one's real motivations as far as this is possible are requirements for such an achievement. The desire to be always right often leads to an overcautious selection of the great variety of ideas floating around in one's mind. By this premature selection process we often lose some of our most valuable ideas. To associate freely, therefore, and permit almost all your thoughts to come out into the open either for yourself or in discussion is one of the prime prerequisites for the development of creativity."—*The Strategy of Desire* (Garden City, N.Y.: Doubleday and Co., Inc., 1960), p. 74.

valuable contributions you should make are questions, short affirmations of belief and approval, even helpful proposals or interpretations of terms—suggestions that enforce or assist in others' contributions without interrupting their flow.

These contributions, however, should be inserted with care, for doing too much may be as detrimental as doing too little. As a cooperative member you want to avoid wordiness, the urge to monopolize, a feeling of defensiveness about your own ideas; at the same time, you want to express friendliness toward other participants without sounding patronizing. Performing these functions is not a matter of adhering to a check list of *do*'s and *don't*'s; it is a matter of judgment. Contributions are helpful *if* they are suited to the immediate situation. While you are volunteering your best efforts, you must avoid throwing the other members of the group off balance by overzealousness.

Although the discussion subject itself should receive your main attention, something in the immediate situation—a phrase, a tone of voice, a facial expression, or a gesture—may alert you to strain in the group about the situation in general or about your participation in particular. It may be, for instance, that your sense of personal responsibility for the success of the group effort has caused you to try too hard; perhaps you have talked too much and too forcefully and the others have withdrawn more and more into silence. If so, you should realize that for the group to achieve its goal you may need to hold back, at least temporarily. You must volunteer your ideas to the group, but you must also use good judgment in introducing them to avoid dominating and thus disrupting the group effort.

You must begin to volunteer early in the session so that the group sees you as a fully participating member. If you wait overlong before making your first contribution, members will begin to speak past you. Moment by moment it will become harder for you to break in and be listened to. From the very outset—through brief assists on the ideas of others as well as more sizable attempts of your own to carry forward the line of thinking—you should take a vigorous part by volunteering.

Resisting pressures to conformity

Many pressures urge the individual to go along with the thinking of others in the group—his desire to be agreeable and cooperative, his desire not to be different, his actual liking and respect for others, a weakening regard for his own thoughts under the impact of a developing group consensus, and so forth.[9] His value in the group, however, lies not only in the affirmation he gives and the substance he provides on ideas with which he is truly in accord, but in the questions he poses when his experience, research, analysis, and basic assumptions give him a different view.[10]

The individual must remember that the contrary information he possesses, the differing interpretations and valuations he puts upon ideas are matters of greatest worth to the group, and that it is up to him to keep from being swept off his feet by the pressures to conformity. It takes fine discrimination to know when to protest against the thinking that the members of the group have built together. As a member of the group you must judge—in the light of the group goals, reality as you know it, and the potentialities of the group—whether you are in accord with the thought-line you and the others have been building or whether your conscience forces you to dissent. You owe this sincerity to the group and to yourself. This obligation does not mean a constant dragging of feet or making of virtue out of nonconformity. It means that you are personally responsible to the group for the straightest thinking of which you are capable, and that, when your ideas differ substantially from those of others, you must not hesitate to make the difference known.

9. Many experimental studies (*e.g.*, those by Sherif and Asch) have demonstrated the general tendency of individuals to conform to group opinion. Other researchers have found this tendency even stronger when the matter of opinion is ambiguous, that is, open to differing judgments; see R. R. Blake, H. Helson, and Jane S. Mouton, "The Generality of Conformity Behavior as a Function of Factual Anchorage, Difficulty of Task, and Amount of Social Pressure," *Journal of Personality*, 25 (March 1957), pp. 294-305.

10. Franz Alexander makes this same point within the framework of a larger view, the individual in society as a whole: "Life need not consist only of obligations to contribute to society; perhaps it becomes most meaningful in the obligation everyone has toward the cultivation and development of his own unique endowments. Man, through the cultivation of his unique self, although indirectly, advances human welfare more effectively than by merely accepting his share in those standardized assignments open to him in different social roles. The latter makes him a useful member of society in maintaining the status quo. Creative change, however, can only come from the not immediately useful realization of individual strivings, curiosities—sometimes even oddities—which may appear idle, playful and non-utilitarian at the moment."—*The Western Mind in Transition* (New York: Random House, 1960), p. 240.

Rebuilding group interaction and atmosphere

A member should also take a responsible part in handling difficulties which arise from time to time within the group activity.[11] If
the thinking has bogged down or if undesirable attitudes—such as
feelings of inadequacy, annoyance, hostility, frustration, and so forth
—have appeared in the group, he needs to make some reconstructive
efforts. Hazarding a quick guess as to the probable cause of the
difficulty, he thinks of actions that might minimize or remove it and
puts the action he thinks most appropriate immediately into effect.[12]
The following are examples of causes he may find and of possible
actions he could choose among on the basis of the immediate situation:

Cause:	**Possible reconstructive actions:**
Poor grasp of essential problem	1. Supply information, examples, experiences that will fill in the member's (or members') inadequate background and understanding; or 2. Raise questions that will uncover aspects and issues not so easily perceived by the less well-informed member; or 3. Define terms that may be troublesome; or 4. Explore in depth those areas in which the poorly informed member seems confident; etc.
Poor motivation	1. Express vigorously his own dedication to the group goal; or 2. Show vividly how the topic under consideration is related to important, highly prized values; or

11. The importance of achieving group-orientation is revealed in a study of
seventy-two decision-making conferences in business and government. The
investigators found that when groups had a high proportion of members
demonstrating self-oriented needs—dependency, status, dominance, aggression,
and catharsis—the members were poorly satisfied with the process as well as
with the results of the discussion. See N. T. Fouriezos, M. L. Hutt, and H.
Guetzkow, "Measurement of Self-oriented Needs in Discussion Groups," *Journal
of Abnormal and Social Psychology*, 45 (October 1950), pp. 682-690.

12. Here the member is applying to these difficulties in group interaction and
atmosphere the same problem-solving steps which he learned in Chapter 6 for
handling the subject problem. He (1) identifies the difficulty; (2) searches
out its most probable cause; (3) thinks out possible means of removing that
cause; (4) selects that behavior with most chance of removing the cause; and
(5) puts that behavior into effect.

3. Emphasize the expected results if the problem is not solved;

4. Link declared purpose of the unmotivated person with the present issue; etc.

Poor understanding of the discussion process

1. Ask the group as a whole what technique would be most efficient for the task at hand; or

2. Explain what method he is employing as he makes a contribution; or

3. Rephrase a member's unsuitable contribution to fall within the bounds of good discussion procedures, asking carefully whether the rephrasing represents the member's intention; or

4. Ask the group whether it might not be wise to stop consideration of the subject momentarily and let all members discuss how the use of the discussion process might be improved; etc.

Notable differences in prestige

1. Show supportive attention to the contributions of less renowned or commanding persons to indicate desire to hear the ideas of all; or

2. Carry the authority's idea forward, subjecting it to the same kind of rigorous investigation as anyone else's idea; or

3. Take direct issue with the pronouncement of the authority in a reasonable, unemotional, respectful manner; or

4. Simply play his own constructive role, regardless of prestige, with greater vigor and sincerity; etc.

Seeking personal (not group) goals

1. Reiterate the group goals vividly, tying them to values that all members would hold; or

2. Emphasize the importance of each individual's full assistance in achieving the common goal; or

3. Initiate group consideration of alternative goals, hoping that the disruptive person will acquaint the group with his personal goals; or

4. Explain the implications of the group's line of thinking so that it poses no hidden threat to other loyalties; etc.

Only your understanding of the immediate situation will help you decide among these and other possible lines of action, but you should choose quickly and put your choice into effect. When difficulties of interaction arise in the group, you have a responsibility to take what reconstructive action you can in order to help the group achieve its task.

Combating injustice, ignorance, and blundering

If a member sees that truth and justice are being sacrificed in the conclusions being drawn by the group, he is obligated to speak up, to make known the additional information, the lines of reasoning that the group is neglecting or misinterpreting. And this he should do with all the clarity and persuasiveness that he can muster. If his best cooperative efforts have failed to prevent the group from moving toward an unjust or unintelligent decision, he should take stronger measures to stop the error. His cooperativeness up to this point will have prepared him for this exigency: the others are assured of his good will, his dedication to their goal, his competence. Now, with all the persuasiveness at his command, he must present material for the group to use in re-examining the faulty conclusion.[13]

He may not be sure, of course, that his interpretation is wholly accurate, but he acts on the basis of what he knows and understands at the moment. It is his personal responsibility to keep the group from making what his best judgment tells him is a serious mistake. This honest effort should not be confused with the disruptive tactics of an individual who has come to the group with his mind made up and seeks to win the others to this preconceived opinion. Rather, without personal bias as to the outcome, he tries to keep the group from adopting insufficiently examined conclusions.

Exposing misuse of group methods

The member of a group also has a responsibility to detect objectionable motivations behind acceptable or common discussion methods.[14] Such abuse of procedures might be suspected if a member's methods repeatedly brought detriment to the group purpose.

Wrong motivations may be partially classified as follows:

13. He will be using the tests explained in Chapters 4, 5, and 8 to detect the possible error.
14. "The last temptation is the greatest treason:
    To do the right deed for the wrong reason."—From *Murder in the Cathedral* by T. S. Eliot. Reprinted by permission of Harcourt, Brace & World, Inc., New York, and Faber and Faber, Ltd., London.

1. Motivation: to put others off balance
Methods:

Inappropriate and inexplicable change of pace, tone, volume, or language level (*i.e.*, formality, technicality, etc.).

Overextension of another's idea so that he (a sincere person) is made to seem to contradict himself or to have been extreme or unreasonable.

Abrupt switch from logic to sentimentality (*e.g.*, "You don't want your children deformed, do you?").

Disparagement of important matters by overcasual reaction to them or by minimizing their importance verbally.

Studied misrepresentation: continued emphasis of a minor point or de-emphasis of a major one; claiming more or less than was originally claimed; treating honest questions as dogmatic assertions.

2. Motivation: to divert attention from the purpose
Methods:

Tangential anecdotes that frequently interrupt the discussion, starting with some tie to the thought-line.

Humor.

Creating minor disturbance (searching for map, dropping notes, etc.) to withdraw attention from ideas he wishes to receive less attention from the group.

3. Motivation: to delay the work of the group
Methods:

Unnecessary summarization at short intervals.

Cautions against moving too fast.

Deceptive show of deliberation and judgment, such as bodily posture and gestures while pondering.

4. Motivation: to induce feelings of inadequacy in other group members
Methods:

Use of unnecessarily technical language.

Insistent and repetitive demands for definition.

Studied disregard of a person's comments, going back to the previous speaker as though nothing had been said.

Repeated usurpation of the leader's functions.

5. Motivation: to control others by building a personal image
Methods:

Collusion, *i.e.*, feeding cues to confederates; the conspirators may not be looking at each other, but they open opportunities for each other to add ideas and gain stature in the eyes of the group.

Overresponsiveness in listening and responding to give a false aura of cooperativeness.

Fostering involuntary imitation, by assuming a homespun simplicity or by inspiring awe.

Using new phrases just catching on in the public vocabulary, thus making self pleasantly conspicuous.

Moving faster than others, with suggestions before others get started.

Taking an extreme position, then centering a little to seem cooperative.

Name-dropping, place-dropping, experience-dropping ("When I had dinner with Leonard Bernstein in New York last month, he said. . . .").

Specious earnestness ("Oh, I'm *so* glad you brought that up; I think it's *enormously* important because. . . .").

Adopting a sage role; *e.g.*, remaining quiet in the early part of the discussion, but coming in when the group has become anxious about him;[15] he then shows himself to be so reasonable, so kindly that members vie with each other to agree with him and neglect to be critical of his contributions.

Many of these actions can occur in the ordinary course of discussion without disruptive motivation; the danger to group judgment and welfare arises when they are done to achieve such subversive purposes as the five listed above. Such motivations animate persons who for some reason want to prevent the decision the group seems likely to make or want the group to be unsuccessful or its leader discredited. These desires may be personal—to maintain a job, sell a product, keep a policy intact; at other times they may reflect a fundamental disagreement with current social or political philosophy.

If you detect that such motivations are at work in your group, you must expose them or thwart them. Should you alone in the group recognize what is happening, you may need to begin by neutralizing

15. E. E. Smith set up five-member groups of college students to play the game of "Twenty Questions" and included in each group two students who, unknown to the others, were to remain quiet during the discussion. He found that this lack of expected participation reduced the productivity and the satisfaction of the others and made them defensive. See E. E. Smith, "The Effects of Clear and Unclear Role Expectations on Group Productivity and Defensiveness," *Journal of Abnormal and Social Psychology*, 55 (September 1957), pp. 213-217.

the undesirable effects on the group—assist the persons put off balance or help the group move on again, and so forth. By becoming more active yourself, more powerful in your own contributions, more helpful in the work of the group, you may be able to offset the subtle destructive influences. Even if such efforts on your part fail, the fact that something is seriously wrong will likely have become clear to enough of the group members that the tactics can be openly challenged. Once such unscrupulous maneuvers are exposed for what they are, their power is lost.

No individual should become suspicious of good actions merely because they can be used to cover bad motives; but, if he values the purposes of the group in which he works and of the society in which he lives, he must assume his responsibility to detect and expose these deceptive practices when they occur.

Summary

For effective discussion members must demonstrate three attitudes: (1) open-mindedness toward ideas; (2) supportiveness toward members; and (3) personal responsibility. Open-mindedness means considering others' ideas fairly—not rejecting or adopting them uncritically—and being neither unduly defensive toward one's own ideas nor too ready to abandon them. Supportiveness means enabling others to contribute to the discussion by accepting them personally and expecting valuable contributions from them. A sense of personal responsibility means volunteering; resisting pressure to conformity; rebuilding group interaction and atmosphere; combating injustice, ignorance, and blundering; and exposing the misuse of group methods.

References

(1) John Dewey, *How We Think* (New York: D. C. Heath & Co., 1933), p. 30.

(2) *The Records of the Federal Convention of 1787*, Max Farrand, ed. (New Haven: Yale University Press, 1937), Vol. II, rev. ed., pp. 641-643.

(3) Norman Cousins and Thomas K. Finletter, "A Beginning for Sanity," *The Saturday Review of Literature*, 29 (June 15, 1946), 9.

Readings and problems

1. Watch for examples of idea-possessiveness in discussions and conversations which you observe or in which you participate. How did the idea-possessiveness reveal itself? What reactions to the idea-possessiveness did you notice?

2. Think of persons you have observed who, on first hearing a new idea, tend to reject it or to accept it without considering it. Bring a list to class of the phrases they used in making such uncritical rejections or acceptances.

3. During your next classroom discussion make an analysis of how idea-possessive the participants are. Stop at any point where an idea is being argued down or an objection is being by-passed, and consider—as a group—what is happening, what caused it to happen, and how such incidents could be avoided.

4. Use the incident described below as the basis of a classroom discussion on *acceptance* and *expectation*. Make two lists in preparation: first, of the factors in the first situation that made the engine-room men feel they didn't belong to the ship; second, of the factors after the blow-by-blow description was started that changed their feelings.

When Navy put to sea right after Pearl Harbor, morale in the engine rooms of the larger ships was often at a very low ebb under strenuous battle conditions. This wouldn't ordinarily be a matter of life and death, except for the fact that there are times when the captain wants an extra five knots, for tactical reasons, over and above the maximum rated speed which is clearly stenciled on the engine-room control panel.

On one particular ship, the Old Man decided he wanted that extra five knots. The executive officer passed the order down the line until it got to the man who had his hand on the throttle. And the word came back up the line to the Old Man: "Can't be done."

The Captain demanded to know, "Why not?" The reply came back from the engine room: "We've got boiler scale." Boiler scale, apparently, had something to do with the rated maximum capacity of the boilers, beyond which you were not supposed to pile on extra steam.

He groused and griped to his exec and to others of his top brass. Finally he mentioned it to the chaplain. The chaplain had an answer for him.

After one particularly strenuous engagement, the chaplain had happened into the mess. The men from above and below decks were filing in for a long overdue meal; the deck men were comparing notes on what they had accomplished. The din of bragging and counterbragging drowned out all other noises.

The chaplain noticed the below decks men, the "black gang." They weren't participating; they were just eating their bean soup. They had nothing to talk about. Indeed, had they not shown up for chow, they wouldn't have been missed.

"Captain," said the Chaplain, "I think that's what's wrong. Those men think they'd never be missed. All they do is turn valves, throw switches, pull levers, watch gauges and oil pressures—no matter what's happening topside. From start to finish in an engagement, they don't know what's going on. They don't tie in what they're doing with winning battles.

"They get orders, but there's no feeling of urgency or importance attached to the orders—none that means anything to them, that is. They never know when they'll be blown to bits, and they have no hand in preventing it, and get no recognition for the part they might play in preventing it. Captain, those men don't feel they belong to the ship."

The Old Man thought about that for a minute. "I see what you mean," he said finally. "What can we do?"

The chaplain suggested they find an officer who'd had news or sports broadcasting experience in civilian life, that they put him behind a microphone on the bridge, and that he give a running account over the public address system of the entire strategic and tactical situation as it unfolded, and of the immediate part their own ship was playing in it. He was to give a blow-by-blow description of each engagement, the disposition of the enemy, and the ship's battle status at every instant. The Captain agreed. They found their man, a lieutenant, jg, and put him to work.

During the next battle engagement the lieutenant did his job well. After it was over the captain said to him, "Lieutenant, give me that microphone. I want to announce the box score." When he had finished he added, over the public address system, "This is peanuts compared to what we could do if we could overtake an enemy squadron to westward. But we need an extra five knots to do it."

He got the extra five. They overtook the enemy and clobbered him. After the engagement the Old Man grabbed the microphone from the lieutenant, "You men down in the engine room," he shouted. "We did it! *You* did it! Thank you for those five knots!"

The chaplain beat the men to the mess room. The usual din of competitive bragging was building. Presently one of the men from the engine room stood up and pounded his coffee mug on the table. When he got things quiet, he said, "Did you hear what the Old Man said? He said that if us guys hadn't found the extra five knots, you guys wouldn't have anything to talk about!" He sat down; the engine crew beamed.

One of the above-deck crowd yelled, "What about the boiler scale you guys have been griping about?"

"Boiler scale?" came the answer. "We licked boiler scale years ago! What the devil are you talking about?"[16]

5. Work out the three *role playing* situations described at the end of this problem in order to experience feelings of acceptance and nonacceptance in discussion groups. First, though, consider carefully the following summary of Grace Levit and Helen H. Jennings' explanation of role playing as a "technique in which people spontaneously act out problems of human relations and analyze the enactment with the help of other role players and observers." —"Learning Through Role Playing," in *Adult Leadership*, 2 (October 1953), 9-16. The summary is largely in the authors' own words.
Steps in the role playing process:
  I. Defining the problem
   A. The problem must be meaningful and important to the whole group.
   B. The problem should be clear and specific, not too complex in structure.
  II. Establishing a situation
   A. The design must depend on the learning outcomes desired or needed.
   B. If skill training is desired, as well as understanding or insight, the design must include an opportunity for new insights to be tried and tested in actual practice.
   C. The situation must provide enough content to make it seem real and to give players and observers a common orientation but should avoid the kind of complexity that will take the group's attention off the problem to be studied and get them bogged down in irrelevant situational facts or history.
  III. Distributing the roles
   A. Assignments should be made on the basis of which persons can carry the roles well and are not likely to be threatened or exposed by it. If the role is unfavorable, it should probably be assigned to a person with status or enough personal security to carry it without stress.

16. "Reaching the Black Gang," adapted from a story told by William Oncken, Jr., at the American Society of Training Directors Annual Meeting in New York, 1956. Reprinted by permission of Mr. Oncken.

B. The role takers must always be willing and not overurged.
IV. Briefing
    A. If the situation is very simple, it is probably better to depend upon an oral briefing.
    B. The briefing should be before the group of observers as well as the role takers or before only the role takers or the individual role taker on the basis of the purpose in mind.
    C. The briefing process should not be used to structure what the role takers are actually going to say or do in the action. Often a little warm-up among the members—talking among themselves about their roles—is helpful.
 V. Playing
    A. The director must see that everyone moves into the role play at the same time; a person talking as himself destroys the mood.
VI. Cutting
    A. Don't let the role play go on too long.
    B. Cut when
        1. enough behavior has been exhibited that the group can analyze the problem;
        2. the group can project what would happen if the action continued;
        3. the players have reached a stop because they don't know how to go on;
        4. there is a natural closing.
VII. Analyzing the action
    A. Director must be alert to see that the discussion relates back to the original problem under study.
    B. Sometimes the players are asked to comment first and sometimes the discussion is started by the observers.
    C. Director must see that observers steer clear of comments that evaluate the acting ability of the players or the convincingness of the players' interpretation of their roles.
    D. Observers should try to bring into the discussion data about *what they saw*, rather than restrict their comments to opinions about what should or should not have been done.
VIII. Replaying the situation
    A. The replaying may be done by the same or different players going over the same scene but making the changes recommended in the discussion.

B. The same or different players may try to play out a probable scene following the one just acted out, illustrating how the recommendations might change the consequences.

IX. Summary and evaluation

A. The group may wish to try a different role playing situation to test out their insights.

B. The director might suggest readings that the group could do to explore the problem further.

Cautions for use of role playing:

Avoid overpersonalization of problems. The director sets the tone for portrayals and analyses in introducing briefing and discussion, by pointing out that the job of the observers is to look at the actors in terms of their *roles.* It should be made clear that each actor is playing a specified role in a specific situation, and is merely giving his spontaneous interpretation of how such a character would be likely to respond in such a situation.

Avoid overuse of role playing. Reserve it for problems involving human relations.

Adapt the situation to the needs of the group. Groups that have gained some experience with the basic technique will want to build new or more complex structures for getting at specific problems. For example, alter-ego techniques, consultants to the role players, and so forth, might be used.

A. Plan a situation that might take place in office, schoolroom, committee room, or home where one member of the group is not being accepted; let the role play reveal how he reacts when he is continually by-passed, when nothing important is expected from him, and so forth. Play this situation and hold class discussion afterward.

B. Plan a situation where someone who has always been by-passed is treated with *acceptance* and *expectation* by the others. Play and discuss.

C. Plan a situation where someone *expects the worst;* play. Then let the person *expect the best;* play. Then discuss the differences.

6. Use the classification of wrong motivations on pages 209-210 as the basis for classroom discussion. Role play any of the behavior that would seem hard to visualize, such as "claiming more or less than was originally claimed"; or "over-responsiveness in listening and responding"; or "taking an extreme position, then centering a little"; and so forth.

7. Organize the class into small, leaderless groups to consider this categorization of *group needs:*

Group Task Needs	*Group Maintenance Needs*	*Group Focus Needs*
Ideas initiated	Members welcomed	Discussion opened
Ideas probed	Members harmonized	Progress encouraged
Ideas developed	Members group-oriented	Participation fostered
Ideas synthesized		Time apportioned
Ideas summarized		Discussion closed

Apply these questions to each of these needs in turn, making a group decision on each (using the term *members* to mean all participants other than the designated leader):

A. Which of these needs can be filled by members? Which, if any, should be left to the leader?

B. What will happen if any of these needs arise in a group and are not filled?

8. Select types of disruptive member behavior frequently found in discussion groups, such as the overtalker, the arguer, the single-point-pusher, the nontalker, the quibbler, the tangent-goer, the eager-agreer, the belittler, the blocker, the dominator. For the type chosen, set up boundaries within which remedial action by other members or the leader could be instituted beneficially; suggest possible causes of such behavior and work out several methods by which members and/or leader might handle such disruptive behavior when it is caused in each of the several ways.

9. Discuss these categories as the basis for evaluating the work of a member in a discussion group:

1. *Objectivity of contributions*
   Avoids finality of statement?
   Genuinely seeks the best idea instead of being defensive of own viewpoint?

2. *Sensitivity to other members*
   Is friendly and encouraging?
   Speaks cooperatively and listens understandingly *to all?*

3. *Worth of information presented to group progress*
   Gives information appropriate in type, frequency, and development?
   Gives information acceptable as to source?

4. *Worth of thinking presented on group (or own) information*
   Is perceptive of idea-relationships?
   Is forward-moving? Not tied unduly to preconceived opinions?

Is interested in clarity, soundness, and significance of ideas?
5. *Acceptance of personal responsibility*
   Contributes own thinking?
   Is concerned over group atmosphere?
   Is concerned over rooting out error?
   Is concerned over group movement toward goal?
        10.   Use such a rating sheet as the following
to evaluate the work of designated members in a classroom discussion:

GROUP MEMBER

	Low					*High*		Comments
	1	2	3	4	5	6	7	Comments
Objectivity of contributions								
Sensitivity to other members								
Worth of information presented								
Worth of thinking presented								
Acceptance of personal responsibility								
OTHER COMMENTS:								

Chapter ten

SPEAKING

AND LISTENING

EFFECTIVELY

"Effective thinking," explained Thomas North Whitehead (1) in the Preface to his book *Leadership in a Free Society*, "is to a large extent a social process; it results from an interaction between members of a group, each contributing his individual experiences and attitudes to the common stock." This interaction, of which Whitehead speaks, usually takes place through speaking and listening. Thus, any analysis of such interaction must concern itself with the use of language in making thought available to others, the voice and manner with which words are uttered, and the listening which completes the communicative circuit.

Using language

In order to participate effectively in discussion, you should choose your words with three purposes in mind: (1) *to make ideas accessible*, that is, to help the listeners come as close as possible to your meaning; (2) *to provide continuity*, that is, to help the group move ahead smoothly from one idea to the next; and (3) *to encourage group cooperation*, that is, to help the other participants contribute to the group effort.

Making ideas accessible

As a discussion participant you have an unusual opportunity to gauge the effect of various types of language. By listening to the contributions of others, you can judge to some extent what kind of language is intelligible to the group; moreover, you can modify your own phrasing—you are close enough to your listeners physically to see pretty well whether they are comprehending and to explain further or illustrate if necessary. Also, anyone who does *not* understand can spontaneously break in to ask for explanation of the point that confuses him.

It is well that you have these advantages in phrasing your ideas in discussion, because you must choose your words on the spur of the moment, often to express an idea that is just forming in your mind as you speak. And it is especially important that your listener understand your idea: he cannot shrug off his confusion as he might in listening to a public speech but must understand your contribution to the thought-line adequately to make his next contribution relevant.

To make your ideas accessible to the group, you need to express them as clearly and appropriately as you can.

Clarity To convey your meaning accurately, your words should be as precise as possible in both *denotation* (literal, dictionary meaning) and *connotation* (emotional associations). Actually this is not so difficult as it may seem: people living in the same culture have a great body of common experience from which meanings derive; as a matter of fact, it is upon this essential sameness of experience that every advertiser, every writer, every political candidate relies. Of course, each person is different from every other, and his unique experiences cause him to see life somewhat differently. These experiences may cause him to attach somewhat different emotional associations to words, but the differences are seldom great enough to interfere seriously with group communication.

To achieve maximum clarity in your word choices, you should try to fulfill these requirements:

1. *Use words as accurately as you can in terms of your understanding of their meaning.* Because of the large body of experience you doubtless share with each listener, simply using words that accurately convey your meaning will assure common understanding in most cases. Where varying experiences cause the members to attach different connotations to a term, these differences often open avenues· for further consideration. Most discussion participants, for example, would agree on the meaning of the term *credit buying;* but if one is a grocer, another a banker, a third an appliance salesman, a fourth a housewife, and so forth, the connotations the word carries for each would probably differ.

2. *Explain complex ideas fully; don't overelaborate simple ones.* A complex idea may not be understood if it is insufficiently explained. Clarity cannot be achieved if a speaker deals too casually with a concept that may be unfamiliar to his listeners. Note how such confusion occurs in this example from a discussion on the question: *How can we best improve our aid to underdeveloped countries?*

> **James Beck** Well, we often give generous outlays of aid, but it seems to me the communication process is faulty; there's not enough feedback.
> **Charles Wright** You mean they should pay us back in some way? In consumer goods?
> **James** No, not that. I mean our capacity to respond to information is limited.
> **Harold Byrne** But it seems to me the United States is eager to gather as much information as

> possible; we're constantly drawing up reports, collecting statistics, sending observers——
> **James**   But the feedback doesn't act as a stimulus very often. We don't adjust our policy to fit what we find out.

If James had taken care when he introduced the *feedback* concept to explain it more fully, perhaps to give a simple illustration of how it works in some familiar device like a thermostat, a self-regulating device that adjusts its behavior in response to information it receives from the environment it is acting upon, he could have prevented confusion due to misunderstanding.

On the other hand, clarity is not served by belaboring a point that is obvious. Note how the discussion is bogged down by the unnecessary elaboration (placed in parentheses) in the following contribution on the question: *How can we best improve our junior high schools?*

> **Mary Feder**   Of course, we would all agree that any school program can be only as good as the teachers who teach it. (No matter how good a program is, no matter what kind of program has been set up—how much money and thought have gone into it—it's what the teachers who actually handle that program in the classroom do, what the teachers who use it do, that makes it successful or unsuccessful.) Just the same, a poor curriculum can handicap the best of teachers, it seems to me.

One should throw "a good descriptive loop around a complex idea," as Norman Cousins (2) so aptly phrased the maneuver. But if the speaker is wordy—if he rephrases uselessly, adds unnecessary details and pointless side remarks, uses several half accurate words to express an idea rather than one more carefully chosen term—the listener simply gets lost. Although such a steady flow of words may give the speaker a false sense of power, it does not usually do much to clarify the idea. You should *come to the point:* with brevity for a thought that is relatively simple and with careful, but not wordy, explanation for a more complex one.

3. *Use words that are likely to be familiar and easily understood.* If possible avoid using technical words when you think the listeners

will not be likely to understand them. For example, don't use the term *Zeigarnik effect* unless it is a short cut to meaning for your listeners as well as for you; substitute such a phrase as *the tendency to recall an unfinished task* if they will understand that better. Unless strictly necessary in the speaker's explanation, technical language and professional jargon are out of place whenever the listeners' knowledge does not prepare them to grasp the meaning of the terms easily and to use them readily also. Should you find that you cannot make your idea clear without using technical language unfamiliar to your listeners, you must recognize that they have a right to have these terms explained clearly and without condescension.

Avoid using difficult, unusual words. Especially avoid those for which there are more familiar, and equally accurate, substitutes. It isn't so much a matter of avoiding *long* words as it is of choosing words in the general vocabulary or, rather, in the vocabulary of the members of this particular group. And also it is a matter of avoiding any showing off with "big words."[1] Most groups would understand *profound* more quickly than *recondite*; and *clear* more quickly than *perspicuous*.

Appropriateness   Not only must your words be clear; they must also be appropriate to the listeners and their common purposes. These standards should govern appropriateness of word choice:

1. *Choose language from the proper level of usage.* Both the composition of the group and the nature of its task will suggest the formality or informality of the language to be adopted. Certainly, profanity of any kind would be in poor taste in most groups; even slang might be inappropriate in some. During a coffee session before the meeting starts, any group will be likely to use more colloquial, unceremonious language than it will adopt during the actual discussion. And the more formal and weighty the subject, the greater the change is likely to be. Of course, if the group contains a particularly distinguished and respected member, even the coffee session conversation may be somewhat formal.

It is regrettable when a participant uses inappropriate language and thinks to excuse himself by asking the pardon of those whose

1. William Hazlitt, the English essayist and critic, wrote, "I hate anything that occupies more space than it is worth. I hate to see a load of bandboxes go along the street, and I hate to see a parcel of big words without anything in them."

taste he feels he has offended. Such apologies simply disrupt group rapport and do not relieve the member of his obligation to choose language appropriate to the dignity of the task and situation.

2. *Avoid using emotion-arousing words to stigmatize or glorify.* Since a discussion aims at a fair, open-minded consideration of all relevant ideas, the participants should avoid introducing personal bias by using emotionally "loaded" terms. Don't try to deprecate a plan by labeling it "skulduggery" or "leftist," or to glorify it by identifying it with "the American way." When a listener responds with emotion instead of understanding, he is no longer weighing the contribution objectively. The speaker needs to be aware of the connotations that words may have for his particular listeners and should not intentionally use words whose connotations will unfairly enlist their approval or disapproval and prevent reasoned judgment.

3. *Avoid trite phrases.* Participants should avoid recourse to hackneyed ready-made expressions like "Let's kick this around a little," "Let's try this on for size," "I'll just toss this into the hopper." By use of these popularized phrases a member characterizes himself as rather flippant and imitative. Such grossly overworked expressions add nothing of value to the discussion and give a note of falseness to the exchange of ideas.

Providing continuity

One of the necessary functions of language in group discussion is to keep the thought-line as unbroken as possible. With one person speaking and then another and another, the developing thought is sometimes in danger of being somewhat disjointed. To prevent this difficulty, the discusser should use these techniques:

1. *Supply transitional phrases.* These phrases should express correctly the relationship your idea has to the thought-line already before the group. There will be times, of course, when the composition and correction of the line of thinking passes so quickly and spontaneously from one person to another that transitional words are not only unnecessary but are likely to impede the idea-development. But members usually supply too few transitional phrases rather than too many; more often, they need to take more care to supply phrases that will pick up the relevant element of the previous idea and link it appropriately with the idea to come.

Sometimes the transition will repeat the essence of the previous idea, as "One reason we haven't been able to obtain the new market may be that . . . ." Sometimes the previous idea is still so clearly in everyone's mind that an opportune relational word or phrase will provide sufficient transition, as "One cause might be that . . . ." Effective transitional phrases are often built around words like these: *result, effect, cause, example, implication, underlying assumption, condition, side effect, exception, application, alternative, supposition, apparent contradiction.*

It is not enough to show that you recognize the need for linkage; you must *express* the appropriate relation between ideas. Such vague expressions as "And along with that . . . ." or "That reminds me . . . ." often merely introduce material of a different kind without clarifying its relationship to what has preceded. Whenever the relationship can be accurately expressed, the beads-on-a-string method does not suffice for effective idea-building.

Suppose that a group is holding an enlightenment discussion on the question: *How is the World Bank assisting economic growth?* Early in its discussion the group talks about the original purpose of the Bank:

Steve Halpern The Bank was established in World War II times to help finance reconstruction in the postwar years.

Though the speaker changes, no transitional phrases are needed because all speakers are occupied directly on the Bank's major purpose

Joseph Brill Mainly in Europe, wasn't it?

Charles Grant At that time, yes. The Bank loaned money for reconstruction in Western Europe.

Joan Sidler But now it's mainly for the less developed countries anywhere in the world, isn't it? To assist in the development of electric power, transportation, industry, and agriculture. Right now the Bank has development projects started on all five continents—that is, it's behind the projects with loans—with the hope of ultimately raising living standards. It's impressive that an emerging country can borrow funds to begin——

Joan has begun to move on, and leader's transition reorients the group

Christine Brown (leader) Before we actually go into the projects the new countries have under way through loans from the Bank, let's suggest where the money comes from.

Paul provides a relational word: source

Paul Warren Well, one source is the member countries. As I understand it, there are about seventy-five countries now that are members of the World Bank, and some additional new African nations have applied to join. Each of the member governments takes part in subscribing the capital stock; and that makes up about a quarter of the total. Then, repayments and earnings from earlier loans add more.

George uses the same relational word and provides a full transition from the line of thinking; if he had said, "Along with that . . . ." the transition would have been less clear

George Adams   Another source of money for the Bank's lending operations is private capital. Commercial banks, savings banks, insurance companies, and other investors all over the world have bought the Bank's bond issues or parts of the loans in the countries that are borrowing the money. And we ought to notice that this private capital makes up over half of the Bank's total.

2. *Develop handles for ideas.* Often the group members discover a word or phrase which seems to embody pretty clearly what they are trying to say. These words should be used as *handles* whenever the group wants to refer later to this particular set of ideas. These handles are valuable because their group-established meaning—that is, a designation of particular details, relationships, and perhaps values—provides for quick and easy recall and because development of a group idiom adds to the group's feeling of cohesiveness.

In the following excerpt a group is holding an enlightenment discussion on the question: *Why do Americans feel insecure?*

John Davis   Well, Professor James Feibleman, professor of philosophy at Tulane University and author of more than twenty books on science, philosophy, and cultural affairs, has an explanation worth considering. He says we have a "split philosophy" but don't realize we have it! He points out our slogans: "Trust God and keep your powder dry!" and "Praise the Lord and pass the ammunition!" And just look at us: we're building new churches all around the country, and yet we're spending billions for nuclear weapons.

Diane Greenholdt (leader)   Does he have a name for it?

John   Yes, Feibleman calls it "idealistic materialism."

Leader echoes the suggested handle to hold it a little longer before the group

Leader   Idealistic materialism——

John   We think conflicts can be settled without going to war, and yet we are good fighters!

Mary Stewart   And he thinks idealistic materialism—even though we don't realize we have it —is the cause of our feeling of insecurity?

John   Yes, and that we must bring this contradictory philosophy out into the open so we can get a chance to heal the split.

Leader suggests that the handle be retained for future reference

Leader   Well, shall we then list idealistic materialism as one of the possible factors that we will want to discuss in detail later? If so, what is another possible cause of our feeling of insecurity?

Encouraging group cooperation

Your beliefs and attitudes about the group and the task are revealed in the words you use in phrasing your contributions. To encourage group cooperation, try to put into practice these suggestions:

1. *Use we, our, and us.* One way to elicit your listeners' interest and understanding when volunteering either a substantive or a procedural suggestion is to include them; for example, "*Our* idea that . . . ." or "Do you suppose *we* should . . . ." Your use of the pronouns *we, our,* and *us* expresses belief in the cooperative enterprise and acceptance of others as partners in the work.[2]

Your use of first-person terms should be the natural outgrowth of your feeling about the group; if you feel idea-possessive or superior, use of these cooperative words will be considered insincere by the group.

2. *Ask the group to test your ideas.* Your words should show your desire to put your idea before the other members for their careful attention. Your suggestion should reach forward in thought but ask

2. Two investigators, after studying interaction in a therapy group and a clinic staff group, have suggested that the members' use of pronouns tends to reveal how adequately the group is carrying out its task. See Dorothy C. Conrad and Richard Conrad, "The Use of Personal Pronouns as Categories for Studying Small Group Interaction," *Journal of Abnormal and Social Psychology,* 52 (March 1956), 277-279.

them to reach with you and then to test the thinking; you must *ask* them, not *tell* them.[3]

Your word choices will indicate the degree of tentativeness you have about your ideas and will largely determine whether the other members will feel free to test them. Note the difference between the dogmatism of the first phrase and the tentativeness of the second in these pairs:

The result will be	This will tend to result in . . . .
My opinion is that	Could it be that . . . .
The way to do it is	One way we might consider is . . . .

This element of tentativeness should run throughout the group's deliberation. Even when presenting a fact from personal experience or from incontrovertible authority, you need to inquire whether the fact might be useful. And in offering conclusions, avoid dogmatic assertions like "These facts obviously prove that . . . ." Ask rather, "Given these facts, might we think that . . . ?" Even when summarizing, you should *inquire* of the group; such a phrasing as "Are we saying then that . . . ?" reveals your open-minded approach to ideas and does much to encourage a high degree of cooperation in the group. This constant use of the questioning form of contribution reinforces the idea of the group as a team whose several energies are needed for the task.

You should avoid such phrases as *Correct me* (or *contradict me* or *stop me*) *if I'm wrong*. By using them, the speaker identifies

---

3. Benjamin Franklin explained his own experience in improving his communication with others: "I made it a rule to forbear all direct contradiction to the sentiments of others, and all positive assertion of my own. I even forbid myself . . . the use of every word or expression in the language that imported a fixed opinion, such as *certainly, undoubtedly,* etc., and I adopted, instead of them, *I conceive, I apprehend,* or *I imagine* a thing to be so or so; or it *so appears to me at present.* When another asserted something that I thought an error, I denied myself the pleasure of contradicting him abruptly, and of showing immediately some absurdity in his proposition; and in answering I began by observing that in certain cases or circumstances his opinion would be right, but in the present case there *appeared* or *seemed* to me some difference, etc. I soon found the advantage of this change in my manner; the conversations I engaged in went on more pleasantly. The modest way in which I proposed my opinions procured them a readier reception and less contradiction; I had less mortification when I was found to be in the wrong, and I more easily prevailed with others to give up their mistakes and join with me when I happened to be in the right."—*The Autobiography of Benjamin Franklin* (Boston: Houghton, Mifflin and Company, 1886), p. 113.

himself so strongly with his comment that he almost dares the listener to find him in error. This transposition of emphasis from the speaker's idea to the speaker himself is inconsistent with a receptivity to honest criticism.

Also avoid *pseudo requests* like these: *I don't know about the rest of you, but I think* . . . ; *I don't know whether we want to go into this, but I'll just say that I* . . . ; *I know we don't have much time, but I just want to say that* . . . ; *I don't know how we want to do this, but I think* . . . ; *I realize we agreed not to go into this, but* . . . . Such phrases are hypocritical because the apparent request in the first element is promptly ignored in the second. Rather than awaiting group permission, the speaker assumes that his recognition of possible differences of opinion frees him to proceed.

3. *Avoid belligerent phrases.* Group cooperation is greatly inhibited when a member uses language that indicates inflexibility, irritation, or defiance. Such language makes other members feel intimidated or threatened and prevents them from participating freely in the discussion. Such blanket statements as *I agree with you!* or *I disagree with you!* indicate a fixed position on the part of the speaker and suggest that he is issuing a personal challenge to the others. You will naturally find some contributions more persuasive than others, but group cohesiveness will best be served if you announce your reaction less sweepingly: *Yes, the facts do seem to indicate that* . . . . or *But are the data available sufficient to show that* . . . .

It is equally rude and disruptive to brush aside a member's reasoned contribution as if it were of little worth, with statements like *You have a right to your opinion, but* . . . . or *Well, sure, a lot of people may think that, but* . . . . Such phrases are often used by those who want to dismiss the weight of evidence or reject logical inferences; they contribute nothing and reduce cooperative attitudes.

If a misunderstanding seems to be arising at some point, tactful phrases should draw attention to it. To bark out defiantly *Define your terms!* or *You didn't understand me!* simply arouses group tension. A less emotional, objective tone is implied by phrases like *I'm not sure I understand what you mean by* . . . . or *I'm afraid I didn't express myself clearly when* . . . . Remember that even under ideal conditions communication is a difficult process and that easy irritation simply compounds the difficulty.

4. *Express your friendliness.* Appropriate word choice and sentence formation and frequent inclusion of phrases that express friendliness,

appreciation of others' efforts, and recognition of others' feelings reveal supportive attitudes toward others. Hostile and abrupt words are out of place. Furthermore, friendly phrases must be honest indicators, sensibly introduced, of true feelings. Used too often—no matter how honestly—they sentimentalize the discussion, making the personal relationships seem more important than the common task. Used as a superficial device by a member who emptily parrots the phrases but lacks the sincerity they express, they are irritating to the members and destructive of the group's cooperative effort.

Avoid making a practice of starting every comment with a saccharine appreciation of the previous speaker's contribution: "I'm sure the rest of the group appreciates as I do your fine suggestions, Bill"; "We all see how you feel, Bill, and we can surely see why you do . . . ." A constant use of such phrases becomes patronizing; a much better practice is to reserve praise for an outstanding effort and, even then, to recognize that it was an effort made *on behalf of the group:* "Sounds good! Now we're moving!"

Speaking

The language of discussion is *spoken* language, a plastic medium that is more flexible than written discourse.[4] The words are accompanied by voice inflections and bodily gestures which are of extreme importance in developing ideas cooperatively and in maintaining attitudes favorable to such cooperation.

No matter how much assistance you give the group by attentive listening, you assume much more direct responsibility the moment you claim the "floor"; you are then carrying the thought-line for the group. On these occasions you should express yourself naturally: the cooperative nature of the discussion process does not call for oratory but for clear and animated expression of your ideas.

Voice

A speaker's voice has much to do with whether following his thought is easy or difficult, whether his remarks are attended or

---

4. "Spoken language," said Oliver Wendell Holmes, "is so plastic—you can pat and coax, and spread and shave, and rub out, and fill up, and stick on so easily, when you work that soft material, that there is nothing like it for modelling."—From Oliver Wendell Holmes, *The Autocrat of the Breakfast Table* (New York: A. L. Burt Company, Publishers, 1900) p. 24.

ignored, whether he encourages or discourages cooperative effort in the group. By watching the reactions of your listeners, you can detect the comprehension or confusion, the interest or restlessness that your contribution is creating. If careful use of the suggestions given below does not bring you the necessary improvement, you should consult a speech instructor or clinician for explanations and exercises that will assist you in breaking poor habits and building better ones.

In order to be effective in discussion, a person's voice should be *easy to understand, unobtrusive, investigative,* and *pleasant.*

Easy to understand Speaking loudly enough to be heard and distinctly enough to be understood by all members of the group is essential. Do not allow the informality of the seating arrangement and of the group atmosphere to lull you into relaxing communication standards. Whenever members have to strain to catch what is being said, the group process suffers and the speaker is at fault. You must avoid, for example, talking only loudly enough for those near you to hear or leaning on and mumbling through your hand or slumping in your chair and speaking without enough volume. Being easy to understand requires an attempt to meet these requirements:

1. Speak with enough vigor so that your words carry easily to every member of the group.

2. Enunciate your words clearly enough so that they are quickly and easily grasped by your listeners.

3. Avoid talking too fast for easy comprehension or so slowly that you waste time and irritate the group or so jerkily—with unnatural pauses and broken sentences—that the listeners find it hard to follow you.

4. Adjust your rate of speaking to the complexity of your contribution and to its importance in view of the time available to the group.

5. Avoid speaking in a monotone. Display your interest in what you are saying and emphasize appropriately the key words in your contribution.[5]

---

5. You should speak with the "full realization of the content of your words as you utter them" and the "lively sense of communication" explained Professor James A. Winans, in *Speech-Making* (New York: Appleton-Century-Crofts, Inc., 1938), p. 25.

Unobtrusive[6]   Your voice is a tool for communicating your thoughts and feelings to your listeners; to the extent that your voice calls attention to itself rather than to what you have to say, your communication has been harmed. To use your voice unobtrusively, you should attempt to meet these requirements:

1. Avoid the insertion of meaningless sounds that distract from your message and annoy your listeners, for instance, *uh, er-uh, and-uh, well, now-uh, then-uh.*

2. Use a pitch level that is appropriate to your sex and age.

3. Correct irritating qualities of voice, such as nasality, huskiness, breathiness, and harshness.

4. Avoid articulation and pronunciation errors. (If you have serious trouble here, you should seek help from a speech instructor or clinician.)

5. Avoid any form of vocal affectation—eccentric pitch level, pattern of intonation, tone, pronunciation, and so forth.

Investigative   How open-minded and how purposeful others in the group think you are depends to a large extent upon your use of voice. No matter how carefully you use the language of investigation—the questions, the tentatively phrased suggestions—you will not be considered open minded and inquiring unless the tone of your voice carries this same impression. A speaker who is genuinely probing for answers characteristically ends his inquiries with upward intonations; he hesitates and pauses while waiting for group assistance. His sentences do not close with a downward inflection of finality, nor do they waver so uncertainly that he sounds confused or half-hearted. Changes in volume and pitch convey his enthusiasm without detracting from the ideas expressed.

Pleasant   How supportive of others in the group you are and how responsible you feel for making the interaction a success will show clearly in your voice. A valuable appropriately worded comment will often be resented and resisted if the tone in which it is uttered is sarcastic or supercilious. A pleasant voice is varied in tone and emphasis, in rate of speaking and length of pauses. These changes are an aid in communication: emphasis on a word or phrase, with pauses before and after, says to the listener,

6. McBurney and Wrage have used the term *unobtrusive* in their treatment of "Goals for Vocal Usage"; see *The Art of Good Speech* (New York: Prentice-Hall, Inc., 1953) pp. 385-386.

"This is important." And a casually tucked-in phrase, like "if we ever get around to it," shares a reaction with him. While expressing varying emphases in content, a pleasant voice is never wheedling or abrasive, never suggests tension or impatience.

Accompanying action

How the discusser looks and moves as he talks is important; his listeners are so close to him that they respond—even unconsciously—to his facial expression, the set of his shoulders, the movement of his hands as he talks. To use bodily communication fully and naturally, you should lean slightly forward and glance at your listeners while speaking, to make it clear that you are offering your ideas to them. Avoid pushing back your chair and regally holding forth to them from a distance or wagging a finger as if remonstrating with them. Looking directly at each of the other participants will help you perceive their understanding, confusion, or disagreement. It will also help them perceive the emphasis, the enthusiasm your facial expressions convey, and will help you to watch for cues that others are ready to pick up and continue the thought-line from the point you are making. Do not hesitate to use whatever gestures may help to clarify your remarks, as long as they do not distract from the ideas they aim to elucidate.

Listening

The quality of listening done in a discussion is one of the most important factors in its success. Fortunately, the average listener can hear and comprehend many more words per minute than a speaker can say—four or five times as many. He needs this time advantage to absorb and scrutinize the ideas offered; but even with this extra time he is sometimes hard put to keep up, for he is also reacting to cues from the speaker's words, voice, and manner and to the nonverbal responses of the other listeners.

Sometimes the personal emotional associations aroused by a remark drown out the information for him; sometimes new ideas are piled on too rapidly by different members before he has finished thinking about an earlier idea. Sometimes he needs to have a point clarified but cannot break in to ask; sometimes he gets interested in a tangential thought and loses touch with the developing thought-line. Sometimes the speaker's voice or manner contradicts his words and confuses the listener. But he must not bow to these distractions. If he does not succeed in listening effectively, he may bring up ideas someone else has already suggested, ask for clarification of points already carefully explained, or lose track of the development of thought.

Hence, he must spur himself on to grasp and evaluate ideas quickly; when necessary he must not hesitate to stop the flow of ideas and request an explanation. He must discipline himself to resist pleasurable tangents, filing them for later musings; he must interpret voice and gesture as shrewdly and objectively as he can. He must reason responsibly because his inner thought-line and the group-developed thought-line need to correspond as closely as possible. Only then are the members of the group understanding each other.

His responsibilities take three forms: *listening to understand, listening to evaluate,* and *listening to provide support for the speaker.*

Listening to understand

As a listener you must understand the speaker's remarks reasonably well before you attempt to criticize or evaluate them; you must be willing to hear him out and ask for clarification if the meaning is unclear.[7] Your study of the processes of reasoning (pages 97-117) and of the uses of language (pages 221-231) has provided you with information you should apply in listening. While absorbing the

7. Carl R. Rogers has suggested that the tendency to evaluate before understanding is the primary barrier to communication and has explained: "Although the tendency to make evaluations is common to almost all interchange of language, it is very much heightened in those situations where feelings and emotions are deeply involved. So the stronger our feelings, the more likely it is that there will be no mutual element in the communication. . . . This tendency to react to any emotionally meaningful statement by forming an evaluation of it from our own point of view, is, I repeat, the major barrier to interpersonal communication.

"But is there any way of solving this problem, of avoiding this barrier? . . . Real communication occurs, and this evaluation tendency is avoided, when we listen with understanding. What does this mean? It means to see the expressed idea and attitude from the other person's point of view, to sense how it feels to him, to achieve his frame of reference in regard to the thing he is talking about."—From "Barriers and Gateways to Communication," *Harvard Business Review,* 30 (July-August 1952), 19.

And F. J. Roethlisberger, considering communication in the industrial context, urges the same view: "The biggest block to personal communication is man's inability to listen intelligently, understandingly, and skillfully to another person."—*Ibid.,* p. 24.

speaker's words, you should be alert to his meaning, measuring his facts and opinions against your own and singling out discrepancies. This kind of mental sorting and rearranging keeps your personal thought-line consistent with that developed by the whole group and suggests to you points to raise, questions to ask, information and insights to add.

As a good listener you must restrain any disruptive feelings of your own. The speaker's words may convey his emotional attitudes as well as his literal meaning, but you should avoid reacting to these implied attitudes in ways that will distract you from the group thought-line or arouse a personal bias against his ideas.[8]

Listening to evaluate

A listener begins to evaluate what he hears as its meaning emerges. Yet you should hold back any firm acceptance of the judgment that is beginning to form until you understand sufficiently well to be

---

8. Adverse and facilitating listener responses have been classified as follows:
The Adverse Factors:
1. Absence of observable response
2. Presence of nonfacilitating responses
a. *Competitive responses,* in which the listener provides competing stimuli that are situationally distracting, such as drawing attention from the speaker by talking to a companion on seemingly unrelated matters;
b. *Threatening responses,* in which the response of the listener too seriously threatens the speaker as a personality or defeats his bid for attention;
c. *Ego-maintaining responses,* in which the listener's response is an overpolite attempt to maintain harmony with the speaker, perhaps at the expense of clarity or progress in the line of thinking;
d. *Anticipatory responses,* in which the listener agrees too readily and vigorously, interrupting the speaker's elaboration of his idea, or in which he evidences readiness to interrupt orally.
The Facilitating Factors:
1. *Meaning-oriented responses,* in which the listener shows that he intends to employ his intellect and experience fully in understanding what the words, voice, and manner of the speaker are communicating;
2. *Initiative-yielding responses,* in which the listener shows that he intends to give the speaker opportunity to set forth his communication, relieving him of the necessity of competing with others for this chance;
3. *Distraction-resisting responses,* in which the listener gives continuing attention to the speaker despite distracting occurrences in the group and elsewhere.
—Quoted and paraphrased from S. Frank Miyamoto, Laura Crowell, and Allan Katcher, "Communicant Behavior in Small Discussion Groups," *The Journal of Communication,* 7 (Winter 1957), 151-160.

reasonably sure of your evaluation. To evaluate effectively, you must observe the following rules: distinguish carefully between facts and opinions; apply the tests of logic to the speaker's reasoning; remember that your own judgment may be wrong.

Listening to provide support for the speaker

As listener you have some responsibility to help a speaker express his ideas clearly; the cues you provide him should increase his power to get his ideas across and encourage him to do his best. To provide such support for the speaker, you should fulfill the following obligations:

1. Give your attention willingly and consistently. If he does not have to strive for your attention, he will have more mental energy to devote to the development of his idea. And he is further encouraged if, when distractions in the group occur, you resist being drawn from his contribution.

2. Make yourself easy to talk to. You should show—by facial expression, turn of head, set of shoulders, and so forth—that you are really trying to understand what he means and are giving him freedom to express his ideas as he thinks best.

3. Avoid responses distracting to the speaker. If he sees dead-pan faces, giving him no reaction at all, or if he observes responses disturbing to his line of thinking or to his self-confidence, he will be handicapped in presenting his ideas well.

Summary

Interaction in the discussion group involves using language in speaking and listening. Using language effectively means making ideas accessible, providing continuity, and encouraging group cooperation. Accessibility is achieved through clarity and appropriateness of word choices; continuity through transitional phrases and handles *for ideas; cooperation by using* we, our, *and* us, *by asking for group scrutiny, by avoiding belligerent phrases, and by expressing friendliness orally. The discusser's voice should be easy to understand, unobtrusive, investigative, and pleasant; the accompanying physical cues should reveal his meaning and his attitudes. When another participant is speaking, the discusser should listen to understand, to evaluate, and to provide support.*

References

(1) Thomas North Whitehead, *Leadership in a Free Society* (Cambridge: Harvard University Press, 1950), pp. viii-ix.

(2) Norman Cousins, "Diary of a Change," *Saturday Review*, 44 (February 18, 1961), 28-29.

Readings and problems

1. Listen to a classroom discussion for instances of unusually effective uses of language. Make a list of words that were particularly high in clarity or appropriateness and analyze the reasons for their effectiveness.

2. Bring examples from some discussion heard in classroom, committee meeting room, or elsewhere of *handles* developed by the group for key ideas.

3. In a classroom discussion make a tabulation of the uses of *we*, *our*, and *us*. Discuss the effect of frequent use of these pronouns on the cooperativeness of the group.

4. What inferences for the discussion process can be drawn from the following occurrence, related by M. L. J. Abercrombie in *The Anatomy of Judgment* (London: Hutchinson, 1960), pp. 105-106?

An illustration of how communication between people can be made difficult by using a word such as *normal* is given by the case of an old man whose illness could not be diagnosed for some days after he had entered hospital. On admission he had been asked if his diet was normal and had replied yes. After some time one of the physicians asked what exactly had he been eating, and when this question was put, the patient said he had been eating little more than bread, margarine and treacle during the last three years. It then became clear that he was suffering from scurvy, a possibility which had not been entertained (although the signs were present, they were not perceived) until it was known that his diet had been deficient in vitamin C. In asking the patient if his diet was *normal*, the questioner had wanted to know if his diet was suitable to maintain health; in saying that his diet was normal, the patient had wanted to say that there had been no recent change from his usual diet.

5. Listen to a discussion in your classroom, club, or living group for the purpose of noticing the voices of the participants. Select one person whose vocal usage interests you and evaluate his voice in terms of these four requirements: easy to understand, unobtrusive, investigative, pleasant. Prepare also to describe the physical acts which characteristically accompany his vocal contributions.

6. Join in a conversation with several of your friends on a topic of mutual interest. Notice which person in the group seems to have the most difficulty in getting his ideas considered by the group; give him strong *facilitative responses* and note any changes in his contributions.

7. In a classroom discussion listen carefully to the speaking of a designated participant. Check the list below to indicate where he needs to improve his use of voice. In some cases none of these descriptions will apply; if so, write general suggestions for his improvement.

General pitch too high	_____	Rate too fast	_____
General pitch too low	_____	Rate too slow	_____
Tone monotonous	_____	Enunciation poor	_____
Tone unresponsive to		Pronunciation faulty	_____
meaning	_____	Uses *uh, er-uh,*	
Hard to hear	_____	*and-uh,* etc.	_____
Too loud	_____	Too dogmatic	_____

General suggestions:

---

8. Prepare to hold a classroom discussion on methods of improving in the use of voice. Give primary attention to the problems most widespread in your class. Your instructor will refer you to appropriate manuals on speech improvement.

9. Keep a list of clichés heard in classroom discussions. For a usable organization, see William W. Watt, *An American Rhetoric*, rev. ed. (New York: Rinehart & Co., 1957), pp. 285-286. His categories, plus two examples of each, are given below:
1. Trite comparisons: *brown as a berry; brave as a lion*
2. Canned adjective-noun combinations: *acid test; budding genius*
3. Overworked proverbs and fragments from literature: *It's better late than never; A rolling stone gathers no moss*
4. Pseudopoetic personification: *arms of Morpheus; Dame Fortune*
5. Miscellaneous: *bolt from the blue; calm before the storm*

   10. Discuss the significance for group discussion procedures of the following statement from the psychoanalyst Theodor Reik in his book *Listening with the Third Ear* (New York: Farrar, Straus & Co., 1948), p. 27:

> The road from thought to speech is shorter than from thinking to writing. It is really a return to the original, because what we think is only what we say within ourselves without pronouncing the words . . . . The spoken words have an emotional quality different from the words that have only been thought. The Catholic Church does not recognize a confession which is only thought or written down. The confession must be *vocalis*, spoken; it must be articulated, vocalized. A comparison between written and thought words shows that the effect of articulate speech is different not only upon the hearer but also upon the speaker himself.

   11. Watch throughout a classroom discussion for instances of adverse and facilitative responses by the listeners. Prepare also to discuss the general effects of such responses on the speakers. Use the organization of responses suggested in this chapter (see footnote 8, page 236):

Adverse responses:	*Facilitative responses:*
1. Absence of observable response	1. Meaning-oriented
2. Presence of nonfacilitating responses	2. Initiative-yielding
a. Competitive	3. Distraction-resisting
b. Threatening	
c. Ego-maintaining	
d. Anticipatory	

12. Listen to a radio or television broadcast discussion, or use scripts of discussion broadcasts, where available. Analyze the participants' (1) use of questions, (2) use of transitional words and phrases, (3) use of words, and (4) use of *handles*. Obtain scripts from programs currently on the air; or make tape recordings of radio or television discussions that seem likely to suit your purpose, for example, the *Invitation to Learning* radio program.

Chapter eleven

LEADING

GROUP

DISCUSSION:

PART I

Leading a group discussion is both an exacting and an exhilarating task. No wonder many a busy executive—whether in government, business, school, community organization, or church—finds the hours spent in conference the most demanding of his entire day. Whatever the subject for discussion may be, the task of guiding the deliberations of a group of diverse individuals demands keen use of a leader's faculties, sensitivities, and skills.

Effective discussion leadership is primarily a matter of helping the members focus their efforts fully on the common task.[1] The good discussion leader helps the group achieve five essentials of effective interaction: (1) free contribution by all members; (2) systematic development of thought; (3) sound development of thought; (4) constructive use of differences of opinion; and (5) effective handling of disruptive factors.[2] In assisting with these functions, the leader does *not* have a preconceived opinion of what the group's decision should be; he is not trying—either openly or subtly—to move the members toward a particular belief or policy. By helping the group look responsibly at all relevant aspects of the subject, he aids it in reaching not his predetermined decision but a group-developed one.

Different group situations require different forms of assistance from the leader. In general, the effective discussion leader today is more likely to be democratic than authoritarian, because he feels that in a democratic environment the creative energies of the members are most fully and cooperatively used; he realizes that only under these conditions can the best results be achieved.[3] But if the group

1. You may have heard of leaderless groups. Groups without designated leaders are frequently used in three situations: (1) in interview sessions for discovery of persons with "leadership potential" in industry, the armed forces, etc.; (2) in research projects on group interaction; and (3) in leadership training programs. The types of groups (problem-solving and enlightenment) about which this textbook is written, regularly have designated leaders.
2. The first two essentials will be developed in the present chapter, the remaining three in Chapter 12.
3. The leader must keep a balance between group accomplishment and individual initiative, as John Stuart Mill has suggested in regard to the state: "A state which dwarfs its men, in order that they may be more docile instruments in its hands even for beneficial purposes, will find that with small men no great thing can be accomplished."
If the act of leadership is so performed as to incapacitate the members for the very kind of behavior necessary from them, it not only fails to accomplish its goal but, at the same time, reduces the value of the participants as individuals.

faces an emergency situation and rapid decision is essential, the leader will need to assume a larger share of the responsibility in making the decision. Or if the group members are accustomed to authoritarian leadership, he, as their new leader, should not shift too far or too fast into democratic procedures—much as he personally might desire to do so—until a readiness for such change has developed in the group.

How the person has become the leader will affect the manner of his leadership. If he has been elected by the membership, he has the good will and cooperation of at least a majority from the outset; if he has been appointed through a recognized procedure (as by the governor, the minister, or the instructor), he probably receives cooperation more or less automatically; if he becomes the leader because of his place in the organization to which he and the members belong, he may receive cooperation but will generally have to win confidence in his leadership.

The size of the group whose discussion he is leading also conditions the form his assistance to the members will take. If the group is unsuitably large for the type of discussion it is holding (see pages 31-35 for optimum size), the members will rightly expect the leader to move ahead without contributions from every participant on every facet of the problem. On the other hand, if the group is unsuitably small for the type of discussion, the members will expect the leader to enter into the substantive work of the group—giving information, developing lines of thought, and so forth—more fully than he does in a group of more appropriate size. Although members of a group of less than optimum size also need focusing action, they probably need it less than they need assistance on the actual composition and testing of ideas.

Thus, the effective leader aims to focus the efforts of the group on its task and suits his assistance to the specific conditions of the immediate situation. He realizes that many of the duties necessary to the effective functioning of the group can and should be voluntarily assumed by the members themselves; therefore, he strives to make it possible and easy for them to assume them.[4] He notices tasks going

4. Temporary and permanent groups are likely to differ greatly in the freedom with which they assume these duties; doubtless in groups of long standing in which the leader has shown his expectation that members will assist in guiding the work of the group, the members will have developed habits of doing so.

unfulfilled and either invites the group to attend to them or handles them himself. It is not that he is surpassingly wiser; but since he is less responsible for contributing materials, he can watch a little more to see whether all materials the group needs are presented. It is not that he makes decisions for the others; he merely takes responsibility for bringing to their attention matters of completeness, depth, and direction toward the goal rather than obliging each member to constantly evaluate them himself. Any of these that they happen to introduce contributes to the group progress, but the leader provides a valuable service in the continuing nature of his check on these matters. On the other hand, if the members are slow at composing and testing the thought-line, the leader will need to assume more responsibility to help with these functions, even though he then has less time to evaluate and guide the general progress of the group.

Preparation

The leader will need to know as much as he can about the task that lies ahead for the group—the information that is relevant, the assumptions that must be made, appropriate lines of inquiry or springboard ideas that facilitate explanation of the subject, and the important values involved. This requires keen research on the subject and the most rigorous attention to developing an outline or agenda of relevant issues.

But the leader also needs to know the persons with whom he will work during the discussion. How many are there in the group? What are their expectations of leadership? What are their relations with and expectations of one another? What relevant opinions and loyalties do they have? How great is the variation in their understanding and effectiveness in the use of the discussion process, as well as in their experience and knowledge of the subject itself? The more of this information the leader can obtain before the group meeting, the more he can adapt his preparation to the actual situation.

Further, he needs to know the time allotment within which he and the group must work. Only then can he estimate the scope that can be reasonably attempted, the segments that must be considered minor and covered quickly, the pace the discussion will have to maintain.

And he must know the physical environment, if possible, within which the work of the group is to be done. If he has been able to choose the room, equipment, and furniture, he will have set the stage as well as possible for the particular task and group. When he can make no such preparation, upon his arrival he can adjust as much as possible whatever factors will increase efficiency of communication and collaboration in the group.

Introducing the group to the task

The opening remarks of the leader are important in building a relationship sufficient to unlock the energies of the group and to direct them toward the common purpose. Such a relationship is based not only upon an awareness of where the group is heading but upon an affirmative feeling toward those with whom the work is to be done. To bring such results, the leader should meet four requirements; he must (1) be informative; (2) be stimulating; (3) establish a favorable climate in the group; and (4) invite the group to begin with an appropriate aspect of the subject.[5]

Information

Whatever the group needs at the outset in order to see its task clearly should be presented—procedures to be followed, length and calendar of sessions, plans for obtaining data or expert assistance, use to be made of the product of the group's thinking, scope of the group's responsibility and authority, and so forth. Such clarification of procedures cannot help but make the members feel that they are starting from a secure footing. The leader, while giving them assurance that all appropriate steps have been taken for using their time and efforts well, yet stops short of giving them cause to feel that their rights have been presumed upon in the making of the plans. Furthermore, he watches that his recital does not clutter the opening of the discussion and take too much time from the group deliberation which is, after all, the real purpose and function of the meeting.

Stimulation

If the group goal is already chosen, the leader must convince the members that it is truly important, a task worthy of their best efforts. If the members are to participate in choosing their goal, he heightens their awareness of the importance of a worthy choice. Of course, he

5. See pp. 14-15 for the leader's opening remarks in a classroom discussion.

must watch that the goal of the group is an obtainable one. If it is too distant or grandiose, it will frustrate rather than motivate and polarize the group. It must be compelling enough to mobilize the members' cooperative efforts, but realistic enough to assure them ·a reasonable chance of success.

Rather than simply declaring the task's importance in a general way, the leader should prepare himself to set forth specific information which will impress the members with the importance of the subject. Although he may arrange to show a brief film, display a chart, exhibit a picture or object, more often he will relate orally a vivid example, a compelling set of statistics, or a dramatic or forceful statement from an authoritative report or a prominent person.

Stimulation is always necessary: it is necessary even though the members arrive at the group highly motivated, for their separate motivations need to be collected into a group-recognized common motivation; it is necessary even though the group has met in a series of meetings on the same task, for group energy needs to be called out and focused anew; it is especially necessary if the members have come stimulated by separate personal goals, for only when they can see beyond the individual goals to the larger common goal will they be ready to cooperate fully in their task. As U Thant, when Acting Secretary of the United Nations General Assembly, told the nations, group members must be ready to "submit to the discipline of the larger good."

Climate

In establishing a climate conducive to effective group work, the leader's own attitude is of basic importance. As he gives information, stimulates, and suggests an appropriate opening, he needs to show himself purposeful, fair, and of good will. His own enthusiasm should invigorate his presentation but must not stifle the contributions of others, either through its emotional intensity or its length.[6] If the members are unacquainted with one another, the leader needs to reduce their isolation by making or arranging for appropriate introductions. Where knowing one another's position and experience will

6. For example, in introducing an enlightenment discussion on the value of life insurance, a leader made the error of confessing to her group that she had lost her husband and that the insurance had made all the difference in bringing up the children; the members were sympathetic and no one thereafter could suggest any drawbacks to the buying of life insurance.

assist in the task at hand, the leader should make these suitably known, taking care not to establish status differences in such a way as to bottle up later contributions.[7] When the group is meeting under emergency conditions whose seriousness cuts down all barriers of rank and experience and it is clear to all that the worth of the ideas presented is the only thing that matters, then a quick explanation of different qualifications is helpful and sufficient.

Throughout the leader's opening remarks he must reveal himself as impartial on the discussion subject and desirous of the most forthright contribution by each of the members. His confidence that the members can and will achieve their goal together must be made clear to the whole group by his words, his voice, and his manner. His evident good will must assure them of their freedom to suggest their ideas without danger of ridicule if the thoughts happen not to be fully developed or useful. If he thus lets them know before they enter the interchange of ideas that he will guide them with friendliness, firmness, and fairness, he will have greatly increased their chances of starting their discussion at a relatively high level of cooperation. He should watch his listeners to note when he has supplied information and built interest sufficiently that they want to begin discussing the subject themselves.

Invitation

The leader then invites the participation of all the members with a welcoming glance around the group and a suggestion of a relevant point to start with if they wish to use it. Note the strengths and weaknesses of these invitations given at the end of opening remarks:
Mary, will you start us off?
> *Strength:* Is a question. *Weakness:* Indicates that the leader may intend to assign the order of contribution and thus eliminate the right to volunteer; establishes prestige for Mary; may worry shy people in the group. *Rating:* poor

Where shall we begin? or *Would someone like to begin?*

---

7. This occurred, for instance, in a group of young widows meeting to organize a local unit of Parents Without Partners. Their chairman introduced them all and then emphasized how fortunate they were to have a certain person as one of their number because she had helped to establish a phenomenally successful group in an Eastern city and would be of invaluable help to this group. All the other members felt stifled by the generous introduction given to a person with this outstanding experience.

Strength: Are questions; are open to the whole group, preserving the right to volunteer. *Weakness:* Run the risk of starting the discussion on a minor point, a matter of less importance, however, than the fact that the members may then get off to a bad start, feel uninterested, contentious, or frustrated. *Rating:* fair

Perhaps first we should list the areas we want to consider. What areas do you suggest?

Strength: A tentative statement which, although it assumes acceptance, yet holds decision open through its tentative words *perhaps* and *should;* suggests that ideas of all are desired and allows someone to volunteer. *Weakness:* If each "area" needed some group consideration before being added to the list, this question would bring in several suggestions at once instead of holding one before the group at a time. *Rating:* good

Since we are trying to describe our problem, perhaps we should start with symptoms. What symptom or evidence of the problem should we begin with?

Strength: Opening clause presents the leader's reason behind the suggestion he is about to make; suggestion is tentative with the words *perhaps* and *should;* question is asked of whole group and the right to volunteer is preserved. *Weakness:* If someone wanted further clarification of terms, and so forth, before starting consideration of symptoms, he might hesitate to make his request or offer his contribution. *Rating:* good

Free contribution by all members

The leader's opening remarks serve initially to orient each member to the task; his establishment of team relationships in the group opens the door to voluntary efforts on their part; and his invitation to begin at a relevant point enables them to start together effectively. But these attempts in the opening remarks only begin the leader's task. Throughout the discussion he demonstrates in his speaking and listening the free and open action he suggests for them, restrains himself from actions that might curtail their freedom, and acts to break down obstacles created by others in the group.

Demonstration

As he speaks and listens, the leader shows that voluntary efforts are desired from all members and are respected:

1. He speaks *to all* and listens *to all;* this group-wide attention on his part tends to encourage similar behavior by other members.

2. He does not, by any proprietary air in his listening, draw the speaker's attention to himself alone; in fact, if he finds a member speaking directly and regularly to him and to him alone, he acts to turn the speaker's attention to others—perhaps by small, hardly noticeable gestures or by his own glance to others.

3. He shows by the inquiring tone of his voice and the timing of his words a willingness to stop at any number of points if another person wishes to take over the composition of the thought-line; at all times his comments sound *interruptable*. Thus, he encourages the members to think concurrently and to take hold when they can.

4. He interjects a word or phrase when it is needed in another's presentation with such obvious good will and helpfulness that the speaker continues without loss of thought or poise.

Self-restraint

The effective leader realizes that his own sincere but overdirective performance could curtail the members' opportunities for free contribution. Therefore, he restrains himself in a number of ways; in general, he tries to:

1. *Avoid speaking regularly after each contributor*. If he responds to virtually every remark made in the group, he cuts off spontaneous building by the members and the consequent expansion of their discussion powers. The participants tend to construe him as teacher or judge and begin to turn to him to assess or rephrase their every idea. Thus, the members never feel the full rigor of having to present ideas ready for the group's use, since they are relatively sure that their ideas will be put into shape anyway (or at least paraphrased) by the leader.

2. *Avoid contributing data too frequently*. If the leader presents his own information too readily, the members tend to neglect sources of their own. Regarding his data as authoritative, they may accept it uncritically or perhaps grudgingly. Any of these results is harmful enough to suggest that if the leader has relevant information, he should put it to two tests before giving it. First, he asks himself: *Does the group really need this particular piece of information?* Then, if he considers that it does, he asks the group such a question as this: *Does anyone remember the experience of the Baxter Brothers Company?* With this kind of question he expects that if someone

does know the instance, he will now put it before the group; if no one does, all will look to him with the implicit or expressed request that he provide the answer, and he will then present the information.

If the leader is the most knowledgeable person in the group, he must find a way to invite the attention of the members to that portion of the problem for which their varied experiences will have best prepared them. He may also "feed in" appropriate data at suitable times, as though such leader behavior was a normal expectation in the situation, as though they were no more remiss in not bringing in the data than in not bringing the conference table and chairs. Lest the members come to think that in every situation the leader should be the one to provide all necessary data, he should make it clear that these are special circumstances, requiring special procedures.

3. *Avoid designating the order of contributors.* The leader should restrain himself from designating *who* shall speak *when*, lest such authoritativeness (or formality) destroy the free offering of comments, the spontaneous building of the thought-line by the cooperative effort of the group. The only time he restrains one and encourages another is when a too-frequent contributor is choking off comments by those less venturesome in volunteering.[8]

4. *Avoid singling out an individual for special praise.* Such commendation actually handicaps the person who receives it. Knowing now what type of contribution is deemed praiseworthy by this chief dispenser of rewards, he tends to make more and more such contributions whether or not they are his best possible offerings. Also, wrong attitudes are now developed in other members: some will vie for rewards of praise for themselves, and others will show resentment over what they consider partiality.

Throughout the discussion the leader will likely wish to acknowledge unusually good ideas and helpful efforts (especially of quiet

8. Reference was made in Chapter 2, page 38, to Steinzor's finding that persons tend to talk more with those seated opposite them in a circle than with those beside them. Other researchers have also reported this oppositeness effect with two members seated on one side of a table and three on the other. See Lloyd T. Howells and Selwyn W. Becker, "Seating Arrangement and Leadership Emergence," *Journal of Abnormal and Social Psychology*, 64 (February 1962), 148-150. Hearn's study, though, tends to indicate that this spatial effect is canceled in groups where the leader functions with the members in providing direction for the group. See Gordon Hearn, "Leadership and the Spatial Factor in Small Groups," *Journal of Abnormal and Social Psychology*, 54 (March 1957), 269-272.

members), but this can be done by the appreciative glance and the quick "Good idea!" done in a manner which accepts the contribution as a part of the work being done together.

5. *Avoid fulfilling needs which members can and should fulfill.* The leader should restrain himself from insisting upon performing too quickly every duty which the group may be expecting of him; if he lets the group depend upon him too much, he will stifle the creativity of others in the group.[9] He must not, by forestalling their efforts, dwarf those alert members who see the next relevant issue and introduce it, who see the need of a summary and make it, who see the interrelationships of material and produce a synthesis. Also, if the members for any reason (lack of personal trust in the group, previous experience with authoritative leaders, recognition of the present leader's knowledge of the issue at hand) rely too much upon his suggestions and judgments, he must as skillfully as he can turn the responsibility and power back to the group by phrase, voice, and manner. If the newly elected officers of a club and the retiring officers meet together at the time of the change of responsibility, there may be a strong tendency to rely overmuch on the suggestions of the former president. If the former president realizes that he should resist the group's inclination to depend overly upon him, he may give any data needed and then raise questions to elicit group interpretation: "Yes, we decided against having a speaker this year at the quarterly business meetings. But I guess that's a decision to be made over again each year. Is there a purpose that a longer business meeting can serve? Or would it be better to shorten the business and hear a brief lecture in addition? We will be wanting to think what purpose we're striving to achieve."

On the other hand, if one unusually energetic member voluntarily assumes so many tasks that resentment grows in the group or confusion over the focus of authority arises (who *is* the leader—this person or the one designated as leader?), the leader should take a larger share in the fulfillment of these needs.

9. Fiedler summarized four investigations of the leader's effect on group creativity. In the study of boards of directors and management of thirty-two consumer cooperatives as well as in the laboratory studies, creativity was found to result from more relaxed leadership in pleasant group situations and from more directive leadership in stressful ones. See Fred E. Fiedler, "Leader Attitudes, Group Climate, and Group Creativity," *Journal of Abnormal and Social Psychology*, 65 (November 1962), 308-318.

6. *Avoid calling directly on quiet members.* The leader should not make an abrupt request for contribution from a quiet member. He should value that person's right to choose whether he wishes to volunteer or not. Furthermore, even if his request elicits a useful contribution, he will have damaged the group expectations; another quiet person may now think grimly, "I'll be next!" and the likelihood of his working whole-heartedly with the group is further reduced.

Instead, the effective leader is alert for physical signs that the retiring member wishes to speak. Then he says, in a questioning tone, "Mary, you had a thought there. . . ." or "Mary, did you have a point you wanted to make here?" If the leader has misjudged Mary's readiness, her denial of such intent is quickly absorbed and passed over. Recognizing the leader's legitimate task of sponsoring the efforts of the members, no other member fears being forced to contribute when he is not ready.

7. *Avoid announcing a point of view on substantive issues.* As explained earlier, cooperative building of a thought-line by a group cannot occur if members speak from fixed points of view rather than from earnest and genuine desire to develop the best understanding or answer of which they, working together, are capable. It is obvious that such voluntary cooperative efforts can never be achieved in a group if the leader himself is partial.

If the leader shows a preference for a certain line of reasoning or for a particular member of the group, he has violated the conditions under which true cooperative action occurs. If the leader presents himself as inviting open-minded efforts at idea-development from the members and then undercuts these efforts by his own fixed opinions or by his unusually strong acceptance of the ideas of one of the members, this lack of integrity will produce little cooperative effort and exceedingly bad group morale.[10]

10. This quality of integrity is considered a central characteristic in managerial leadership. Field Marshal Sir William Slim, Commander in Chief of the 14th Army in World War II and later Governor General of Australia, in an address to the Sydney Division of the Australian Institute of Management, November 25, 1953 (page 5 of a pamphlet published by the Institute), named five qualities as essential in a leader: courage, will power, flexibility of mind, knowledge, and "the last quality, on which all the others have to be based, is integrity— the thing that makes people trust you."

Peter F. Drucker refers more than a dozen times in his book *The Practice of Management*, (New York: Harper and Brothers, 1954) to integrity as the one quality most necessary in a manager.

8. *Avoid tying ideas to their initiators.* If the leader labels an idea by its initiator's name, as *John's idea* or *John's suggestion* (or does not remove such a designation when used by members of the group), he may restrict not only John's voluntary contributions but those of the other members as well. Such labeling may make John feel responsible for the idea as he first suggested it; this situation tends to make him defensive of the idea even if he has not been so up to this point. In addition, it virtually deprives him of the chance to shift and modify his idea with the work of the group; he is, in a sense, immobilized at the point at which he introduced the idea.

And others, hearing the idea called *John's suggestion,* may find it hard not to invest the idea with the attributes they see in John, such plus values as good looks or good sense, or such negative values as aggressiveness or superficial thinking. The ever-present problem of seeing the idea in its own colors—neither deriving its coloration from its contributor nor coloring the contributor with its hues—is intensified by such labels.

But such labeling harms the rational thinking of the group in still another way: a designation is not efficient which asks the listener to think: "Just what, after all, is *John's suggestion?*" If the leader consistently labels the idea by its meaning, as "Our idea of Big Brother Clubs in every neighborhood," he will not only tend to free John of the idea and free the idea of John but will also recall the gist of the suggestion to everyone's mind more expeditiously.

Reconstructive action

Should it happen that the members begin to address their remarks too exclusively to some person of high prestige—prestige resulting either from eminence outside the group or from behavior in the group—the leader should take action to preserve the group process. In such a situation the number of persons making voluntary contributions drops sharply and the desired diversity of opinion is lost.[11]

11. When one person talks far too much, he tends to develop unwarranted influence on the group decisions. For example, Riecken's experiment with thirty-two groups demonstrated that the "biggest talker" obtained acceptance for a good solution (supplied to him secretly by the experimenter) over two thirds of the time, whereas the "small talker" (provided with the same solution) did so less than one third of the time. See Henry W. Riecken, "The Effect of Talkativeness on Ability to Influence Group Solutions to Problems," *Sociometry,* 21 (September 1958), 309-321.

Since the prestige person, in what has become virtually an interview situation, makes every other contribution and tends naturally to reply directly to those who have addressed him, the opportunities for others to enter the discussion are restricted and a "communication squeeze" has developed. Recognizing this tendency toward progressive exclusion, the effective leader should take steps to widen participation:

1. He encourages everyone to get into the discussion in the first few minutes of the meeting. By inquiring looks and quick response to signs of growing readiness to enter the exchange, the effective leader tries to elicit contributions from those who seem less likely to contribute voluntarily. The interchange is more likely to remain general (as it should be, most of the time) if everyone's voice has been heard early and his team membership acknowledged.

2. If a "communication squeeze" begins to develop, the alert leader interposes quickly and firmly by directing attention to persons who seem eager to enter the exchange; he may say, looking in the general direction of such a person and letting him volunteer, "I believe there was an idea over here. . . ." or he may catch the line of thinking from someone who is active in the discussion and then look around to the others with words like these: "Just a minute; let's not move away from that idea quite so fast. What other implications need consideration here?"

Another threat to group process lies in the varied treatment ideas receive when brought before the group. To the extent that the ideas are weighed on the basis of *who presented them* rather than on the basis of their meaning and value to the group, the whole process of idea-development, as well as the morale of the group, is endangered.[12] The leader needs to counterbalance this tendency as well as he can: usually he moves in quickly to identify an idea with the group (*our idea that . . .*), to forestall its being undervalued if suggested by a member of lesser prestige or overvalued if suggested

12. Torrance, in a study of B-26 combat crews, analyzed how often the person with the correct answer to a problem failed to secure its acceptance by the other two crew members. Only 6 per cent of the permanent-crew pilots (with final authority as aircraft commanders) failed in gaining acceptance when they had the correct answer; 20 per cent of the navigators (also commissioned officers) failed when they had the correct answer; but 37 per cent of the gunners (enlisted men) failed when they had the correct answer. See E. Paul Torrance, *Research Studies*, State College of Washington, 22 (1954), 130-140.

by one with high prestige. He then invites all members to test the idea impartially.

A further danger to effective group process lies in the distortion of communication produced by stressful situations. When a member does not feel that he can rely upon the good will or sincerity of another member (or other members), he will tend to withhold his contribution or to conceal his true opinion by speaking compliantly, evasively, or aggressively.[13] Since the group is thus deprived of his genuine thought, the leader needs to take remedial action where possible:

1. The leader may show the importance of the group task so compellingly that its accomplishment overrides any interpersonal considerations.

2. He may help the group to bring personal motivations out into the open so that greater understanding and sincerity of contribution will result.

Systematic development of thought

One of the most important services the leader performs in the group is his assistance in the systematic development of thought. Since the group thought-line is constructed by the addition of diverse elements whose importance may be differently evaluated by each member, the individual efforts to assist in its growth must be coordinated. The effective leader tries to keep the development of thought systematic by helping the members know where they are in their subject at any one time, by making transitions and summaries, by echoing, retracking, and pacing the ideas.

Clarifying present status

If the group has become confused among the ideas members are presenting, the effective leader is quick to clarify what the line of

13. A study conducted in a large governmental organization devoted to medical research revealed that the primary goal of a person who distrusted another's motives was not to transmit ideas accurately but to reduce his own anxiety. Two factors were found to affect the extent of the damage to effective communication: the disparity in status of the two persons involved and the nature of the issue. See Glen D. Mellinger, "Interpersonal Trust as a Factor in Communication," *Journal of Abnormal and Social Psychology*, 52 (May 1956), 304-309.

thinking has become at the moment, its present status. He says something like, "Are we saying, then, that . . . ?" Or he himself may be in doubt and say openly to the group, "Let's see; what are we saying?" The members have to know the present status of the thought-line they have produced before they can move on together.

Making summaries

The leader should not wait until the end of the discussion to summarize the group's decision or insights. At many points within the discussion the group needs to know just what has been accomplished in order to move forward. In attempting to reach agreement in one portion of their task, the members need a summary of their achievement thus far and a list of any remaining issues, so that they can complete that aspect and then move smoothly to another part of their subject. Indeed, at any point in the discussion when ideas so far developed by the group seem to be slipping away from the members, the leader gathers them up; his summary clears out of the way those aspects already handled and makes it easier to see what must yet be done. Of course, if a member wishes to summarize for the group, the leader willingly allows him to do so.

The leader restates ideas in *group terms* as much as possible, using any "handles" developed by the group (see page 227), and phrases them as questions so that any errors he makes in interpretation or emphasis are more likely to be noticed and remedied. He says: "We said, then, didn't we, that . . . ." or "Our proposal has three parts—do I have them right?—one was . . . ." Furthermore, he lists the items in the precise order in which they were developed by the group so that they will be most easily recalled by the members.

The effective leader sees that his summary includes only what is immediately relevant on each point; it is not the wanderings of the group in its process of idea-development that he recapitulates, not the scaffolding through which the resulting thought was constructed, but the essential thought-line. He should summarize the substance of the ideas ("We have agreed, then, that new sources of food supply are not immediately available and that the amount of living space is permanently limited by the dimensions of our planet; now shall we . . . .") rather than generalize about the areas discussed ("We have talked about food and land; now perhaps we should . . . ."). If he neglects the substance, the members lack a common foothold for taking the next step.

At the close of the discussion, the leader should summarize the conclusions reached and the issues remaining unresolved, if there are any. In his summary he should recognize the result as a cooperative product and encourage a sense of common achievement.

Making transitions

The leader may assist the group greatly in the systematic unfolding of the subject by suggesting a succeeding inquiry that it may wish to make. After an appropriate summary he may say, for example, "Perhaps we are now ready to suggest causes of the problem as we have found it to be; what might we say is one of the causes operating here?" His question bites into an area appropriate for group examination and prompts a smooth transition into it. He avoids asking a question that suggests no direction, like "Well, what shall we take up now?" Rather than offering too little guidance, he centers the attention of the members on a specific forward inquiry and lets them decide whether they wish to undertake it.

The effective leader suggests movement to a different aspect of the subject when he judges that the group has achieved enough accord on the aspect under discussion; or when the time is running out and important issues remain to be considered; or, especially in enlightenment discussion, when group interest has seemed in danger of waning. Suggesting transitions to *appropriate* areas at *appropriate* times is one of the leader's most important functions. Often, of course, members make transitions voluntarily; if the leader thinks, in such instances, that not all members have noted the transition, he asks clarification with such a question as, "Are we talking now about . . . ?"

Echoing

Sometimes a member's contribution is incomplete or lacks forcefulness in language, voice, or manner; in such cases it is likely to be passed by without due consideration. To hold it before the group the necessary moment longer, the leader may echo its key words tentatively:

> **Mary Quinn** Doesn't that phrasing carry a negative presumption?
> **Peter Linde (leader)** A negative presumption?
> **Mary** Yes. I'm suggesting that . . .

The leader's manner should indicate that here is a point for the group to consider but should not suggest advocacy or rejection. He thus enforces an underlying assumption of the discussion method, that every idea voiced in the group merits fair attention from the members.

The leader should notice any particular phrasing of ideas that the members seem to find meaningful as they develop the idea together and use it in synthesizing that segment of thought, even though he may not have echoed this "handle" at the time it initially appeared.

Retracking

The leader should take action, without rebuke or undue emphasis, to help the group to *return from a tangent* to the main thought-line. He knows, however, that he should avoid exposing the tangent too soon, especially if its initiator or chief advocate is someone who needs special encouragement—a new member, a person who seems to feel rejected by the group, or someone who needs the approval of those in authority. Usually the group can afford the time consumed by the tangent and will profit later from the tangent-goer's added sense of acceptance.

When the situation allows straightforward treatment of the tangent, however, the leader usually raises the issue to the group at once to conserve time and energy, with some remark like "I wonder if we're moving away from our analysis of present efforts?" If the idea which is tangential is likely to be of value at a later stage of the discussion, he files it away mentally and suggests its reintroduction at an appropriate later time. Instead of an abrupt "I think you're off the track here!" he says, "I wonder whether we're getting off the track a little here. We were trying to . . . ." or "I wonder, could we hold up a minute with this point? We need right now to . . . but let's not forget to bring that idea back when we get to . . . ."

When ideas branch far off from the main line of thinking, they are easily labeled as tangents and the retracking is quickly achieved. But slight deviations—large enough to be important but slight enough to go unperceived—are a different matter; in fact, no leader is astute enough to know always whether such an idea actually constitutes a tangent. But his alertness to the possibility of tangents and his retracking in question form are of great assistance to group movement.

Pacing

If the leader feels that probably enough has been done with the idea at hand—that present comments are making less and less difference in the modification of the idea—he needs to synthesize the idea as developed and suggest moving to another issue. Or perhaps he realizes that, in view of the portion of the task remaining to be undertaken, the group must move more quickly and says, "Do you suppose we could move a little faster here? We have three areas still to examine in the time we have left." In general, he needs to assist the group to move speedily through the resolution of less important issues in order to save time for the more important or more complex ones. He must help the group, then, to move efficiently and with speed befitting the situation without seeming hurried and without continually referring to the shortness of time.

The leader can do a great deal by the pace of his own contributions. If the members are so slow to pick up cues and build on one another's ideas that interest wanes during the pauses and the whole investigation moves in a labored fashion, he demonstrates by the alertness of his own contributions that ideas can *catch fire* from one another. He often increases the tempo of the entire group movement by the speed of his own reactions and by his expectation of swift-moving responses from others. Someone with good thoughts but a slow pace of expression must not be cut off, however, unless his frequent contributions at this rate take up too much time or influence others to fall back unnecessarily to a time-consuming pace.

On the other hand, the movement of the group may be too hasty. If the thought-line is borne away too swiftly by one member while the others remain uncomprehending, or is being constructed erratically by numerous jabs of uncoordinated thought, the leader should break in and, by his own more deliberate pace, reduce the tempo of the group. He can tactfully suggest that the members slow down, saying with entire good will, "Just a minute! I wonder if we're not moving a little too fast here. Could we take a closer look at this one idea about . . . before we move on?"

Modifications for exploratory discussions

In the exploratory form of enlightenment discussion—where the group is able to move off more freely in many directions from a common body of material—the leadership function should be performed somewhat differently:

1. The leader's opening remarks should articulate but not pre-empt the members' feeling of anticipation for the discussion. On occasion he may, after an introductory sentence or two, guide the group in

outlining quickly and without comment the main ideas in the common body of material.

2. He must exercise self-restraint (see pages 254-258) with special care, realizing that the spontaneous surge of interest in new and unpredictable directions succeeds only in a very free atmosphere.

3. Since an exploratory group is usually a large one (see pages 32-33), he does not expect *everyone* to participate but does move to break a "communication squeeze" if one develops.

4. Although he synthesizes ideas where necessary, he usually omits summaries, because thought-lines in the exploratory group should be left open for further pursuit rather than summed up as completed.

5. Since there need be no continuity between successive spring-board ideas taken up by the members, the leader helps them move (on the basis of *interest*, not *relevance*) to a new topic if they do not themselves initiate the transition when they have gone as far on a line of thinking as they can with any depth or with the interest of the majority of members, or when they are spending an exorbitant amount of time on one line, thus ignoring others of similarly high interest. He then suggests: "Shall we move to another idea?" or "Did anyone notice that idea about . . . ?"

6. He generally does not retrack the group unless tangents multiply so fast as to be confusing.

7. Since the pace of exploratory discussion depends entirely upon the degree of interest the group generates, the leader usually tries to keep the interest high rather than to change the pace.

Example of leader's systematizing function

In problem-solving discussion and in all forms of enlightenment discussion other than the exploratory form, the leader should attempt to use the suggestions given above for assisting the group in systematic development of thought. Suppose that a group is engaged in an enlightenment discussion of the evaluative type on the question: *How dangerous is our use of insecticides?* The group has started to discuss the dangers being claimed, and Jim Adler has mentioned Rachel Carson's book *Silent Spring*.

Echoes to hold new idea	**Carol Dexter (leader)** *Silent Spring?*
	Jim Adler Yes, I guess the title comes from— at least, it seems to me anyway—from that part

about the elms. She says—and I copied it down because I thought it was, well, eloquent in a way —"We spray our elms and the following springs are silent of robin song, not because we sprayed the robins directly but because the poison traveled step by step, through the now familiar elm leaf-earthworm-robin cycle." Now, that's *down-to-earth* truth; that's the way it happens.

Warren Marx "Down-to-earth"—that's good! Nothing quite as down-to-earth as a worm!

General laughter

Retracks in question form

Leader Let's see—we're pointing out that the use of insecticides tends to break up the inter-relationships of nature—is that it?

Allen McCoy The *indiscriminate* use, or *over-use*, didn't we say?

Leader Yes, the indiscriminate use of insecticides breaks up the interrelationships of nature. Perhaps now we should ask ourselves: how does this affect us other than killing our birds?

Suggests a transition

Paul Willis One very grim way is through our food. When bees get nectar from forests that have been sprayed, they make poisonous honey!

Janice Halleck Yes, and the rain falls on the forests that have been sprayed and the water runs off into the rivers and out into the oceans, and, of course, the dangerous chemicals are in it.

(The group continues to give examples of dangers through food; the leader notes that much time has been expended in this procedure and alerts the group.)

Paces group interaction

Leader So far, we've mentioned the upsetting of the interrelationships of nature—that it despoils our environment and endangers our food sources. Perhaps we should turn to the question: if they are so bad, why do we use them?

Tom Spohr They're tremendously effective. We want to destroy gnats and mosquitoes and weeds, of course. So we use DDT and stronger chemicals, without knowing what harm they really do.

Paul Willis But we mustn't sell DDT short. Think how we've moved in all over the world to conquer pests that have crippled whole societies; DDT has done immense good in underdeveloped areas.

Janice Halleck   But maybe we've introduced dangers too wherever we've used it, and the dangers might be worse than the flies or mosquitoes we were fighting.

Leader defers idea until an appropriate later time

Leader   Could we hold up on balancing the achievements and the dangers until we've taken a careful look at both angles separately? Let's take a look at the achievements first, shall we? What valuable results have insecticides brought?

Summary

The effective discussion leader provides himself with knowledge about the subject, the participants, the time allotment, and the place of the discussion. His opening remarks to the group are intended to (1) be informative, (2) be stimulating, (3) establish a favorable climate in the group, and (4) invite the group to begin with an appropriate aspect of the subject. Two of the essentials of interaction he helps the group achieve are: (1) free contribution by all members and (2) systematic development of thought. In fostering free contribution by all members, he demonstrates the desired characteristics in his own speaking and listening, restrains himself from actions that might curtail the members' freedom, and acts to break down obstacles created by others in the group. He helps the group in systematic development of thought by clarifying the present status of ideas, by making transitions and summaries, by echoing, retracking, and pacing the ideas. These techniques must be modified somewhat by the leader of an exploratory discussion.

Readings and problems

1.   Analyze what you yourself expect of a leader in discussion groups in which you participate. Think of the most effective leader you have worked with in a discussion group up to this time and evaluate his fulfillment of each of the expectations you have listed.

2.   Note the opening remarks of the leaders of two discussions in which you participate. Contrast the effectiveness of these two leaders on the four requirements: be informative; be stimulating; set a favorable climate; and suggest an appropriate starting point.

3. From among the suggestions for the leader given in this chapter list those that you yourself find hardest to carry out successfully. Analyze why these points cause you difficulty.

4. Keep a count of the contributions of each participant in a classroom discussion by making a seating chart and noting the number of contributions that each member makes in the first fourth of the time, the second fourth, and so on. Use the information as the basis of a class discussion on the problems involved in getting wide participation.

5. Prepare to hold a class discussion on the making of summaries in a discussion group. Use sentences from the chapter for springboards; for example:

"At any point in the discussion when ideas so far developed by the group seem to be slipping away from the members, the leader gathers them up."

"If a member wishes to summarize for the group, the leader willingly allows him to do so."

"He should summarize the substance of the ideas . . . rather than generalize about the areas discussed."

6. Define these terms used in this chapter, and relate them to the functioning of an effective discussion leader: interruptability, communication squeeze, handles, integrity, present status of ideas, echoing, retracking, pacing.

7. Set up role play situations (see pages 215-217 for suggestions) based on these circumstances:

A. The leader emphasizes status differences by the manner of his introduction of the members.

B. A quiet person is asked directly and abruptly for a contribution.

C. A proposal is referred to repeatedly by its initiator's name.

D. A communication squeeze is stifling the cooperative work of the group.

8. Hold an exploratory discussion on "leadership," using these materials as springboards:

A.

"One of the most fundamental of all human qualities necessary for leadership appears to be tact. The tactful person seems to possess a sense of the state of mind of other individuals and is able to make the proper approach to them and establish agreeable relationships. On the other hand, the tactless person is constantly jeopardizing his plans by his irritating activities. . . .

"Tact begins in specific external manners and ends in a sort of realization of a completely integrated life. It involves a vivid awareness of one's own experiences, a constant self-criticism of these experiences, and a precise measuring of their values for oneself. The practice of tact has been considered by some writers as a test of intelligence and imagination."—Henry L. Smith and Levi M. Krueger, "A Brief Summary of Literature on Leadership," *Bulletin of the School of Education,* Indiana University, 9 (September 1933), 32.

B.

"The fact is that a leader should have a high capacity to vary his rate of activity; he must be active at one moment and passive at the next."—George Homans, *The Human Group* (New York: Harcourt, Brace and Co., 1950), p. 439.

C. A résumé of Napoleon's chief mental traits as recorded by his biographers:

"An imagination of wonderful force, a power of calculation that embraced everything, and yet grasped the smallest details; the master faculty of always perceiving the dominant fact in what was before him, of separating it from what was subordinate, and of seeing how it could be turned to account; and admirable celerity and keenness of thought."—Abdul Majid, *The Psychology of Leadership* (London: T. Fisher Unwin, n.d.), pp. 52-67.

D.

"This is pre-eminently the leadership quality—the ability to organize all the forces there are in an enterprise. Men with this ability create a group power rather than express a personal power. They penetrate to the subtlest connections of the forces at their command, and make all these forces available, and most effectively available, for the accomplishment of their purpose."—*Dynamic Administration: The Collected Papers of Mary Parker Follett,* Henry C. Metcalf and L. Urwick, eds. (New York: Harper and Brothers, 1942), p. 283.

E.

"Know how to put fire into your subordinates."—*Gracian's Manual,* Martin Fischer, trans. (Springfield, Illinois: C. C. Thomas, 1934), No. 265.

Chapter twelve

LEADING

GROUP

DISCUSSION:

PART II

As we have seen in the previous chapter, the effective discussion leader helps elicit voluntary contributions from all members and also guides them in a systematic development of thought. We will now consider the other important functions he performs in maintaining a sound development of thought, making constructive use of differences in opinion, and handling disruptive factors effectively.

Sound development of thought

To assure development of a sound thought-line, the leader gives the members assistance in correcting faulty handling of ideas, faulty understanding of ideas, and questionable reasoning.

Faulty handling of ideas

Sound thinking cannot occur if members are talking about two ideas as if they were one or about one factor as if it were two, or have allowed contradictory elements to slip into their thinking unnoticed. "Do you suppose we are really talking about two different cases here?" says the leader; or "Could it be that these two ideas are really about the same after all, just expressed in different terms?"; or "I wonder how this idea can be reconciled with what we were saying earlier . . . ?"

Suppose that a group is setting up criteria for a voluntary course in home safety; the members have been suggesting what should be included:

> **Mrs. A** Probably we would want to be very sure that all matters of importance were included. Our planning of the units and procedures should revolve around this consideration.
>
> **Mr. B** Yes, all matters of importance and probably on the basis of their *relative* importance. Our point seems to be that all the factors that seem of interest to the group should be included.
>
> *(Notice the shift here—from matters of importance to matters of interest. The underlying assumption is that what is of interest will be of importance. While this should ideally be true, no doubt it often will not be.)*
>
> **Mrs. C** We surely have to keep our members interested; so it is a very good idea to keep our

plans geared to the particular interests of our own group.

(Note how far afield this comment takes the thought-line. The idea now is that the selection of factors to be included should be based on their degree of interest to the members of this particular group.)

Mr. D But some interesting things aren't important!

(He has seen the shift of focus but has not provided a way for the group to break out of the tangle.)

Mrs. C You've got to keep things interesting or no one will come! You'll have to admit that after a day at the office you will expect the evening to be interesting.

Mr. E (leader) Yes, something that will hold your attention easily. But do you suppose that we might be talking about two different aspects here: one, what is included—the important things, on the basis of their importance—and, two, how they are to be treated—in interesting fashion?

(The leader has seen that the group is talking about two things at the same time without realizing it, and he suggests to the group a way of breaking the log jam.)

Mr. A Well, could we establish two criteria here: one, covering the important things in due proportion in the course, and two, handling them in an interesting way?

Leader Does it seem so to all of us? O.K., let's divide it this way then. Our first criterion is to be: The course must include all matters of importance in proportion to their relative importance—does that say what we mean? And the second: The course materials must be handled in an interesting way—there, does that do it?

(The leader recognized that phrasing the criterion is a separate logical task from developing the idea to be phrased; hence, picking up terms from the group, he tried out a phrasing to check its acceptability to the group. Often the phrasing will not arise so directly from the work of the group as it

*did in this case; then the exact phrasing will have
to be chosen with deliberation by the full group.)*

Faulty understanding of ideas

Sometimes the members will think that they understand each
other when they actually don't; they may have handled an idea so
generally that each is still a captive of his own interpretations. On
the other hand, sometimes they will mistakenly think that they are
saying different things and become vociferous in their explanations
and declarations without realizing that they are fundamentally
in agreement.

In either case, the leader should bring the faulty understandings
into open view. If the members seem content with some ambiguous
generalization, he should pose specific questions that will reveal
the relevant differences in their interpretations. Suppose, for example,
that a discussion of status differences in American society seems
to be breaking down because several members have asserted that
"it is natural for people to stick with their own kind," a generalization that the others quickly accept. Seeing the variety of personal
interpretations possible, the leader attempts to bring these into the
open and to revitalize the discussion by asking questions such as
these: "When we say *natural,* do we mean in the biological sense,
psychological, cultural, or what?"; "By *their own kind* do we mean
those like them physically or like them in birth or money or occupation . . ."; "When we say *stick with* do we mean live together in the
same neighborhoods, join together in political blocs . . . ?"

When the opposite situation develops and members are shooting
statements past one another without sensing their basic accord, the
leader should strip away superficial differences and reconcile variant
phrasings in order to reveal the members' fundamental agreement.
To achieve this, he may use questions such as these: "But even though
we seem to be emphasizing different aspects, don't we basically agree
that . . . ?"; "Whether we call it population growth or population
explosion or the baby boom or something else, do we agree that the
figures indicate . . . ?"; "Although we seem to be having difficulty
defining *natural,* could we perhaps essentially mean that . . . ?"

Questionable reasoning

If the leader notices a segment of the reasoning to which the
members seem not to be applying the relevant tests, he should

(1) suggest an appropriate test to the group in question form; (2) start orally and by slow stages to apply the appropriate test, enlisting their efforts for the completion of the job; or (3) if the group is well versed in logical method, suggest the results of the test for the group's consideration. Which of these he will consider suitable in a particular instance will depend upon the time available and the group's previously demonstrated willingness and competency to apply critical thinking.

To move quickly to the appropriate test or tests, the leader needs to have the program of tests clearly in mind:

1. Is the idea relevant? clear? complete?
2. Is the line of reasoning (a) facts-to-conclusion? or (b) expert opinion-to-conclusion? or (c) premise-to-conclusion?
   If (a), are the facts true? Is the reasoning sound?
   If (b), is the expert a qualified authority? Is his reasoning sound?
   If (c), is the premise acceptable? the conclusion logical?
3. Is the significance given the idea appropriate?[1]

Suppose that in the discussion on insecticides in Chapter 11 (see pages 261-263), the group proceeded as follows:

He is pointing out that the group has been relying strongly on an expert opinion-to-conclusion line of reasoning, and he casts doubt on the soundness of the conclusion	**Paul Willis** I wonder if we're going too far here. Rachel Carson writes a book and we swallow it whole. Do you think we can really rely on her conclusions that much?
Leader poses a test of authoritativeness	**Carol Dexter (leader)** Yes, let's examine how much belief we ought to be putting in her opinions. Her book came out this spring, didn't it? **Janice Halleck** Yes, it's a 1962 book.
Suggests other qualifications of the authority	**Jim Adler** She used to be a government biologist. Now she does research and writes. She's the one who wrote *The Sea Around Us*, you know. This book, *Silent Spring*, is the result of four and a half years of research.

1. See Chapters 5 and 8 for full explanation.

Affirms the authority's data	**Tom Spohr** Well, there are a couple of other things that tell us we'd better take her conclusions pretty seriously. When the agricultural chemical industry tried to find errors in her book—you can imagine how threatened they felt—they couldn't refute a single fact or case history that she reported.
Affirms the authority's reasoning	**Allen McCoy** Well, she's not radical about it; she's not saying we ought to do away with these pesticides, only that they—that we—ought to use them more carefully and investigate their possible effects more thoroughly. That certainly doesn't seem too much to ask.
Cites another influential opinion	**Tom** And when the President announced at a press conference recently that the government was starting to examine the long-range side effects, he mentioned her book.
The leader checks with the group to see whether all members understand the results of the testing in the same way	**Leader** Are we satisfied, then, that her conclusions are worthy of our belief since her research has withstood all the tests the chemical industry set up and her conclusions from her research are responsibly drawn?

The effective leader also prevents the rejection and loss of ideas which are not being given fair consideration by the group. He finds a way to keep the members' attention from sliding away: he may simply rephrase the unnoticed or unappreciated idea and invite their attention to a relevant aspect of it. Thus, the potentially good but currently unpopular idea gets fairer consideration.[2] On the other hand, the leader should not allow an idea to assume disproportionate weight simply because of its reiteration. Members who have heard one persistent individual continue to bring in a certain view may, out of sheer weariness or a desire to placate the person, begin to give it more attention than it deserves. A. Lipsky (1) has explained the danger in this situation:

2. Two researchers found that more valuable results were reached in groups with leaders who stimulated consideration of divergent views than in those without such stimulation. See N. R. F. Maier and A. R. Solem, "The Contribution of a Discussion Leader to the Quality of Group Thinking: The Effective Use of Minority Opinions," *Human Relations*, 5 (August 1952), 277-288.

It is no doubt true that one man who holds his belief tenaciously counts for as much as several men who hold theirs weakly. Yet it is well known that the intensity with which an opinion is held is in no wise proportional to its truth or to the depth of the mind that entertains it. The shallowest and the most ignorant are the most violent in their opinions. All we know of the intensity of an opinion is the fierceness with which it is expressed and the doggedness with which it is clung to— qualities not of opinions but of temperaments. Fierceness and tenacity go far in getting opinions accepted by others partly because of the natural dislike of most men for controversy, partly owing to the presumption that an opinion sincerely and strongly held is more apt to be true than one indifferently defended.

To prevent these forces from coming into play adversely, the leader should urge critical evaluation of an idea as soon as he notices its frequent reappearance.

Constructive use of differences of opinion

Differences of information, interpretation, and value judgment among the members of a group should enrich the work they do to- gether. If, however, such differences arouse tensions and rivalries that prevent the group's progress, the leader must attempt to prevent them from exerting a destructive influence on the discussion. He should remember the comment of Wendell Johnson (2), that there are differences that make a difference and differences that don't make a difference. When differences threaten to undermine group judgment or to injure interpersonal relationships, the leader should help the group use them constructively to achieve a wider range of opinion. This is particularly necessary in the problem- solving discussion, where unresolved differences pose a greater ob- stacle to group achievement than they do in the less confined enlightenment discussion.

The leader should be skilled in the use of a number of different methods of handling opinion conflicts. Whichever method he adopts, the effective leader treats the conflict as a disparity in honestly held beliefs rather than a matter of interpersonal discord. There are four basic approaches that leaders often try in handling conflict: (1) examine the data and lines of reasoning behind the divergent views; (2) increase understanding before attempting evaluation; (3) examine the difference by easy steps; and (4) restrict the means by which conflict may be expressed.

Examine data and reasoning

In this widely useful approach the leader helps the group to look at the relative value of the opposed ideas: he moves in quickly to state the issue clearly and to invite all members to cooperate as a team in examining the evidence and reasoning behind each. Enlisting the critical aid of those who have drawn a different conclusion and resisting all tendencies to let the opposed view obscure the one being considered, the leader focuses the group's effort on testing the validity of one conclusion at a time. It may turn out that there is a difference in the use of terms, the interpretation of facts, the reasoning from facts, or the values sought. Sometimes the alternative view will disappear when the first view withstands an honest, cooperative testing. If, however, the second interpretation is not absorbed or dissipated in the exploration of the first, the same concentrated group attention should be turned upon the evidence and reasoning underlying it.

Such a procedure may eliminate the conflict entirely or may merely reduce or localize it. In the latter cases, the disparity between the two views may become so small that it matters very little in the group's work, and the members may move on to the next segment of thought. If the difference is still great, the leader should restate the remaining controversy and again guide the group through critical examination of each view in turn. In extreme cases the group may have to put an issue aside as unresolved, hoping that a later portion of the discussion may give them new insights into solution.

Suppose that a group is holding an enlightenment discussion on the question: *How do twentieth-century social mores differ from those of the past?* At one stage a difference of opinion develops:

Max Bruhn   Marriages, for example, seem to be more realistically contracted in terms of the expectations of the partners. They are alliances of individuals rather than families.

Gordon Villard But they are less stable than ever before. Look at how the divorce rate has multiplied! Right here in our city about one out of every four marriages ends in divorce—and this is true of most urban centers—whereas in the nineteenth century divorce was rare. Surely this indicates that marriage doesn't mean what it used to. A lot of people are entering into irresponsible unions, it seems to me.

Randy Masters (leader) Let's see now. We agree, I suppose, that a high divorce rate is a relatively recent phenomenon? Now the question seems to be whether this rate indicates that marriages are becoming less stable, that is, are entered into more lightly?

Charles Rodriguez Well, the rate simply reflects a change in laws, doesn't it? I mean, in recent times it has become relatively easy to get a divorce, but in the past it was very hard—

Max Yes, if the laws regarding divorce were the same in the nineteenth century as now, I suppose the figures could be compared, but, since this isn't so, can we really judge? And besides, isn't it a difference in social mores? That is, there was a social stigma attached to divorce then that is largely gone now.

Gordon Hmm, yes. The change in the law has something to do with it, and I see the point about the social stigma. A person may want to do something, but if society opposes it, he probably won't. But look, doesn't the change in the law itself reflect a weakening in the marriage bond? *(Gordon has been drawing his conclusions by interpreting evidence differently from the others; when this is discovered, the difference begins to clear away. Of course, Gordon may still feel that his initial inference about contemporary marriages is correct, but now his reasoning will be free of faulty use of statistics and the participants will be better able to use conflicting viewpoints constructively.)*

Increase understanding before evaluation

When it seems likely that a point of view is being overstated—whether because of long or close personal commitment or temporary emotional charge—a leader may encourage the group to hear fuller explanation before evaluating the position. If all members yield the opinion giver their full attention, demonstrating their interest in seeing what he really means and how he feels about it but indicating their desire to consider it critically, he may, in explaining more precisely, modify his extreme position. In the few instances where such supportive attention may make a member self-conscious and cause him to abandon his view too readily, the leader should quickly identify it as a *group* idea and thus retain it for constructive use by the group.

Carl Rogers (3), whose client-centered approach to counseling is well known, has suggested that listeners must refrain from early evaluation of an idea being presented, that communication is fostered when they try to understand the idea *as the speaker means it,* sometimes rephrasing it themselves *to his satisfaction,* in order to test their understanding. Such a method, initiated by the leader if not by the members, helps to guarantee fair examination and constructive use of divergent views. A careful and unbiased attention to all ideas encourages members with minority views to express themselves freely and thus enrich group resources.

An example of how the leader can foster understanding occurs in an enlightenment discussion on the question: *What should be the role of the United States in the economic growth of the developing countries of Africa?* The members have just described our present role in developing countries around the world as large and increasing:

John Patterson But we make such mistakes overseas! It isn't wise to keep expanding our role and making more and more mistakes.
(John is making a premise-to-conclusion inference from his generalization.)

No one speaks for a moment, then with tone of true inquiry
Don Stokes Would you explain about our making mistakes, John, a little further?

John Yes. We use a country for our benefit, as a base for military operations or something, and then we pull out and the country's whole economy collapses.

Gives him support in continuing his explanation but makes no judgment

Carl Piekot (leader) Umhm——

John I'm thinking of Samoa. You know, the Samoan Islands were used in World War II as a staging area for our stand at Guadalcanal; so the Islanders worked for the Navy at our installations there, and everybody had money. Then the Navy pulled out in 1951 and the Department of the Interior took over and the economy went to pieces —not enough money for administration, and not very clear goals either. So the Islands are a shameful example of our country's actions abroad: poorly staffed and equipped schools, poor roads, poor agriculture, not enough medical service. Our treatment of Samoa condemns us in the eyes of every new nation—or at least every nation that is looking for our mistakes——

Testing the extent of his actual meaning

Leader You're thinking of Samoa, then, as a real mistake?

John Yes, I wouldn't say we always make it, but this time we surely did.

(John has now abandoned his generalization; doubtless he will move ahead with the group in developing a plan to safeguard our country against any repetition of this example he feels so strongly about.)

Examine by easy steps

When the conflict is complex or deep seated, the problem is often better approached by a series of steps, rather than directly. The leader verbalizes the basic difference and breaks it down into the smaller issues of which it is composed. He may make statements like these, for instance:

Leader We seem to differ, then, on the propriety of religious observances in public schools. First of all, perhaps we should decide what we mean by *religious observances*. Would the singing of Christmas carols, for example, be a religious observance? [raises the issue of definition] . . . Should we examine the financial base of our public school system [raises the issue of affiliation] . . . Might it not be useful to know how our courts have ruled on such matters? [raises the issue of Constitutionality].

In cases where it is clear that some subissues are thornier than others, the leader first poses those which the group can resolve more easily. Then, with a backlog of successful cooperative work on these issues—and the resulting sense of group confidence—the leader helps the group to move on through the more controversial ones to the crux of the difference.

Major Charles Estes (4), the former Commissioner of the U.S. Mediation and Conciliation Board, developed a "conditioning" procedure which he used for difficult labor-management sessions. In this method the whole group participates in explaining a series of aspects of the problem *without taking a point of view* on any of them. Then the leader raises the easier issues for the group's consideration, and only when the members have moved successfully to accord on these do they move on to the hotter issues.

Restrict means of expressing conflict

If none of the previous methods brings accord, the leader may formalize the rules of contribution temporarily. Irving J. Lee (5) suggested that the leader invoke a period of "Chairman's Privilege." During this interval no expression of a difference of opinion is in order. The chairman invites a proponent of the view that started the controversy to state or restate the position. He is not to be interrupted; no denials or rebuttals are allowed. Then his opponents can ask him questions of these three types only (examples quoted from Lee):

1. *To clarify*

   What did you mean when you said . . . ?

   Did you say . . . ?

   You said . . . ; did you mean this . . . ?

(Information is sought here as to what the speaker actually means as distinguished from what the listener may have assumed that he means. Sometimes as a consequence the speaker corrects his own earlier statements.)

2. *To examine uniqueness*

   In what way is this different from other situations or proposals we have faced?

(Information is sought about certain differentiating characteristics to allow comparison with previous experiences or opinions.)

3. *To find means of testing*[3]

Can you tell us any way of testing your assumptions or predictions?

(Information is sought on a way by which listeners may check these claims with reality, for example, a trial run or a test with a small sample, and so forth.)

Lee pointed out that in his use of this method these results occurred:

1. The discipline of questioning halted the tendency toward immediate opposition.

2. The questioning sometimes caused a proponent to re-examine and subsequently withdraw his proposal.

3. Tensions were reduced as members became aware that they were fighting common problems rather than each other.

4. Cooperation among members increased.

The leader must not make the mistake of thinking that differences should not arise in good discussion. He must realize that the building of a valid thought-line requires a continual influx of new ideas, with the sounder interpretations of facts or values winning out over the weaker, less desirable ones. This sifting of ideas—and the discovery of the most desirable and feasible idea at each turn—involves the most vigorous opposition of ideas that the combined efforts of the whole group can produce. This does not mean, however, that a conflict of *persons* should accompany a conflict of ideas; in fact, when members identify themselves personally with ideas they present, they make it difficult for the group to evaluate the ideas fairly and unemotionally. The leader, then, should recognize conflict as essential to the production of a valid thought-line but should work to keep the conflict of ideas from becoming a conflict of persons.

When a group has worked together, with the full energies of each member invested in arriving at a common understanding, there is little need for the leader to ask whether they "agree." In fact, it is often detrimental for him to do so; it interrupts the flow of cooperative achievement and raises an unnecessary procedural question. He should recognize that full investment of the energies of the members

---

3. This type of question is not applicable in a purely theoretical discussion since it presumes an actual specific problem.

at every stage in the task assures that any points troublesome to a particular member have already been posed to the group and ironed out in the cooperative building of the thought-line. On other occasions, however, when confusion or uncertainty may remain among members who have not entered fully into the discussion or when time pressures require moving on to another point before all possible differences have been aired, the leader may legitimately check the group's accord by asking, "Are we then agreed that . . . ?"

Effective handling of disruptive factors

The leader needs to take corrective action against factors that destroy the cooperative work of the group; such factors may be environmental conditions or actions of the members.

Disruptive physical conditions

If the leader discovers that some physical factor has a detrimental effect on the well-being of the group, he attempts to remedy it. He takes steps to increase or reduce the room temperature or lighting, to secure additional necessary equipment or handle a technical breakdown, to stop an unwarranted disturbance or interruption. He takes these steps only when group or individual action is sufficiently harmed by these conditions to make the confusion occasioned by his remedial action the lesser of two evils. For example, if the light is annoyingly strong for the persons on one side of the table, the leader's suggestion that all rise and move the table over a bit is an appropriate solution, that is, appropriate insofar as it eliminates a sizable disturbance to some by a small disturbance to all.

Disruptive actions of members

Handling disruptive members is usually a harder task than handling unsatisfactory physical conditions. But the effective leader needs to deal capably with poor group climate, disruptive acts of individuals, use of stigma words, evasions, and so forth.

Poor group climate Sometimes the leader discovers that the whole group is lethargic, with the building of the thought-line practically at a standstill. Or he may find it overbrash, moving in a reckless, headlong fashion, ignoring alternatives or failing to test its facts or conclusions. Whenever the discussion climate is poor, the leader should avoid rebuking the members; rather, he should remind them of the overriding importance of their goal, linking it vividly with values they hold—linking the insecticide menace with the safety and welfare of future generations and our handling of our African policies with national survival.

Goal enhancement should be a continuing concern of the leader who is striving to obtain cooperative effort of a high order from members with different personal motivations, different histories of group association, and different reference groups. If the leader can show repeatedly the compelling significance of the group's common goal, he can mobilize the members' efforts toward its achievement. The relative importance of ideas becomes easier to see; thus, lesser concerns are subordinated and rivalries for status are set aside and each man's ability is highly prized for the part it may play in the interdependent efforts ahead.[4] An additional method of mobilizing group efforts is to verbalize the difficulty and to enlist all to assist in its correction. In such a request for group effort, the leader should imply confidence, not rebuke or impatience.

Disruptive acts of individuals Sometimes one member or a few members become disruptive in word or manner. The leader should analyze the cause of such behavior and attempt to remedy it. Often the individual is behaving disruptively because of unstated loyalties or beliefs; the other members are puzzled or irritated. For the good of the individual as well as of the group the leader should encourage a forthright expression of these motives. If, for example, the group is urging the adoption of a proposal which a person feels threatens his status, his income, his religious beliefs, and so on, the leader clears the air for honest evaluation of the proposal by encouraging the member's explanation of the true source of his reluctance or opposition.

---

4. For example, during the Korean War, a captain in the Navy, two lieutenant commanders, a lieutenant, and an ensign were called to Washington, D.C., to meet as a committee on a vital military matter. Walking down the corridor to the conference room, the captain led the way. At the rear of the little procession, the lieutenant leaned back to say half under his breath to the ensign, "They won't get a word out of me!" But the captain, as he reached the door of the meeting room, took off his hat and tucked it under his arm. Turning to the others, he said genially, "Off with the rank. Come on, men, we have a job to do." Even the ensign talked in that committee.

As the leader initiates a remedial step, he carefully respects these boundaries: he must not harm the member's feelings of self-confidence or cooperativeness, causing him to abstain from subsequent participation; he must be careful not to take an undue amount of the group's time from its task nor harm the general interpersonal relations in the group.

The disruptive member's actions may take a number of forms. His damage to group action or atmosphere may take the form of overtalkativeness or of no participation at all, of overaggressiveness or excessive timidity in presenting his ideas, of constant digressiveness or a plodding preoccupation with minute details, of belittling responses to some ideas or contributors or uncritical acceptance of certain views and their contributors, and so on. When a member repeatedly responds in such a fashion, the harm he does to group action must become someone's vital concern. Of course, if another member notices the disruptive behavior, discerns its probable cause, and attempts to institute a remedy, the leader should always welcome such efforts, because reconstructive action by members often strengthens their sense of group competence more than action instituted by the leader.

When a disruptive act occurs but once, the leader need not devote much time to its likely cause. In such a case he removes or minimizes as well as he can the harmful result of the act. On the other hand, if disruptive actions are repeated, the leader should isolate the most likely cause and seek to remedy it. In his analysis he should be alert to the possible importance of very small factors, even minor physical factors, like lighting or seating arrangement, which may distort or inhibit a person's response to nonverbal cues. If the leader strongly suspects that such factors are the cause of disruptive behavior, he should attempt to correct them as inconspicuously and as quickly as possible.

Use of stigma words A member may arouse tensions in the group and inhibit free discussion by using emotionally charged words to stigmatize a concept being considered; in such a situation, the leader should restate the idea, neutralizing the "loaded" statement. Mr. Denny, long the director of the American Town Meeting of the Air, demonstrated the deft removal of stigma in a London broadcast on the welfare state, with both Englishmen and Americans on the panel. In the forum period which followed the initial statements by the panel members, a member of the London

studio audience addressed a highly-explosive question to one of
the Americans:

> **Questioner** Mr. Byfield, how do you account
> for a country with millionaires on the one hand
> and paupers on the other? With the Star Spangled
> Banner on the one hand and Buddy, Can You
> Spare a Dime on the other?
> **Moderator (Mr. Denny)** Mr. Byfield, would
> you care to comment on the disparity in the dis-
> tribution of wealth in the United States?

Sometimes, of course, the neutralizing of charged language will not
clear the air; at times, the stigma term raises an important issue so
cogently that it precipitates a valuable investigation by the members
themselves. Here the leader should be alert to see that analysis remains
focused upon the issue instead of becoming an attack upon the initial
user of the term.

  Evasions When members knowingly or un-
knowingly inhibit development of the thought-line by evasive measures, the leader should move to cancel any debilitating effect if he
can do so. Some of the most common ways by which members
evade the idea at hand are:

  1. Deprecating the use of figures: "You can find statistics to prove
anything!" or "Figures don't prove anything!"

  2. Labeling an idea and dismissing its relevance, significance, and
validity: "That's a generalization!" or "You're making an assumption."

  3. Overplaying open-mindedness instead of actually considering the
idea at hand: "Of course, you have a right to your own opinion," or
"There are two sides to everything," or "There's probably as much
good on the other side, only we don't know about it."

  Although these statements may sometimes be true, they are often
used to evade rational analysis by substituting combative attitudes.
When they act as thought-stoppers, the leader should help the group
to pursue the examination they attempt to sidetrack.

Other assistants to the group

  Although the leader is the chief assistant to the members in working together creatively to solve problems or to enlighten themselves

on some subject, other assistants may also be used, such as a recorder, a resource person, or an observer.[5]

Recorder

When the results of the group's deliberations must be presented to a larger assemblage—often very soon after the close of the discussion —the group needs a *recorder*. This person assists the members by taking notes during the discussion so that he can report faithfully on the work of the group.

If you are to act as recorder for your group, keep in mind the following suggestions:

1. Be brief. Do not try to include all the ideas brought up in the discussion, but only those which received enough consideration to become important in building the group thought-line. Make use of the leader's summaries as indexes to these ideas. If there are significant points which remain unresolved, keep a list of them as a guide to further discussion.

2. Be accurate. If you are in doubt about some point, check with the leader and group before attempting to record it.

3. Be objective. Avoid injecting personal interpretations of the group's ideas. Don't label an idea by the name of its initiator; treat all ideas as group contributions.

4. Write legibly. Make sure that your handwriting and system of organization will be comprehensible to you or to any other person making later use of your notes.

5. Additional assistants are sometimes suggested. Irving J. Lee in *How to Talk with People* (New York: Harper, 1952), pp. 162-168, has suggested the *reminder* as a helper who would call the leader's attention to procedures and ideas he had overlooked. Some books on leadership recommend the use of co-chairmen. Herbert Thelen explains that the co-leader "may operate to 'spell' the leader. . . . He may be a sort of supermember, presumably identifying himself with the group and formulating some of the questions other members hesitate to ask. He could also have a group protective function in that he would feel freer to demand more adequate explanations by the leader." From *Dynamics of Groups at Work* (Chicago: The University of Chicago Press, 1954), p. 327. Nevertheless, Thelen does not recommend the use of co-leaders because of the ambiguity of authority that is likely to result, and he concludes: "It is our impression that the concept of equal leadership as a goal is unrealistic and stultifying. The second person should be an assistant, or handyman, or apprentice, or anything else that accurately assists the role relationship."

Neither of these uses is recommended in this textbook which you are studying, that is, neither a reminder nor a co-leader.

5. Be alert for questions. Be ready to supply information from your notes if it is requested by the group.

6. Be audible. If you present an oral report to a larger group from these notes, make sure that your voice can be heard by all.

It is important to understand the relationship of the leader to the recorder. Even though the group has a recorder, the leader must take sufficient notes to help him make his own summaries, retain the handles developed by the group, return to unfinished points, and so on; he should ask the recorder to read his notes to the group only when the formal or exact wording of a point is necessary. The leader should, on the other hand, help supply information if the recorder has failed to catch an essential point. And the leader should summarize clearly and with sufficient frequency to indicate to the recorder the essential pattern of group thought.

Resource person

When a person with specialized knowledge of a particular subject is asked to sit with a discussion group, he is rightly termed a *resource person*. Despite his special competence on the question, he must always think of himself as a *resource* person rather than as an active participant; he must remember that he has been invited to contribute knowledge, not make decisions.

A resource person in order to be of most value to the discussion group should abide by these suggestions:

1. Await the request of the group (channeled appropriately through the leader) before offering information.

2. Be brief. Keep to the point; avoid unnecessary and overly technical details. Try to gauge the need behind the question and make a suitable answer.

3. Be clear, orderly, and direct.

4. Show respect for the purposes and work of the group; avoid seeming to attack, rebuke, or belittle the participants.

5. Avoid drawing the conclusions or making the interpretations which are the rightful work of the group.

6. Avoid becoming one of the discussers; don't let the members feel you expect them to adopt your ideas uncritically.

7. Turn the discussion back to the leader voluntarily when the immediate need for your resources has been satisfied.

The leader should strive to help the group use the skills of the resource person most fully. He should avoid letting the resource person be asked for judgments on issues that the group itself should make. He should also tactfully assist the resource person in concluding his remarks when they become too lengthy. And he should express sincerely the group's gratitude for the help.

Observer

The group observer is a person assigned to watch *how* the group operates and report back to the group what he sees. He stimulates the group to examine how it conducts its affairs. Just as one member may act as a recorder of *what* is decided, so the observer is concerned with *how* the decision is made, with the process the group uses in making its decisions. Any group that wishes to improve its discussion procedures can bring in a trained observer from outside or designate one or more of its own members to act in this capacity.

When you act as group observer, keep in mind the following suggestions:

1. Take notes during the discussion on the procedures of the group in such areas as participation, leadership, progress, and atmosphere.

2. Raise questions about why the group acted as it did at certain points in the discussion and hazard some possible explanations. Try to avoid observations that might be personally embarrassing to any of the members. If your report is made at some point during the discussion, limit yourself to only two or three observations that might help the group as it continues. If the group seems unready to hear certain observations, withhold them until a more propitious time.

3. Point out some of the effective work of the group; do this first as often as possible. When you suggest points where improvements can be made, include yourself as part of the group, saying *"Our* group . . . ." and *"We* seemed to feel . . . ." Avoid finality of statement; use phrases such as: "I wondered about . . . ." and "Could we have handled . . . a better way?"

4. Strive to make yourself clear through specific illustrations so that the group can put your suggestions to work. Try to stimulate the leader and members to seek additional ways of improving group functioning.

5. Do not criticize or attack the group; if the group becomes defensive or angry at you, you won't be able to help, no matter how correct your observations are. Demonstrate in your comments, your voice, and your manner that you are fair minded, sincere, and straightforward.

The leader should help the group accept the services of the observer by explaining his purpose and by demonstrating a sincere desire to consider the observations. He may arrange to have the observations presented at a point part way through the session, during the final minutes of a session, or at the beginning of each new meeting of a series. Whatever arrangement is chosen, the leader turns the meeting over to the observer and lets him talk directly with the group.

Summary

In addition to encouraging free contribution by all members and systematic development of thought, the leader also assists in maintaining sound development of thought, constructive use of differences of opinion, and effective handling of disruptive factors. To help in sound development of thought, the leader calls the members' attention to faulty handling of ideas, faulty understanding of ideas, and questionable reasoning. He employs various methods to handle conflict constructively: (1) examining the data and lines of reasoning behind the divergent views; (2) increasing understanding before attempting evaluation; (3) examining the differences by easy steps; and (4) restricting the means by which conflict may be expressed. He takes steps to handle disruptive physical conditions and disruptive interpersonal factors, such as poor discussion climate, disruptive acts of individuals, use of stigma words, and evasions. Besides the leader, other assistants to the group may be the recorder, the resource person, and the observer.

References

(1) A. Lipsky, *Man the Puppet* (New York: Frank-Maurice, Inc., 1925), pp. 48-50.

(2) Wendell Johnson, *People in Quandaries* (New York: Harper and Brothers, 1946), p. 38.

(3) Carl Rogers, "Barriers and Gateways to Communication," *Harvard Business Review*, 30 (July-August, 1952), 19.

(4) Charles Estes, "Speech and Human Relations in Industry," *The Quarterly Journal of Speech*, 32 (April 1946), 160-169.

(5) Irving J. Lee, "Procedure for 'Coercing Agreement,' " *Harvard Business Review*, 32 (January-February, 1954), 39-45.

Readings and problems

1. Bring several examples from discussions in which you have participated of strong differences of opinion, strongly expressed. Explain in each case whether the conflict was used constructively or destructively by the leader and members. Make suggestions for improvements wherever possible.

2. Discuss these categories as the basis for evaluating the work of a leader in a discussion group. Which functions do you find most difficult to perform satisfactorily?

1. *Opening discussion effectively*
   Stating problem clearly and provocatively?
   Inviting participation of all?
   Initially establishing effective group attitudes by example?

2. *Securing effective functioning of all members*
   Encouraging participation but restraining monopolization?
   Appreciating contributions?
   Providing hospitable reception of all viewpoints?
   Stimulating growth of group's confidence in its leader and itself?
   Sensing and fulfilling group's need for change of pace, moment's relaxation, or light touch?
   Proceeding by group agreement rather than by his own decision?

3. *Keeping discussion moving toward group purpose*
   Discerning and checking irrelevant excursions?
   Getting all important matters considered?
   Recognizing agreements and encouraging group exploration of differences?
   Summarizing before moving to new point?
   Providing a sense of overall direction by transitional questions?

4. *Maintaining sound reasoning*
   Probing generalities for underlying data?
   Scanning sources of opinion for competency and bias?
   Assessing single instances as to their representativeness?
   Neutralizing emotionalized statements?

5. *Bringing discussion to a satisfying close*
   Closing on time?
   Restating principal issues considered, agreements reached and areas to be further explored?
   Articulating group's sense of achievement?

3. Use a rating sheet such as the following to evaluate the work of the leader in a classroom discussion:

Group Leader								
	Low					*High*		
	1	2	3	4	5	6	7	Comments
Opening discussion effectively								
Securing effective functioning of all members								
Keeping discussion moving toward group purpose								
Maintaining sound reasoning								
Bringing discussion to a satisfying close								
Other comments:								

4. David Krech and Richard S. Crutchfield in their book, *Theory and Problems of Social Psychology* (New York: McGraw-Hill Book Company, Inc., 1948), pp. 417-422, present a list of the functions of the leader. Consider how many of these functions are applicable to the leader of a discussion group:

1. The leader as executive
2. The leader as planner
3. The leader as policy maker
4. The leader as expert
5. The leader as external group representative
6. The leader as controller of internal relationships
7. The leader as purveyor of rewards and punishments
8. The leader as arbitrator and mediator
9. The leader as exemplar
10. The leader as symbol of the group
11. The leader as surrogate for individual responsibility
12. The leader as ideologist
13. The leader as father figure
14. The leader as scapegoat

5. Discuss this incident described by George D. Halsey, Personnel Officer, Third District, Farm Credit Administration, Columbia, South Carolina, in a talk entitled, "Motivation: An Important Ingredient of Good Leadership":[6]

> I came into the office that morning a few minutes late and my secretary greeted me with this enthusiastic comment:
>
> "I have a pleasant surprise for you this morning, Mr. Halsey. Your royalty check is here and it is larger than it was last time."
>
> She knew that an insurance premium was due and that a check somewhat larger than usual would be *most* acceptable.
>
> Now this is what I should have said:
>
> "That's fine. It surely came at the right moment, didn't it?"
>
> But there is one part of the story which my secretary did not know. Royalty checks come on time each six months so that the arrival of this check, though most welcome, of course, was certainly no surprise. Also I knew the amount due. So my answer was *exactly* what it should not have been:
>
> "Oh, that," I said. "I knew that was coming. I thought at first that you had a real surprise."
>
> "Oh!" she replied, and I knew she must have felt about like a toy balloon does when you let the air out of it.
>
> I went on into my office thinking about the incident and worrying about it, for it was one of those things one does worry about because he knows that it would be made worse by apologizing.
>
> Suddenly, as I was thinking and wondering why in the world I had done such a stupid and tactless thing, the idea came to me that right here in this incident was an answer to my question which was definite, simple, concrete, and clear. The quality most important in pleasing and influencing people is just this:

6. Given at the North Carolina Annual Extension Conference in May, 1954; duplicated for use in leader training by Jewell G. Fessenden, Division of Extension Research and Training, Federal Extension Service, United States Department of Agriculture.

The willingness and the ability to control the natural tendency always present in each one of us to say and do those things which will increase his own feeling of importance, without thinking about what the effect may be on the other person's feeling of importance.

You might say that this does not apply at all to the incident I have just related. Surely I did not say that I knew about the royalty check with any conscious desire to "show off." Of course, I did not!

But it is a fundamental fact of human nature that the want everyone has for an increased feeling of importance is so strong and so continuously present that we all are constantly doing things—often unconsciously—which will in some measure satisfy it. It would not seem, however, that such a silly little thing as knowing some trifling fact which someone else does not know would satisfy this hunger at all—*but it does.* So it was a desire to satisfy this fundamental hunger for a feeling of importance—a desire not consciously felt or identified by me at the moment, it is true, but there nevertheless—which caused me to blurt out the remark I made.

And it is the replacing of just such thoughtless remarks with remarks that thoughtfully take into account the fact that the other person, too, has a desire for a feeling of increased importance, which is the largest single factor in pleasing and influencing people. It is, I believe, the most important single personal quality needed for any large measure of success in the leadership of voluntary groups.

Let me illustrate how easy it is to forget this fact. If someone tells a joke we have previously read, we will probably make some such remark as:

"That's a good one, isn't it—so true to life." And that would be excellent if it would only stop there.

But after we have made this polite and pleasing comment, all too often we just cannot resist the temptation of showing that we, too, have read the magazine, and so we spoil it by adding:

"It was in last Sunday's *Times*, wasn't it?"

6. Set up a role play situation (see pages 215-217) to examine the requirements of leadership in a cooperation-enlisting task (see pages 10-11).

Situation. Business firm operating on six floors of a building; employees have been clogging the elevators as well as returning late from their morning coffee breaks (between 10 and 11 A.M.); management, facing production losses, has sought advice of a team of experts who have made their recommendation.

Plan. Floors 1 and 3 will have coffee break 10:00-10:15. (No congestion on elevators should result because coffee shop is on first floor.) Floors 2 and 4 will have coffee break 10:15-10:30. (The workers on floor 2 will walk down the one flight to the coffee shop.)

Floors 5 and 6 will have coffee break 10:30-10:45. (The sixth floor has few employees since the space is largely used for storage.) It is to be noted that the employees are now allowed a 15-minute break instead of their former 10-minute one.

Leadership. Leader is floor manager on third floor of the firm; group members are his staff from third floor.

Role play. Contrast an autocratic leader with a democratic one by having the third floor workers informed of the plan in a meeting led by the autocratic leader; then let another group of students represent the workers on the third floor and be informed of the plan in a meeting led by another person in the role of the democratic leader.

Autocratic leader: will describe plan and ask for questions. He will answer some queries by saying that the matter has already been taken care of, others by saying that experts have devised the plan and workers would be unable to improve it, others by saying that certain suggestions fail to show a good worker attitude, others by saying abruptly that any problems will be handled by the authorities, and so forth.

Democratic leader: will describe plan and ask for questions. He will answer queries by careful explanations, though without changing the plan. He will honor the workers' rights to question and to comment and will seek areas for small decisions which they could assist in making. He does not short-change management or his co-workers.

Consequent discussion: All class members will discuss the feelings demonstrated by the workers on the third floor under the two types of leadership and relate them to the differences in leader behavior.

Chapter thirteen

PUBLIC

DISCUSSION

"There has never been, nor can there be," declared David E. Lilienthal in his volume entitled *This I Do Believe,* "any good substitute for the all-around common sense of an informed public." One of the most effective ways of helping the public to become informed on subjects of importance and interest is the *public discussion*—usually in the form of a panel discussion or a symposium.

Public discussion differs from what has been called *group* discussion in one fundamental respect—the presence of an audience; indeed, the major purpose of the public discussion is to communicate ideas to an audience. Sometimes the listeners are merely to be enlightened on a subject; sometimes they are to hear the marshaling of evidence and reasoning to lead them to decision and action. Whether the listeners are physically present before the discussion group or form an unseen radio or television audience, they exert a strong influence upon the conduct of the discussion.

When men discuss subjects anywhere, they should assume responsibility for being well informed, for genuinely desiring to recognize all possible alternatives, and for reaching conclusions by logical means. But when men discuss subjects before audiences, intending thereby to develop understanding and to stimulate thinking, these three other responsibilities take on increased importance: (1) to be audible to all those assembled; (2) to be clear; and (3) to be interesting. Although these are also responsibilities of members in a small group discussion, they are crucial requirements for speakers in a public discussion, who should accommodate themselves to the capacities and expectations of a large listening group.

Public address systems and the equipment of radio and television studios have made it easier for a speaker to be audible, but, even with such assistance, the discussion participants need to speak in such a manner as to make listening both easy and pleasant. Making ideas clear is more difficult in public discussion than in group discussion because of the variations of knowledge, orientation, and interest among the members of the audience. When specialists in the medical profession hold a public discussion on the subject of arthritis, each speaker knows that his examples, explanations, and terminology will have to be intelligible to a wide variety of listeners. In addition, he knows that interesting subject matter and effective presentation are essential if he is to gain and hold audience attention. Unless the specialists present interesting ideas in an interesting fashion—using direct, coherent sentences and providing clear transitions—they will

lose the attention of their listeners and will fail in the purpose of
their discussion.

Public discussions are of two major types: the panel discussion and
the symposium. Both are usually followed by an audience-participa-
tion period, customarily called a forum. When a forum is impossible
because the speakers are in a broadcasting studio and the audience
is elsewhere, provision is sometimes made for small group discussions
among the listeners wherever they are.

Panel discussion

In a panel discussion the members exchange ideas spontaneously.
Seated on a platform or at the front of a room before an audience,
or in a radio or television studio, they talk over the subject among
themselves with the audience listening in. The listeners hear active
interplay of ideas among the participants, hear ideas challenged and
modified through the presentation of different experiences and points
of view.

If the purpose of the panel is to extend the knowledge and insight
of the listeners, the panelists will focus on those aspects of the subject
particularly needing explanation and exploration. If the purpose is to
assist the audience in evaluating a plan (or theory, activity, person,
and so forth) or in comparing the relative merits of several plans,
the panel members will move through a series of logical steps that
illuminate the subject.[1] They may discuss the impact of Marxist
doctrine on Asian cultures, seeking only to enlighten the audience.
Or they may discuss the virtues and defects of the state's court system,
hoping to help the listeners decide whether to vote for or against
a proposal for judicial reform.

Panelists

Since the purpose of the panel discussion is to give the audience
added insight, the members should be capable of presenting a variety
of views on the subject. Their experience and training should prepare
them to present information and interpretations derived from significantly different approaches to the topic. For example, the Community
Counseling Service sponsors a public discussion on juvenile delinquency and arranges for the following persons to participate on the

1. See Chapter 6 for explanation of these steps.

panel: Dr. M. S. Clark, psychiatrist; Dr. L. E. Sumner, physician; Miss Dorothy Woodward, director of a home for delinquent girls; Mr. Bruce Wayland, Juvenile Court commissioner; and Reverend Upton Blanchard, minister. The sponsoring agency asks Dr. J. Holmes, mental health expert, to act as moderator and invites ministers, lawyers, doctors, social workers, and senior high school youth leaders from the area to attend.

Often panelists are chosen because of specific experiences which will throw light on the subject. A panel set up by a chapter of the American Association for the United Nations to discuss the plight of the Indian villager included a nursing consultant who had worked with a World Health Organization program in India; an economics professor who had long been interested in the development of agricultural projects in the Far East; a sociologist who had done field research on cottage industries in rural India; a home economics expert who had specialized in the dietary problems of overpopulated areas; and a physician who had served with the American Friends Service Committee in India. Under the guidance of an anthropologist with much experience throughout the Far East, the group examined the interrelated problems in health, agriculture, industry, and diet.

If the purpose of the discussion is to help the audience reason toward a decision on a problem, the panelists should be qualified to present all the major divergent opinions. For example, if the regents of a university are trying to decide whether or not to switch to full-year operation on a three-semester schedule, they may invite a panel consisting of a financial adviser, a faculty spokesman, an administrative official, a specialist in educational theory, and one or more student representatives. By gaining a clearer insight into the views expressed by these panelists and the reasoning behind each, the board would be better prepared to reach a decision.

The panel members should also be relatively equal in experience and knowledge of the subject and in the skills of oral discussion. The audience will get a distorted impression of the topic if they are markedly unequal in these respects; ideas whose initiators are most articulate will be given disproportionate weight. Of course, it is unrealistic to hope to assemble a panel completely equal in experience and oral skills. But one participant's practical experience with a subject can be balanced by another's academic training or wide and varied insights into related areas. And individual differences in verbal expression will be largely unnoticed if each of the panelists attempts to adapt his illustrations, level of language usage, and speaking manner to the needs of the listeners.

Preliminary meeting

Usually the panel members and the chairman should hold a preliminary meeting to decide upon the general scope and the main issues of their discussion. Experienced panelists will need only a brief list of these issues, whereas less experienced panelists will likely benefit from a detailed outline. The participants on the American Association for the United Nations panel needed to know only that they would talk about (1) present conditions in the Indian villages, and (2) attempts presently being made to alleviate medical, agricultural, industrial, and dietary problems. On the other hand, if a panel of students or a community group wished to inform themselves on a relatively unfamiliar subject and then discuss their findings before an audience, they would do well to develop a more detailed outline to guide them in their public presentation.[2]

The panel should not get into extended discussion of the subject at this preliminary meeting, however, for such a rehearsal reduces the spontaneity of the actual presentation. If members of a discussion class, for example, are to participate in a classroom panel on the improvement of science teaching at the high-school level, they should agree on the relevant areas to be considered and an agenda of questions but should refrain from exchanging ideas on the subject before the time of class presentation.

Presentation

A panel usually consists of four or five persons, with one of them acting as chairman and discussion leader. Sitting in a semicircle or behind tables placed in an inverted-V formation, they can speak directly with each other and yet can be seen and heard easily by the audience. The audience is, as it were, listening in on a committee at work, although the presence of the audience will, of course, change that work somewhat.

The leader should open the session with remarks that (1) reveal the significance of the subject and state the informative or problem-solving purpose of the discussion; (2) identify the panel members

---

2. Such study guides as those illustrated in Chapter 7 would serve this purpose effectively.

and their specific qualifications, if these are relevant; and (3) explain the procedures to be followed in the discussion (and in the forum, if one is planned).

The discussion among the panel members may be begun in several ways. The leader may invite voluntary comments immediately, focusing attention on the first issue and letting the panelists respond freely, or he may ask each member to make a clear, brief statement on the subject before he invites general comments. Lyman Bryson,[3] long the moderator of the CBS program entitled "Invitation to Learning," introduced a discussion of A. W. Kinglake's *Eöthen,* on September 18, 1955, in this way:

> **Bryson** One always includes a travel book in a discussion of books on nature, but this one presents a problem because it gives you very little landscape, it gives you very little nature background, and yet somehow it keeps you fascinated as very few travel books do. Can you pin down precisely what the charm of Kinglake is?
>
> **Smith** Well, here is a young man on the prowl in the world with his senses all developed. The world was his oyster and he was going to eat it, but he found his own mind and his reactions to the world much more interesting.
>
> **Bryson** I think that's right. And he was a young man, Kinglake was.
>
> **Smith** In his twenties.
>
> **Adam** Perhaps the really interesting thing is not just that he was a young man, but that he was a young man of a very definite character and of a very definite period. He was a young Victorian Englishman, an upper-class Englishman, running around in the undeveloped Arab world of the early nineteenth century.

On the other hand, Dr. Shepherd L. Witman, introducing four members of the Foreign Affairs Committee of the House of Representatives on the ABC program entitled "Town Meeting of the Air," on March 18, 1956, gave each several minutes at the outset to present

3. Lyman Bryson at the time was Professor Emeritus of Education, Teachers College, Columbia University.

his position. After these opening statements on the question *Do we have effective leadership in our foreign policy?* Dr. Witman was justified in saying to the assembly: "Now, there you have it. You have four statements and four points of view, and there is plenty of meat in these four positions to continue a discussion for a long, long time."

With a noncontroversial subject, the first method will ordinarily be more useful. With a controversial subject on which the panelists' viewpoints differ widely, the second method will probably be better as a means of orienting the audience. But if the panelists are not thoroughly committed to fixed positions and are somewhat flexible in their interpretations, an immediate turn to ideas rather than an assertion of points of view may produce a more fruitful exchange of thinking even with a controversial topic.

During the discussion of the subject, if the audience is small, the panel members should speak up spontaneously and address each other directly; if the audience is large, the panelists may need to be recognized by the chairman before speaking so that the audience can more readily follow the shift from speaker to speaker. The chairman should assist the panelists in examining divergent interpretations and should see that time and opportunity to speak are fairly distributed among the members. He should provide necessary transitions, syntheses, summaries, and, mindful of time limitations, should focus the panel's efforts on the areas determined in the preliminary meeting. He should also close the presentation with a brief but precise summary of the ideas and agreements developed during the interchange; on occasion he may call upon the panelists for brief summaries of their conclusions.

The following excerpts from a series of discussions of books about the out-of-doors show moderator Lyman Bryson at work. The first excerpt is from the July 31, 1955 broadcast discussion of Robert Frost's *Collected Poems*. The panelists were Eric Larrabee, then associate editor of *Harper's Magazine*, and Charles Poore, joint editor of *Books of the Times* (daily book column in the *New York Times*).

Focuses attention	**Bryson** Well, now, what's he after? You've said that he has a moral in his poems. In a real sense, he has.
	Poore All great art has.
	Bryson I quite agree. But what is his moral?

He has certain attitudes—we've talked of some of them.

Poore   I think you've stated it: keep cool!

Makes transition   **Bryson**   Keep cool? It may be, but there's humor here, too. Is that intended?

Larrabee   Yes, I think it's definitely intended. His way of joking, even with his own meanings, is part of the meaning. That's also what he wants to say: "Don't take me too seriously."

Poore   As in that long poem about the wonders of New Hampshire, in which he does with other states what we must never do with poets: he runs them down. But then the last line is: "At present I'm living in Vermont."

The second excerpt is from the July 10, 1955 broadcast discussion of Mary Webb's *Precious Bane*. The participants were Bryson, Chaim Raphael (author and then director [Economics] of the British Information Services in the United States), and Marchette Chute (author of *Shakespeare of London* and *Ben Jonson of Westminster*).

Seeks information for   **Bryson**   But what's the machinery of this story?
benefit of audience   When we speak of violence, what are we talking of?

Chute   Well, the story in general describes the "precious bane" of the title—bane in the old English sense of destroyer. That sense of longing for position and money drives Gideon Sarn to put the wheat crop above everything else; he forces his mother and sister to slave on the land; in the end the wheat is set afire by the father of the girl he's going to marry. And he goes, in time, insane.

Bryson   His ambition leads him so far that when he's thwarted, life is impossible for him. Well, then, what happens to Prudence?

·   ·   ·   ·   ·   ·   ·   ·   ·   ·   ·

Uses the special   **Bryson**   Do you know Shropshire, Mr. Raphael?
knowledge of the   **Raphael**   I do indeed, although when one talks
panelists   about regionalism in English literature, one has to be very precise as to which street or which village one is talking about. Any reader of this book feels the tremendous absorption with Shrop-

shire, or rather with South Shropshire, which is the area where Mary Webb spent much of her life. Shropshire is very close to Wales, and anyone reading this, I think, does feel the echo of Wales —of the fairies, the harps, the legends.

Bryson But you can't make me think that there's no other romanticism in the British nature —that they get it all out of Cornwall and Wales!

Raphael I think we do feel, in England, that each little area, each county and each part of a county, has its own character. Shropshire, as we know from another Shropshire man, Housman, has a special quality. The Shropshire people feel that they wouldn't like to be confused with Wales or Cheshire or Straffordshire or Worcester or any of the adjoining counties, each of which has its own character.

Chute In Mary Webb's case, particularly, she was striking her roots very deep in the past; she went around and talked to people who remembered the old days and the old ways. I'm working now on the seventeenth century, and I noticed a great many things in this book that would seem natural in the seventeenth, even though she's writing about the early nineteenth.

The participants in the July 3, 1955 broadcast discussion of La Fontaine's *Fables* were Bryson, Leo Gurko (then Chairman of the English Department of Hunter College, New York, and author of *Heroes, Highbrows and the Popular Mind*), and Henri Peyre (Sterling Professor of French at Yale and author of *The Contemporary French Novel*).

Gurko Many of his fables deal with the vanity, greed, selfishness, and smugness of human nature. And just as one is ready to believe that La Fontaine is truly a La Rochefoucauld disguised in the form of a fabulist, one comes to a fable in which he talks about the admirable sides of human nature. He has a kind of well-balanced view of humanity, which is one of the enjoyable things about him.

Tests a judgment   **Bryson** I think I'd quarrel a little on the bal-

ance. I just read a long selection of the *Fables*—
I wouldn't say I'd reread all of them—and I was
struck by the fact that he weighs down a little too
heavily on the stupidities, the vanities, the selfishness. As a matter of fact, I was very much dis-
turbed by one of the later fables, the one about
the old man who was planting an orchard. . . .
. . . .

Peyre It is, of course, a wonderful device to
show not only that men are animal in part of
their nature, but also that they have got to learn
from animals how they have become men—and
try to be worthy of what a man is or should be.
Gurko Yes, the moral comments at the end of
the fables, which are generally filled with a kind
of homespun wisdom, flatter us as readers because
we recognize in them substantiation and support
of what we have already discovered.

Synthesizes and
elevates at close
of discussion

Bryson In that little trick, La Fontaine shows
his great artistry. Instead of flattering us, a lesser
man might make us feel that he was condescend-
ing—but La Fontaine is so perfect an artist that
he can put the moral in and make us feel that
we share his wisdom.

In the fourth excerpt, from the July 17, 1955 broadcast, the discussion
participants were Bryson, Walter Cohen (critic and lecturer), and
Anne Fremantle (then associate editor of *Commonweal*, editor of *The
Age of Belief*, and coauthor of *Europe: A Journey with Pictures*).
They discussed Percy Bysshe Shelley's *Shorter Lyrics*.

Cohen He couldn't bear to read universal history. There's that wonderful legend that before a
soul could cross to the Isles of the Blessed it must
go through the waters of Lethe, the river of
forgetfulness, until the past is forgotten. And that,
of course, is a thought which Shelley develops in
the last chorus of *Hellas:* as long as we carry the
old world with us, we'll never attain the new one.
That's still a new idea. It's not old hat.
Fremantle But he had a great feeling for
individual people in history. No one was more

influenced by, as we just said, Lucretius or by Plato or even by Condorcet.

Takes quick action to clarify a misunderstanding

Bryson Mr. Cohen, I'm sure, didn't mean to indicate that because he thought we should go through the waters of Lethe everything in the past was to be thrown overboard—because he was a thorough Platonist and, as you say, a thorough Lucretian. But he thought the crimes of the past ought to be forgotten so that one wouldn't commit them again.

Use of panel discussion

The panel discussion is especially valuable when the subject allows alternative approaches and interpretations, when different views will help truth and relevance emerge. Not only may the panelists consider a common body of material from different viewpoints (as in the Invitation to Learning examples above), but they may find opportunities for the airing of different viewpoints in the study and mutual discussion of subjects like: *What will be the effects of today's radiation on unborn generations? Are we becoming a nation of conformists? What kind of education does today's youth need?* With such subjects, the varied experiences and beliefs of appropriately chosen panelists can be very valuable for the listeners, whether the purpose of the panel is to provide enlightenment or to assist in decision making.

Best results are usually obtained when the panelists can decide before the actual discussion exactly what areas of the subject to concentrate on, when the panelists are as equal as possible in prestige and in discussion skills, and when they take pains to make their comments audible, their terminology understandable, their lines of reasoning clear, and their presentation interesting.

Symposium

The distinctive feature of the symposium is its series of planned talks, which may sometimes be followed by a brief discussion among the speakers. Usually approximately an hour of speaking time is divided equally among three to six persons, and each speaker uses his allotted time to speak directly to the audience on his portion of the topic or on his solution of the problem. Instead of addressing one another as in the panel form, each symposium speaker comes to the lectern in turn and addresses the audience.

The general purposes of the symposium are the same as those of the panel discussion—to enlighten the audience or to assist them in problem-solving tasks. Enlightenment might be provided by a group of qualified speakers discussing the question *How may increased industrialization affect our community?* with individual speakers concentrating on special aspects of the community—business, employment, education, or law enforcement. Assistance in problem solving might be provided by a symposium in which the chairman analyzes the problem and the subsequent speakers suggest answers.

Participants

The symposium member should either be especially well informed in one particular phase of the subject or be willing to become well informed. For example, in Session IV of the Symposium on Basic Research[4] held in New York City on May 15, 1959, each speaker presented a paper on a topic on which he was uniquely qualified. The chairman was Dr. James A. Shannon, Director of the National Institutes of Health; and papers were presented as follows: "Basic Research in Government Laboratories" by Dr. Allen V. Astin, Director of the National Bureau of Standards; "Basic Research in Industrial Laboratories" by Dr. James B. Fisk, President of the Bell Telephone Laboratories; "Basic Research in Private Research Institutes" by Dr. Merle A. Tuve, Director of the Department of Terrestrial Magnetism, Carnegie Institute of Washington.

When such experts have a general knowledge of the field as well as mastery of their special area, their participation is especially valuable. The speakers must plan their talks to suit the occasion, the audience, and the time allotment. As in a panel discussion, they should be comparable in reputation, knowledge, and appropriate speaking skills. If they are notably unequal in these qualifications, the audience will not give the various presentations equal weight, and the purpose of the symposium will probably be less fully achieved.

Preliminary meetings of participants are sometimes held to determine the areas each is expected to cover and the general arrangements

4. The Symposium on Basic Research, held on May 14-16, 1959, was sponsored by the National Academy of Sciences, The American Association for the Advancement of Science, and the Alfred P. Sloan Foundation. See *Symposium on Basic Research*, Dael Wolfle, ed. (Washington, D.C.: American Association for the Advancement of Science, 1959).

Note the use of the term *symposium* to refer to a three-day conference.

for the symposium and the question period. But, in general, preliminary meetings are less necessary for a symposium than for a panel discussion.

Presentation

As in a panel discussion, the chairman in a symposium attempts in his introductory remarks to arouse the audience's interest in the topic, to acquaint them with the special competency of the speakers, and to clarify the procedures to be followed. Sometimes the chairman needs to inform the audience only about the procedures to be followed. For example, suppose that the voters of a town are to decide at their next election whether or not to incorporate an additional area. A symposium is arranged, with individual twenty-minute talks by three men espousing the major opinions held by the citizens—one advocating incorporation, one opposing it, and one urging further study before making the decision. To facilitate the public discussion, the planning committee secures as moderator an adult educator from a nearby university, a man whose fair-mindedness is widely known in the community. The listeners are interested in the subject and know in general the viewpoint of each speaker, but they need to know the arrangements for their own later participation.

The chairman may prefer to introduce all the speakers at the outset so that once the consideration of the topic has begun there will be little break in bringing forward each speaker. In any case, he should establish time arrangements with the speakers before the meeting, and if any of the speakers talks longer than his allotted time, the chairman should call this to his attention firmly and courteously. As the speeches proceed, the chairman should usually make short, appropriate transitions between the presentations. When the series of planned speeches is followed by a brief, informal discussion among the speakers, he acts as the leader.

Use of symposium

Under certain conditions the symposium offers advantages which the panel discussion lacks:

1. *Some subjects require unified presentation with each subtopic fully and systematically treated.* If the members of an audience want to hear about the effects of the European Common Market upon our mines, our factories, and our farms, they will usually gain more information from a symposium than from a panel discussion.

2. *Some audiences are so large that listeners have difficulty in seeing the speakers clearly.* In such cases, there is a clear advantage in the speakers' addressing the listeners directly, rather than addressing one another, as in a panel discussion.

3. *Some groups of speakers cannot be assembled before the time of the public meeting.* Lacking such a preliminary session, the participants in a panel discussion are likely to be scattered in their approach and superficial in their treatment of ideas; symposium speakers, on the other hand, have less need for such preparation.

Despite these advantages, the symposium tends to be less effective than the panel in stimulating the listeners' thinking. Uninterrupted presentations of fifteen or twenty minutes by each speaker rivet the audience's attention upon one interpretation or area at a time rather than engaging it in a lively interplay of ideas. Symposium speakers, however, can do much to foster comparison of ideas in problem-solving topics by responding directly to each other's claims. On the whole, though, the symposium seems to fulfill the informative function better than the panel but seems less likely to evoke the audience's active thinking.[5]

Symposium-panel discussion

Sometimes the planners of a public discussion think it useful to combine the symposium and panel forms. This combination does not refer to the symposium in which a brief interchange among the speakers occurs at the end of the talks and before the forum begins. That interchange is brief, in the nature of clarification, and not a major portion of total discussion. Nor does it refer to the panel discussion in which brief individual statements are sometimes made by members before the actual interchange is begun. Such remarks are simply statements of viewpoints and serve as introductions.

Occasionally, however, a genuine combination of the two forms is arranged. Such was the plan used at the Symposium on Basic Research held at the Rockefeller Institute, New York City, in May 1959. At the regular sessions the sequence was as follows: presentation of three papers on a particular aspect of the subject, then a panel dis-

5. It should be recognized that in popular usage the term *panel* often refers to any group speaking before an audience, without making any distinction between the interacting group (here called the *panel*) and the group of separate speakers (here called the *symposium*).

cussion with four members joining the three speakers to form the panel and with the chairman of the session acting as the leader. For example, in Session II, Dr. John S. Dickey, President of Dartmouth College, was chairman of a *symposium* in which papers were presented as follows: "Basic Research and the Liberal Arts College" by Dr. Laurence M. Gould, President of Carleton College; "Basic Research and the State University" by Dr. Conrad A. Elvehjem, President of the University of Wisconsin; and "Basic Research and the Private University" by Dr. Lee A. DuBridge, President of the California Institute of Technology. In the subsequent *panel discussion* Dr. John S. Dickey was the discussion leader and the panel included (in addition to the speakers) Dr. David R. Goddard, Chairman, Department of Botany, University of Pennsylvania; Dr. William V. Houston, President of Rice Institute; Dr. Deane Montgomery, Professor of Mathematics, Institute for Advanced Study; and Dr. William E. Stevenson, President of Oberlin College. These presentations took place before an assemblage of some two hundred persons distinguished in government, industry, and education. Both clarity of presentation and vivid, spontaneous development of ideas were possible through combining the symposium and panel formats.

Forum

Both the panel discussion and the symposium are usually followed by a period in which the audience is encouraged to ask for additional information or explanation and to raise additional speculations.[6] Sometimes a member of the audience inquires further about a fact or opinion mentioned by one of the speakers; sometimes he reports a piece of information supporting or calling into doubt some assertion made during the discussion; sometimes he presents for the speakers' consideration an idea that seems significant to him. Such inquiries and contributions give evidence that the discussion has stimulated the listeners to think actively about the subject and, to this extent, has succeeded in its purpose.

The audience should be told before the discussion that they will have an opportunity to ask questions and offer comments. Aware of

6. Other presentations—such as the lecture, interview, debate, and so forth—may also be followed by a forum period. The suggestions for use of the forum after the panel discussion or the symposium are applicable to these other situations also.

this later chance for participation, they are more likely to follow the discussion closely and to frame questions they want to raise.

The moderator's responsibilities

The chairman of the panel or symposium usually serves as the moderator for the forum period. To give the audience as full opportunity as possible to draw upon the knowledge and insight of the speakers, he should keep in mind the following responsibilities:

1. He should advise the audience before the presentation (by the panel or symposium speakers) of the arrangement for their participation during the forum period. If questions are to be written, cards for this purpose may be distributed. But questions asked orally of some particular member of the group or of any member who cares to answer have a spontaneity that is lacking in written questions; for this reason the written method tends to be used only when the situation is charged with emotion or when, for some other reason, it is desirable to select with especial care the questions to be answered. Sometimes it is useful to restrict oral questions in length in order to prevent them from becoming extended commentaries; at other times less formality is necessary, and the forum period becomes a relatively free interchange of ideas between audience and speakers. Whatever arrangements seem suitable to the purpose, the size and temper of the audience, and the wish of the panel or symposium members must be clarified by the moderator and adhered to with firmness and good will.

In an ABC Town Meeting of the Air radio broadcast[7] of March 11, 1956, on the subject *Where does the Free World stand today?* the moderator, John C. Metcalfe, began as follows:

> Ladies and gentlemen, let me begin by explaining to you the format which we will follow. We will present discussions under an agenda of items which have been agreed to by the participants in this miniature United Nations Security Council. Any speaker may interrupt another one by simply raising his hand. If the speaker who has the floor is willing to yield, I will then permit him to make his statement, point of information, or whatever

7. These weekly broadcasts of discussions on vital issues of the day were published in the *Bulletin of America's Town Meeting of the Air.* The March 11, 1956 discussion was the 913th broadcast and appears in Volume 21, Number 46.

> he wishes to present and then we will go back
> and continue his statement. With that, let me
> introduce the participants on this program. . . .

2. The moderator should start the forum period with enthusiasm for and confidence in the interchange that is to follow; the spirit of his comments at this point often influences greatly the tone and accomplishment of the forum. In the weekly radio broadcasts of the Town Meeting of the Air (totaling over 800 programs when it closed in 1954), the turn from the speakers to the forum period was made with phrases like these: We have come now to "the most stimulating portion" of America's Town Meeting; or "one of the most provocative portions," or "the most interesting aspect," or "our traditional question period."

Sometimes, if the listeners are likely to be slow to speak, the moderator may break them up into buzz groups[8] for a few minutes of conversation before opening the floor for questions to the speakers. Sometimes, also, he may ask for a question for each of the panel or symposium members before he opens the forum to queries addressed freely to any of the speakers.

3. If questions from the audience are slow in coming or are not very provocative, he should be quick to cite an interesting illustration, raise a stimulating inquiry, and so forth, to motivate the participation of the audience and to set standards for its conduct. In the Town Meeting broadcast of January 5, 1954, on the question *Does wire tapping violate the right to privacy?* the moderator, finding a lull in the forum questions, said: "As a point of inquiry for our listeners, Mr. Dilworth, what is done customarily with wire-tapped tapes after they have been discarded? Are they destroyed under the supervision of the court, for example?"

4. The moderator should receive the questions from the audience—whether written or oral—and transmit them audibly and coherently to the appropriate person. If a reply has not been requested of a particular speaker, he usually turns to the group with the query and lets one or more of them offer a reply.

---

8. Buzz groups refer to quickly designated temporary groupings of persons sitting near each other for brief consideration of specific topics. When used in a forum period, they help individuals to clarify questions they want to ask and to gain confidence to voice them before the large assembly.

Dr. Shepherd L. Witman clarified a question of some length and ambiguity in the March 18, 1956 Town Meeting broadcast on the question *Do we have effective leadership in foreign policy?* as follows: "I wonder if I have that question correctly, which is, Does Mr. Morano approve the idea of a convention of the leading countries in the NATO organization?" In the April 1, 1956 broadcast on *Foreign Aid: how much and how long?* he broke in quickly when a questioner and a speaker were not understanding each other: "I wonder if I may step in here and see if I can reformulate this question. I think the young lady is asking a question along these lines. Is the American aid program in any sense colored by a colonial objective, or is it entirely a selfless program designed for the interests of our allies and friends? Is that correct?"

5. Although he must not keep himself too much in the center of the interchange, the moderator must preserve sufficient control of the situation to rule out irrelevant questions tactfully, prevent monopolization of the questioning privilege by a few persons, and keep tensions from arising.

As moderator, Mr. Back restrains one participant and brings in another in the Town Meeting broadcast of May 8, 1955, on *How much should public opinion influence foreign policy?*

Questioner Dr. Witman, how far do you think the government should go in releasing military and diplomatic material for the public to form opinions on?

Dr. Witman That's a very tough one. I'm not competent to make that judgment at all, being a civilian citizen, but I do think that there must be an area of restricted information. It has to be decided by the chief executive, in connection with his advisers, his military advisers. In short, I put myself in the position of advocating the permission of having secret material which is not revealed to the people. This is not because democracy doesn't call for everything being said, but because foreign policy is too intricate, it is too full of subtleties—I'd like to go into that but I guess Mr. Back is going to stop me.

Mr. Back I think Mr. Chamberlin wants to go into it for a moment.

Dr. Witman, acting as moderator on the November 13, 1955 broadcast on *What is the future role of France in Europe?* terminated a series of spirited assertions and counterassertions with a brief explanation and a new questioner: "Now we must go on to be sure we don't make this simply a debate between the French and Indian problems. This lady right here, please."

6. He should preserve interest by the pace of the interchange; he should be relaxed and exploratory where such an attitude is useful, and quick and efficient where time pressure and group momentum require a faster pace. For example, Mr. Back, moderating the May 22, 1955 discussion on *What influence should the churches have in politics?* sought assistance from a speaker in meeting the time limitation: "Congressman Fountain, I know you want to comment on that. Our time is racing against us, so if you could make it fairly short."

7. The moderator should neutralize any emotionally charged questions, calmly rephrasing them to indicate their literal meaning.[9] By his imperturbable respect for all persons present and for all ideas offered, he can do much to maintain the dignity and purposefulness of the forum period.

8. He should draw the forum period to a close when the appointed time has arrived or when questions seem to be diminishing in number or interest. If time is running out with interest still high and questions animated, he often indicates how many more questions can be entertained or closes the general questioning with an invitation to those with further inquiries to come forward to talk directly with the speakers afterward.

He should express gratitude to appropriate persons and characterize briefly the thinking that has been done. Dr. Witman spoke as follows at the close of the foreign aid discussion (April 1, 1956):

> May I thank our speakers, Mr. James Roosevelt and Mr. James L. Wick, for their very helpful and enlightening discussion of a subject which is before the public mind of America today in a very significant and important way.

In closing the October 2, 1955 discussion on *Are our colleges suppressing individualism?* he included the audience:

9. See Chapter 12, page 282, for an example of effective handling of an emotionally charged statement.

Well, that's a nice balanced point, however, in
which to bring this broadcast to a conclusion and
I want to tell you how very much we appreciated
your contribution, Professor Root, and your contribution, Professor Wilmeth, and the fine help
of all of these people who had questions to ask.

The panel or symposium members'

responsibilities

Although the moderator assumes many essential responsibilities in
the forum period, a large share of the burden for its success necessarily falls upon those to whom the questions are addressed. During the
forum, each of the members of the panel or symposium should keep
in mind the following obligations:

1. If the moderator has not already repeated an inaudible question
or rephrased quickly and casually any unclear question, the person
answering should do so. Frequently the Town Meeting speakers repeated the heart of the question, as Dr. Witman did in the May
8, 1955 broadcast:

> **Questioner** Dr. Witman, since the percentage
> of people who are well informed on foreign affairs
> is very small, do you think much weight should
> be given to the views of the public in deciding
> foreign policy?
> **Dr. Witman** I think that's about what I've
> been talking about all evening. If I understand
> your question, and that is, Since the number of
> people in the public is very small who have com-
> petence in the field of foreign policy, do I think
> much weight should be given to public opinion?
> Isn't that your question? I think that you have to
> give weight to public opinion. Let's look at it
> this way. . . .

2. Make a brief, organized, direct reply to the question, taking
some account of the larger issues involved but providing a clear
answer to the specific question. If the question concerns areas that
cannot be considered in the time available or are not particularly
relevant to the immediate purpose of the meeting, the speaker should

indicate the necessary exclusions and reply fully on the applicable portion.

The speaker gives a direct reply to a question in the April 24, 1955 discussion on *Are we becoming a nation of conformists?*:

> **Questioner** Dr. Valentine, assuming that conformity is natural in that it is always easier to think the way everybody else does, and easier not to think at all, have you analyzed the recent trend toward conformist thinking that you speak of, and what do you consider the fact that has brought it back?
>
> **Dr. Valentine** I think, with all their virtues, our improved system of communication, our media of expression, have contributed toward the conformity. I think that our economic system, with all of its values and it has them, which concentrates on producing standard goods—I think that our extreme emphasis on materialism which removes other senses of values of the materialistic from us are three of the major contributions. As a former educator, retired therefrom, I also have the feeling that our school system is not so much engendering humane values and ideas and standards as it should be, because it's emphasizing vocational preparation and adjustment rather too heavily in proportion.

3. He should reply to the question in the sense intended, finding the point the questioner wished to make despite poor phrasing or fumbling presentation. To belligerent or persistent questions, he should make a noncontentious answer with evident good will; he must keep in mind always the purpose of the meeting and the necessity of maintaining a fair-minded attitude. Note Mr. Dilworth's handling of a combative question in the broadcast of January 5, 1954:

> **Questioner** Mr. Dilworth, do you think that any spy or a hunted criminal will be stupid enough to use the phone, knowing that wire tapping is legalized? Why endanger the privacy of the entire population to get a criminal or a spy who probably will never use the phone?

313

Mr. Dilworth I am afraid your premise is wrong. Experience has repeatedly shown in every big city and in every community that they use the phone repeatedly, even in cases where they know that that phone is tapped. It is amazing, but they do it. . . .

4. The speaker should avoid replying to the questioner only; the forum should not become a one-to-one conversation, because extended questioning by one audience member (1) presumes upon the time of other members also eager to ask questions, and (2) often takes on a dogmatic and contentious tone.

5. He should volunteer an additional reply to a query addressed to another member of the panel or symposium if such an explanation will make differences clear or otherwise enrich the understanding of that particular point. Representative Vorys, in the March 18, 1956 discussion on the question *Do we have effective leadership in foreign policy?* stated: "I'd like to comment on that. I'm quite familiar with the Kefauver resolution, exploratory resolution, to which the gentleman refers. . . ."

In any situation the purposes of public discussion seem to be most fully served if the panel or symposium members set forth their lines of thought vigorously and clearly and if the members of the audience then participate actively and thoughtfully in the forum period that follows.

Summary

In public discussion, speakers must take special care to be audible, clear, and interesting. The two major types of public discussion—the panel discussion and the symposium—differ in that the members of the panel exchange ideas with each other before an audience whereas the members of the symposium give talks directly to the audience. On occasion the two types are used together. For effective public discussion, members should include people capable of expressing all relevant aspects of the topic with the required skills in oral discussion and public speaking. The panel discussion may be more stimulating than the symposium in engaging the audience in active thinking; the symposium, however, may give the listeners more detailed information and insight. The forum period allows the audience to participate and to draw further on the knowledge of the speakers.

Readings and problems

1. Prepare to participate in a symposium on the question *What are the activities of the World Bank in Asia?* Four students should prepare five-minute talks on the work of the bank in one of the following countries: Burma, Ceylon, India, Japan, Malaya, Pakistan, Philippines, or Thailand. Another student should prepare to act as moderator during the symposium and as chairman in the subsequent forum period in which the entire class will participate.

2. Attend a panel discussion or symposium held on your campus, and assess its effectiveness in terms of these criteria:

audibility of speakers

clarity of speakers' contributions

general interest

effectiveness of moderator

effectiveness of forum period

3. Collect for a week all announcements in the local newspaper of forums, panel discussions, and symposiums. Attend one of these and be prepared to comment on its purpose, the selection of participants, the effectiveness of the moderator, the character and worth of the forum period.

4. Assume that you are to arrange a panel discussion on *How has United States society changed since 1945?* Decide which faculty members you would ask to participate on such a panel, explaining each choice. Prepare a discussion outline that you imagine might be agreed upon in their preliminary meeting.

5. On an agreed-upon date, listen to a specified radio or television panel discussion. Be ready to discuss the moderator's efforts to keep the program interesting and clear for the radio or television listeners.

6. Consider your class a problem-solving body on some subject in which the group is interested, one which may be approached in very different ways; for example, reducing automobile accidents; caring for homeless dependent children; increasing interest in voting; improving television programing; curbing air pollution. Hold a symposium with a moderator who presents the nature and size of the problem, then four speakers, each presenting a different proposal for handling the problem. The entire class will participate in the forum period following.

7. Arrange to hold a symposium for all interested speech students on *problems of campus leadership.* Invite appropriate student leaders to give ten-minute talks on each of the following aspects of the subject:

Relationships with students

Relationships with faculty

Relationships with administrative and counseling staff

Or use a problem-solving format, with four speakers talking on these aspects:

Problems of campus leadership: what are they and
    why do they arise?

Handling problems through careful *selection* of leaders

Handling problems through careful *training* of leaders

Handling problems through careful *counseling* of leaders

In either situation provide a moderator and allow adequate time for a forum period at the close.

8. Hold an exploratory discussion on the following article: "The Quaker Way Wins New Adherents," by Morris Llewellyn Cooke.[10]

To persons who are not initiated in politics, a decision reached by the processes of debate and majority vote acquires an aspect of sanctity as the ultimate expression of democracy. But those in Washington who deal with the complex problems of statecraft inevitably come to see grave short-comings in the honored old way of settling issues. Increasingly, these men and women are resorting to a subtle and effective method long used by the Quakers to arrive at essential unanimity in their business sessions—the process known as taking "the sense of the meeting."

The technique is being adopted by numerous directors of public and private organizations in various parts of the country. It has in recent years helped to settle policy on several national issues of great consequence. Already one can detect the small but significant beginnings of this approach in some actions of the United Nations. Doubtless quite a few of those who are starting to employ the technique are not even aware of its Quaker origin, but they are all too familiar with unfortunate results developing from the great reliance on the reaching of decisions by majority rule.

The faults of the conventional parliamentary procedure arise from its basic assumption—that there exists a divergence of interests rather than a common purpose. The introduction of a resolution for a yea-and-nay

10. Reprinted by permission from *The New York Times Magazine,* June 17, 1951. Copyright 1951 by The New York Times.

vote is conceived as a kind of contest between opposing forces, each going into battle armed with fully formed conclusions which it then attempts to put over on the other side. If a group cannot force acceptance of the whole program, then it proceeds, by a process of barter, to swap point for point—often without regard to the right or wrong of the individual points.

The outcome of the vote, then, is a victory for one side and a defeat for the other, which leads to grudges. It is likely to represent no group decision based on the intrinsic merits of the case but a sort of ledger sheet showing the result of bargaining negotiations. And it imposes on the minority a course of action in which they do not concur and which they may positively resent. At its most extreme the tenor of this method may be described in the words of a prominent businessman in the Twenties, who told a stockholders' meeting: "We will vote first and discuss later."

The Quaker practice of "taking the sense of the meeting," on the other hand, is a combination of free discussion and quiet thinking. "The Quaker form of church government," says Howard H. Brinton, director of Pendle Hill, Friends' Graduate School at Wallingford, Pa., "is the most complete democracy ever devised. Not only do the Quakers refuse to admit the imposed authority of any individual. They do not even admit the authority of a majority. All decisions must be made on the basis of unanimity, reached by a process that considers the opinion of every person, both expert and inexpert. Therefore, a Quaker committee sometimes appears to be amateurish and time-consuming."

It is well worth this time, in the Quaker view, to develop in a group the willingness to accept unanimously what appears to be the balanced judgment of the majority or the best informed.

First, according to this procedure, a subject is introduced not by presenting a resolution but by "reading a query." This is usually done by the chairman—or "Clerk of the meeting," as he is known in Quaker groups. Such a departure from parliamentary order is by no means a petty one, for by this simple device, the issue seems to come from the group as a whole instead of being sponsored by one faction within it.

Various points of view on the subject are expressed by individual members—whoever wishes to contribute. But strong words, provocative language and repetitive discourse are taboo; members are encouraged to speak just once on a given point, and only after careful thought. And, most significant of all, the individual speaks not simply as a man expressing his own conscience but as the voice of the group addressing itself to the issue at hand. If a contrary viewpoint is raised, it is considered as if it were one's own for the purpose of treating it objectively. "Getting under the weight" of the other man's doubts is the term the Quakers sometimes use to describe this attitude of respect for a minority viewpoint.

If conflict at any point becomes so heated as to make an agreement doubtful, the Clerk may halt discussion and ask the members to consider

the subject for a while in thoughtful silence. The value of such a deliberative period was shown during World War II, when a group meeting in a
mid-city Philadelphia office attempted to settle a troublesome strike. All
interests were represented. The president of the concern was high in the
councils of the Episcopal Church. The discussion having become bitterly
deadlocked, he said, "My partner is a Quaker from Delaware County and
I propose that after the manner of Friends we settle down to a period
of silence and see if we cannot get some light on these troublesome
differences."

After five minutes of a profound silence the meeting was called to
order and the discussion resumed in a different atmosphere. In a very
short time an agreement satisfactory to all was reached.

There is never any voting. When a positive program of action appears
to have been indicated by the evidence brought to bear on the subject,
the Clerk sums it up by "presenting a minute," expressing what he takes
to be "the sense of the meeting"—the consensus, the course of action
which would take into account the most significant pieces of evidence
contributed by all the members. At that certain point "you can almost
hear the meeting 'click,'" as one experienced Clerk describes this phase
of the proceedings, "and that's the clue for the Clerk to present his minute."

The "sense of the meeting" stands as the group's decision unless some
challenge is made by an unsatisfied individual. In this case the Clerk may
suspend the subject for the time being—true unanimity obviously being
out of the question—to permit more careful consideration and perhaps to
gather more facts. A committee may be appointed for research and to
prepare a report for the next meeting, when a new attempt is made
to attain unity.

Much of the success of this technique depends on the skill and the
character of the Clerk. He must not only be acute, intelligent, sensitive
to the meanings expressed by the members, but he must take care to
refrain from being domineering; in fact, must frequently suppress his own
attitudes. From the membership as a whole the system requires thorough
frankness, sincerity, and a cooperative spirit.

Beyond these there are two principal elements in the practice. There
must be a belief on the part of all or most of the participants in the
meeting that agreement is desirable. Secondly, the belief must be entertained that in any decisions taken the way should be left open for the
unconvinced, ·or for the skeptics, eventually to join in the view reached
by the main body of the group.

If these two convictions are held by a substantial number of those
present in the meeting, the Quaker practice has been known to surmount
very great initial differences of opinion.

How successful is this temperate method when serious differences exist?
The best answer lies in a recital of some important cases where agreement

is, or has been, attained by the Quaker principles of unanimity.

(1) The President's Water Resources Policy Commission recently published its report under the title "A Water Policy for the American People." The findings were concurred in unanimously by the seven commissioners. The commission, of which I was chairman, never took a vote and no record was kept of its proceedings. The report itself is its record. Even though its assignment from President Truman involved reaching decisions on many highly controversial questions affecting water and land, everything was talked out in conference until a meeting of minds was arrived at.

(2) The Acheson-Lilienthal atomic energy report was drafted by a group which tried to operate after the Quaker fashion. A helpful factor in creating the necessary deliberative quiet was that meetings were held in a storage warehouse on the outskirts of Washington, and no one but the participants knew of the project until the work was completed.

(3) The Joint Committee on the Organization of the Congress in 1948-49, commonly known as the La Follette-Monroney committee, drafted—without taking a vote—the voluminous report on the basis of which Congress was fundamentally reorganized.

(4) The present Senate Republican Conference, of which Senator Millikin is chairman, and to which all Republican members belong, takes no votes and such conclusions as are reached are stated by the chairman to be his interpretation of the committee's joint thought.

(5) The International Monetary Fund operates in accordance with this by-law: "The chairman will ordinarily ascertain the sense of the meeting in lieu of a formal vote" unless a vote is specifically called for. Frank Coe, the secretary of the fund, tells me that during the four or five years since it was organized decisions have been reached on over a thousand issues and that on only twelve or thirteen of them have votes been taken.

(6) The Committee on Economic Development, one of the major organizations studying public finance, carries on its discussions and frames its findings Quaker-fashion. At the conclusion members of its committees are recorded as voting for or against, with the opportunity accorded for explanatory footnotes.

(7) Finally, because it is frequently said that the Quaker method can be used only where relatively small groups are concerned, it is worth while to note that the First National Conference on Aging held in Washington during August 1950, under the auspices of the Federal Security Agency, with an attendance of 816, used the group process of discussion and decision. Clark Tibbetts, who acted as chairman of one of the principal committees, thinks that the success of the several sections was "almost in direct proportion to the use made of the group method."

For all these striking examples, it would be false optimism to conclude that the "sense of the meeting" technique could be applied successfully to the deliberations of major political bodies, such as a Congress in full session. Here the limitations of the method must be acknowledged. For by its very definition it requires not only utter frankness, sincerity, and mutual trust but also a suppression of any personal, factional, partisan, or sectional interests.

There is no room in the Quaker practice for unreasoned obstinacy in the face of sound evidence, nor for resistance to unity on a particular issue based merely on traditional antagonism. Some Friends themselves go as far as to say that the practice cannot be applied with much hope of success in any group composed of elected representatives who must report back directly to a constituency, for often the constituency holds some minute but unshakable special interests that are contrary to the interests of the group as a whole.

This also raises the question whether anything can be gained from the Quaker method in the way of peaceful and effective deliberations among the United Nations. It must be recognized that the necessary frankness and trust between Eastern and Western nations are unfortunately lacking at present. We could not be sure, for example, that "evidence" presented by the Soviet Union and her satellites would be anything more than a disguise for her real purposes or a calculated move undertaken for propaganda value.

Still there is a direct relationship between the Quaker practice and methods of securing agreements on disputes before the U.N. Assembly, once these disputes have been handed over to conciliation commissions or to mediators. Because it is possible for these commissions to operate in private, without the glare of press and radio publicity and without the necessity for individual members of the commissions to record their points of view, the way seems open for utilization of the Quaker practice.

In the case of the U.N.'s subsidiary agencies, those smaller nonpolitical organs in which a group of nations represents the total membership, there is also good opportunity for using the "sense of the meeting," for in these cases the members are not expected to reflect only their own national interests. The Economic and Social Council, the Trusteeship Council and their subcommissions are examples in point. There have been occasions in each of these bodies when the chairman has been able, because of the thorough discussion that has taken place, to make voting a perfunctory step.

Do these instances of successful use of the Quaker method, and examples of public bodies which might try it, indicate a wider usefulness for the "sense-of-the-meeting" technique in the future? That they do. If the executives of organizations dealing with public affairs, from the municipal level up through the councils of the United Nations, will test this technique they will find that important decisions can be arrived at with less partisanship, more harmony and with greater faith in the results achieved. That much, in these irascible times, would be a great deal.

Chapter fourteen

DISCUSSION:

METHOD OF

DEMOCRACY

If we are to see clearly in what sense discussion may be character-ized as a *method of democracy*, we must first consider what we mean by democracy. When men say, "We believe in democracy," they are likely thinking of liberty and equality, those principles based on the assumption that man has choices to make by which he may attain a fuller life; when they say, "We live in a democracy," they no doubt have in mind the political system of self-government by which we aim to secure liberty and equality to all citizens of our country; and when they say, "Democracy is a way of life," they are probably referring mainly (although somewhat vaguely) to the freedoms we enjoy in other than strictly political spheres of life—in our occupation, in our family and friends, in our enjoyment of leisure time pursuits, and so forth—freedoms which are dependent, however, upon a democratic framework of government. And all these—democracy as a philoso-phy, democracy as a form of government, democracy as a way of life—are interlocking aspects of the general concept; once we have recognized them as a theory-means-end continuum, it matters little which one we have in mind.

The discussion process, as it has been explained in the preceding chapters, clearly embodies the principles of democracy. When we recall the right of the individual member to contribute when and as he wishes and the responsibility of the others to avoid pressure on him for consensus beyond his true belief, we realize that the principle of liberty (as freedom of belief and action) is in operation in the group. When we recall the effort to keep lines of communication open so that all can contribute freely and so that all ideas will have a fair hearing, we see the elimination of privilege, the utilization of valuable differ-ences, and the respect for other persons which characterize the demo-cratic principle of equality. When we recall that members work together as a team, building on each others' ideas and accepting individual responsibility to combat injustice, ignorance, and subver-sive motivation in the group, we are noting the individual participat-ing with others for the general good through making choices responsibly, that is, through self-government and majority rule.

This embodiment of democratic principles in the discussion process is of tremendous importance.[1] Since every person spends a large

1. Explanations of the discussion process in this chapter are made from the point of view of the small group; these would apply with certain modifications to the panel discussion, and in some respects to the symposium.

portion of his waking hours participating in group activity, the characteristics of such activity have significant influence on his development as man and as citizen.

Effective uses of the discussion method

Laurence Stapleton (1) has set forth in his book *The Design of Democracy* the responsibilities of the citizen in a democracy:

1. "consider and understand the underlying principles of democracy";
2. do his part "in the choice of government";
3. "strive to change [laws that are wrong] rather than to disobey them";
4. avoid identifying democracy only with his own community; rather "seek the good of other communities and modify the demands of his own";
5. "search for the ablest statesmen and support the best in them";
6. "accept the responsibility of office if he is needed."

If an individual discusses with others the subjects involved in carrying out these responsibilities, he helps to assure the rationality and practicality as well as the idealism of the actions he and perhaps they also subsequently perform. And, furthermore, in the very act of discussion which has led to these more effectively founded opinions as bases for action, the individual has been practicing the arts of democracy—responsible use of his power to make choices and respect for the equal rights of others. Thus, both substantively and procedurally, the individual in such discussions has been readying himself for more effective social action.

When a person participates, for example, in a Great Books discussion session on Milton's *Areopagitica,* he is learning concepts that may help him form more soundly based opinions on today's question of "managing the news"; thus he is receiving substantive value. Also, as he sits down with others somewhat different from himself in experience and outlook, differing in good-humored fashion over meanings and interpretations, over problems that rend society, and over the current proposals that promise to alleviate them, he experiences the mutual trust, the willing helpfulness, the subordination of personal preference that makes cooperative social action possible.

The woman who joins the League of Women Voters not only studies deeply the problems of her community and the world, but learns a particular meaning of the word *consensus*. When a unit follows its discussions with a report of its consensus to be used with the reports from other units in deciding the League *stand* on an issue, it attempts to report the context of opinion, not only the belief of the majority and that of the minority but the depth of conviction with which these beliefs are held.

Groups interested in enlightening themselves on subjects of current importance abound in every community. Or, if they do not, any individual has many opportunities to initiate one of the established programs in his community or to turn some social, occupational, or recreational group to which he belongs into such a discussion group.[2] The following programs are examples of some of the possibilities:

Great Books Discussion Program—a program of twice-monthly discussions based on the reading of designated "timeless" books which consider "the persistent questions that each man asks himself, every society is forced to deal with. . . ." Two trained leaders cooperate to raise pertinent questions and focus the contributions of the members. Recordings of the Great Books are now available for use by discussion groups for the blind. (Great Books Foundation, 5 South Wabash Avenue. Chicago 3, Illinois)

Great Issues in Education Program—a new program started by the Great Books Foundation. Its purpose is to assemble people interested in studying and talking about some of the basic questions in the field of education. (Great Books Foundation, 5 South Wabash Avenue, Chicago 3, Illinois)

The Delphian Society—a bimonthly, three-year series of discussion programs for "women over 25 years of age, qualified for college-level study, and not engaged in business or the professions." The aims of the series are to help the adult woman develop her understanding of psychological, political, and cultural patterns of living in the modern world. (The Delphian Society, 105 West Adams Street, Chicago 3, Illinois)

Great Decisions Program—a program of eight sessions to be set up locally by interested persons to discuss national issues of the cur-

---

2. These enlightenment groups are in addition to the problem-solving groups in which the individual may be participating in his business, his profession, his church, his club, and so on.

rent year. Information, maps, and so forth, are assembled by the Foreign Policy Association and are usually made available through a local educational institution. Frequently radio and television programs are provided by community stations as further stimulation to the group discussions, usually during February and March. (Foreign Policy Association, 345 East 46th, New York 17, New York)

League of Women Voters Program—a women's organization which aims at providing each member with a sound basis for drawing individual conclusions on the subjects studied and discussed. It is organized in small groups (called *units*) which meet regularly for discussion and decision. The League holds that "the experience of stating a problem in our own terms, of using our own minds in search of a solution, of acting on our own decisions, makes League membership and national citizenship an active rather than a passive experience. It puts quality into our League product and it upgrades the political wares of our democratic government." (League of Women Voters, 1026 17th Street N.W., Washington 6, D.C.)

Society for Individual Responsibility—a loosely knit (by intention) group of locally established chapters made up of persons who study and discuss questions of national importance. Emphasis is on getting reliable information: members operate in task-force fact-finding groups to obtain and present reliable information to the group-at-large. Emphasis is also placed on giving public officials "constructive support for constructive policies." (Society for Individual Responsibility, 25 West 45th Street, New York 36, New York)

In addition, there are the myriad discussion programs set up by churches, Y.M.C.A. and Y.W.C.A. groups, retired persons' organizations, divisions of continuing (or adult) education at universities, state agricultural extension divisions, community development associations,[3] and so forth that study public problems.

Of course, not all such groups talk about concerns that would be classified strictly as political. But whatever the subjects discussed, the members' experience in exchange of information and interpretations and in mutual accommodation of viewpoints for mutually accepted constructive ends is highly valuable in its demonstration of the

3. For example, the community development programs conducted by the Community Development Bureau of the University of Washington are of the self-study type, basing the work largely on local discussion groups. Richard Poston's book *Democracy Is You* (New York: Harper and Brothers, 1953) outlines the basic structure of the study programs.

freedom and equality of individuals and of coordinated efforts for general welfare.

But in addition to the gain in knowledge and understanding on public questions and the values in democratic association with others for a common purpose, there is an inestimable personal enrichment for the participants. No individual can participate in effective discussions without becoming more sensitive to the needs and aspirations of other people, more capable of communicating his own ideas and experiences, and more keenly responsive to nuances of thought and behavior.

Note that the attainment of these valuable results is predicated upon participation in *effective* discussions. All of us know that many discussions fall far short of being effective—the group has inadequate data, or the efforts of the members are not focused cooperatively on the subject, or the time is too short for the task, and so forth—and, therefore, the substantive goal is not reached, the practice in democratic processes does not occur in any significant fashion, and the individuals are not greatly enriched.

Sometimes groups wishing to improve their uses of discussion method set up a workshop and ask experts on human relationships, group processes, psychology, and so on to give them help on theory and practice. Or certain of the members arrange to attend a training conference on leadership or group methods, such as the annual summer sessions of the National Training Laboratory (affiliated with the National Education Association) or one of the regional laboratories. Other groups call in trained observers at some of their regular sessions in order to achieve more fully the values to be derived from effective handling of the discussion process.

Misapplications of the discussion method

The discussion method is frequently misapplied in two separate ways: as a *panacea* and as a *scapegoat*. No doubt it is the wish to secure the most tangible benefits of the discussion method—a superior solution and strong loyalty to it—that leads men sometimes to use it in situations to which it is clearly not suited. And it is likely the high esteem in which the method is held that leads men sometimes to use it as a scapegoat.

As a panacea

We should not use the discussion method in emergency situations; when an answer must be forthcoming quickly, the discussion process is usually not appropriate. Of course, the members of a group with a history of cooperative achievement and with a competent and confident way of working together can attack a new problem more swiftly than can a group without such working relationships. But even the experienced, successful group needs time to build its decision by the play of idea upon idea. When time for such mutual interaction is not available, the process we call *group discussion* simply cannot take place and should not be relied upon to provide the answer.

Nor should we expect to use the discussion method on problems whose answer will be clear once the relevant facts are known. When it is information that is needed rather than the interplay of minds upon that data, discussion is usually not an appropriate means of approach. No amount of group thinking will produce the data that could be obtained through such methods as the questionnaire, interview, observation, experimentation, and so on. This does not deny the value that some researchers have found in a team attack upon projects, but in such cases the value probably stems from the cooperative conceptualizing that precedes the experimentation or from the speculation that follows rather than from the process of data-gathering itself.

As a scapegoat

When a person in authority—an executive in a business organization, an administrator in a public agency, a supervisor in a factory—who is faced with the necessity of making a judgment for which he will rightly be held solely responsible assembles his subordinates to share with him the decision making and consequent responsibility, he is using the discussion method as a scapegoat. *Advisory* discussions might be legitimately helpful to the man ultimately responsible for the decision, but his subordinates must not be made accountable for weighing factors that their position gives them no chance of knowing in any adequate fashion.

As we all know, there are times when individuals wish to defeat a proposal without seeming to do so; in such cases, they often, as they say among themselves, *bury it in a committee*. Such disposition would upset their intention, of course, if the committee had opportunity, motivation, and power to consider the proposal and to recommend a decision. It may be that the proposal is premature or awkward, that is, generally unattackable but not suited to their immediate purposes; or it may be that it is supported by an influential faction whose enmity must be avoided. The individuals do not want a decision but they hope that any opprobrium for the defeat of the proposal will fall on the committee. Here the discussion method is clearly being used as a scapegoat.

Creativity in the discussion method

Obviously the misuses of discussion arise out of the very recognition of its frequent successes. But let us not deceive ourselves. Even when the group is of appropriate size and composition and its members have sufficient time to address themselves to a suitable subject, they do not always bring into being that responsible interchange of thought and feeling which make the group a highly creative instrument. Clear thinking and wise choices are never easy. And when men attempt the tasks together they provide themselves with both increased power and increased risk—more ideas and more ability to shape them, but greater danger of misunderstanding, disruptive personal motivation, and easily offended pride.

Hence, we should seek to improve our use of the discussion process —by additional training, perhaps, and certainly by continued self-evaluation of day-to-day experiences in its use. By such improvement we will be able to use more fully the increased power and to minimize or handle the increased risk produced by group interaction.

Summary

Discussion is a method of democracy in that it embodies the principles of liberty, equality, and self-government. Participation in effective discussion gives an individual both substantive and procedural assistance in his role as a citizen and also enriches him as a person. The discussion method is often misapplied as a panacea and as a scapegoat. Group discussion can attain creativity when its users have learned to handle its risk and utilize its power.

Reference

1. Laurence Stapleton, *The Design of Democracy* (New York: Oxford University Press, 1949), pp. 120-122.

Readings and problems

1. Prepare to participate in an exploratory discussion on democracy, using these excerpts as springboards.

1. Democracy "enlarges the scope of our experience by enabling us to acquire insight into the needs, drives, and aspirations of others. Learning to understand how life is organized by other centers of experience is both a challenge and a discipline for our imagination. In aiding the growth of others, we aid our own growth."—Sidney Hook, "The Presuppositions of Democracy," *Ethics*, 52 (April 1942), 288.

2. "In a democracy, liberty depends on liberalism—defined as faith in change by reason and persuasion rather than by force or violence. By placing its primary emphasis on the individual, democracy becomes an open society, in which individuals can challenge any and all traditions; in which private experience is the ultimate criterion of truth and value; and in which informed public criticism is the primary means of improving our heritage." —Henry Ehlers and Gordon C. Lee, eds., *Crucial Issues in Education*, rev. ed. (New York: Holt, 1959), p. 4.

3. "A popular government without popular information or the means of acquiring it, is but a Prologue to a Farce or a Tragedy, or, perhaps both. Knowledge will forever govern ignorance; and a people who mean to be their own Governors must arm themselves with the power which knowledge gives."—James Madison, Letter to W. T. Barry, August 4, 1822, in *The Complete Madison: His Basic Writings*, Saul K. Padover, ed. (New York: Harper and Brothers, 1953), p. 337.

4. "Democracy is a regime which to be successful demands the greatest intellectual maturity, for not only is it based upon reasoning but upon the willingness to let others reason."— George Boas, "The Century of the Child," in *The American Scholar Reader*, Hiram Hayden and Betsy Saunders, eds. (New York: Atheneum, 1960), p. 85.

5. "In short, it is essential to the effective working of democratic government that the great majority of citizens should be sufficiently easy in their present circumstances and sufficiently secure in their future prospects to afford certain intangible luxuries— the luxury of good will, of tolerance for opinions not shared and of consideration for interests not their own, the luxury of be-

lieving in the value of rational discussion and of entertaining the conviction that their common interests can be better served, in the long run, by relying upon the methods of persuasion than by appealing to the methods of force."—Carl Becker, *New Liberties for Old* (New Haven: Yale University Press, 1941), p. 105.

6. "The case for democracy is that it accepts the rational and humane values as ends, and proposes as the means of realizing them the minimum of coercion and the maximum of voluntary assent. . . . The essence of that faith is belief in the capacity of man, as a rational and humane creature, to achieve the good life by rational and humane means. The chief virtue of democracy, and the sole reason for cherishing it, is that with all its faults it still provides the most favorable conditions for achieving that end by those means."—Carl Becker, *New Liberties for Old* (New Haven: Yale University Press, 1941), p. 151.

7. "A lively temper of mind and spirit can set the clumsiness of institutions at naught. But men must solicit this better self. It does not come by plan, neither does it come unasked. It is not born of the outpourings of a press and radio dominated by commercialism. The mountebank tricks of advertisers, of commentators seizing on conflict as an easy source of drama, the taste for gossip and triviality which hinders us from learning more seriously the resources of human character, are unworthy of our intelligence."—Laurence Stapleton, *The Design of Democracy* (New York: Oxford University Press, 1949), p. 159.

8. "In the ultimate ideals of the classless, stateless society of abundance, there are several affinities in Marxism with the ideals of traditional liberal and democratic theory. But one—the vital one—is absent: the importance of politics, and with it the need for government. All political and governmental problems vanish in the classless society, and we are left with virtual anarchism. The contrast between dream and reality is given by the Soviet Union, where politics and democracy are not so much assumed away as frankly suppressed in favor of the absolute, the governmental, and the administrative."—H. B. Mayo, *An Introduction to Democratic Theory* (New York: Oxford University Press, 1960), p. 281.

9. "What the principle of democracy does is to provide a criterion or set of criteria that enables us to discriminate certain politically vital from other (and therefore, in this context, subordinate if

still precious) liberties, and thereby to determine which of the many restraints or deprivations of power we are prepared to tolerate. For while all restraints involve a limitation of some freedoms, the creation of means necessary to the elimination of some of those restraints may involve a restraint on other, and more important, freedoms. Thus, the paradox is affirmed that some restraints—even such as might otherwise be deemed an abuse of power—may, in an indirect fashion, further rather than restrict the preservation and enjoyment of the vital liberties."— David Spitz, *Democracy and the Challenge of Power* (New York: Columbia University Press, 1958), p. 170.

10. "Liberty and equality essentially are not exclusive but complementary. The recognition of the equality of human personalities involves their freedom to develop, and freedom of choice is, indeed, the very condition for the unfolding of the personality and its progressive development. It is possible to reconcile these diverging elements, and this task is particularly appropriate for a democratic society."—Charles E. Merriam, *What is Democracy?* (Chicago: The University of Chicago Press, 1941), p. 84.

      2. Examine the contribution of the following sources to your understanding of discussion method, taking note of the explanatory statement quoted from the preface or the introductory chapter:

1. Beal, George M., Joe M. Bohlen, and J. Neil Raudabaugh, *Leadership and Dynamic Group Action*
   (Ames, Iowa: The Iowa State University Press, 1962).

"This book is for the millions of people who make up the myriad of groups operating within democratic societies—who are searching for ways to enhance the results of their group activities. Much of what is known about individual and group behavior has not been integrated and translated into meaningful terms so that it can be used by individuals in democratic groups to help them perform more efficiently and effectively."

2. Berlo, David K., *The Process of Communication: An Introduction to Theory and Practice*
   (New York: Holt, Rinehart and Winston, Inc., 1960).

"This is a book about the way people communicate with each other. Essentially, it is concerned with the scope and purpose of communication, the factors involved in the process, and the role of language in human behavior. It is about people's behaviors and the relationships between the talker and the listener, the writer and the reader, the performer and the audience. It explores the complex nature of the communication process. It identifies and describes factors affecting communication and its results. It attempts an approach to the process that will increase understanding and effectiveness, and yet avoid distortion or oversimplification."

3. Bonner, Hubert, *Group Dynamics: Principles and Applications*
   (New York: The Ronald Press Co., 1959).

"As the subtitle indicates, we are concerned with both theory and empirical example. Accordingly, we offer first a systematic presentation of those aspects of group behavior which have come to comprise the central subject matter of group dynamics, namely, group structure, group cohesiveness, intergroup tensions, group learning, group problem-solving, and group leadership. Having laid down this theoretical framework, we then trace its important emergent applications to the vital areas of industry, community relations, political behavior, group psychotherapy, and education."

4. Chase, Stuart, and Marian Tyler, *Roads to Agreement: Successful Methods in the Science of Human Relations*
   (New York: Harper and Brothers, 1951).

This book is "an experiment in *integration*. Specialists 'know more and more about less and less' as science advances, and a liaison service is needed to keep them in touch with one another. Even more, perhaps, a service is needed to keep the intelligent layman in touch with the advancing front. . . . So far as I know, this is the first attempt to integrate techniques of agreement from widely distant sources. I hope it may serve as a useful map for better equipped expeditions in the future."

5. Klein, Josephine, *Working with Groups: The Social Psychology of Discussion and Decision*
   (London: Hutchinson and Co., 1961).

"Working with groups requires three skills: an understanding of theory, a knowledge of its application, and trained experience in its use."

6. Lee, Irving J., *How to Talk with People*
   (New York: Harper and Brothers, 1952).

"In this book I report an attempt to look at some human troubles— those that come when men and women talk together. The committee room is far from being the most important scene of human interaction. It is, however, convenient and confined. In it one can see on a reduced scale the way conflicts begin and go on."

7. Maier, Norman R. F., *Principles of Human Relations*
    (New York: John Wiley and Sons, Inc., 1952).
"This book is written for persons who are interested in human relations problems, and as such it concerns itself with overcoming communication barriers, preventing misunderstandings, and developing the constructive side of man's nature. . . . The examples and applications are pointed toward industry, but the principles apply to all situations where leaders must deal with groups or individuals."
8. Olmstead, Michael S., *The Small Group*
    (New York: Random House, 1959).
This is "a survey . . . of propositions and findings in the study of small (and of primary) groups, focusing on major approaches, assumptions, and problems, and organized in terms of a conception of social science deriving ultimately from the work of Talcott Parsons and Robert F. Bales."
9. Thelen, Herbert A., *Dynamics of Groups at Work*
    (Chicago: The University of Chicago Press, 1954).
This book analyzes group practices found effective in six areas—citizen participation, classroom teaching, in-service professional training, administration and management, human relations training, and public meetings—then presents "a development of ideas beginning with the meaning for individuals of group membership and then considering in turn the processes of experiencing by individuals, the kinds of facts with which a group operates, the nature of group control, the problems of leadership, and, finally, the community as the context for group activity."
10. Thibaut, John W., and Harold H. Kelley, *The Social Psychology of Groups*
    (New York: John Wiley and Sons, Inc., 1959).
This book offers what the authors "believe to be a rather new approach to the old problems of interdependence, attraction to the group, power and control, status evaluations, social norms, etc."

        3. Examine the contribution of the following sources to your understanding of group discussion leadership, taking note of the explanatory statement quoted from the preface or the introductory chapter:
1. Bass, Bernard M., *Leadership, Psychology, and Organizational Behavior*
    (New York: Harper and Brothers, 1960).
"The intention of this book is to gather together some of what we

know about leadership and to organize this knowledge into a set of generalizations held together by reason as well as experiment."

2. Bellows, Roger, *Creative Leadership*
    (Englewood Cliffs, N.J.: Prentice-Hall, Inc., 1959).

"Creative leadership involves arranging the situation so that mutual goals and understanding meld people into harmonious teams."

3. Gordon, Thomas, *Group-Centered Leadership*
    (Boston: Houghton Mifflin Co., 1955).

"Part One presents the philosophical and theoretical foundations of a particular kind of leadership, one in which the basic aim of the leader is to tap and develop the creative resources of his group members. Part Two describes an experience in which the leaders of a single learning group plan and carry out this leadership approach and observe and record the process of change and development within the group." Part Three "is a description and an evaluation of an industrial leader's attempt to try out group-centered leadership in an industrial organization."

4. Haiman, Franklyn S., *Group Leadership and Democratic Action*
    (Boston: Houghton Mifflin Co., 1951).

"To our knowledge there has been no attempt to bring together in one place the philosophical-scientific background and the practical techniques of democratic group leadership. This book is such an attempt. In it an effort has been made to strike a healthy balance between theory and practice—a balance which we feel has been lacking in previous works on leadership."

5. Laird, Donald A., and Eleanor C. Laird, *The New Psychology for Leadership*
    (New York: McGraw-Hill Book Co., 1956).

This book presents basic findings from 22 research centers without the technical terms. "Our part has been merely to tie the researchers' findings together, and point out how the active leader can be guided by these findings."

6. Lindgren, Henry Clay, *Effective Leadership in Human Relations*
    (New York: Hermitage House, 1954).

"The purpose of this book is . . . to stimulate self-examination and to promote self-understanding on the part of that large and varied group of people we have designated as leaders. In attempting to achieve this purpose we have tried to present some typical examples of problems that occur when leaders work with subordinates or group members. We have tried to suggest some of the reasons why such problems occur; and we have given a few suggestions as to how some of the basic problems of leadership may be met."

7. Maier, Norman R. F., *Problem-Solving Discussions and Conferences: Leadership Methods and Skills*
   (New York: McGraw-Hill Book Co., 1963).
"Groups have two assets that exceed those of any individual in the group: they possess more knowledge, and they can think in a greater variety of ways. These potential assets may cause the group to be in conflict, or they may lead to a superior product and increased satisfaction. For the latter to occur, the principles of group behavior must be skillfully used by the leader. What these principles are and how they may serve to improve meetings is the subject. . . ."

8. Petrullo, Luigi, and Bernard M. Bass, eds., *Leadership and Interpersonal Behavior*
   (New York: Holt, Rinehart and Winston, Inc., 1961).
This book reports a symposium whose purpose was "to take stock of the current status of achievement. . . . Where a field is expanding, it is desirable to take periodic panoramic views without sacrificing the minute inspection of details."

9. Ross, Murray G., and Charles E. Hendry, *New Understandings of Leadership: A Survey and Application of Research*
   (New York: Association Press, 1957).
"The purpose of this book is to provide for those who carry day-to-day responsibilities for leadership training and development in business, educational, or social organizations, a relatively simple summary of recent thinking and research on the nature and meaning of leadership."

10. Tead, Ordway, *The Art of Leadership*
   (New York: McGraw-Hill Book Co., 1935).
Aware of the desirability of controlled scientific experimentation, the author states that "if a book were to wait upon such formal scientific corroboration, none would appear, perhaps, for another decade."
"The purpose of this book is to set forth the meaning and methods of leadership as contrasted with the concept and methods of command which have so long prevailed in organized human affairs. . . . A second and complementary purpose is to provide organizations which recognize the importance of helping executives to become leaders, with a volume that supplies the essential subject matter for a study of this relatively unexplored art."

        4. Prepare to explain briefly the design and major findings in several recent research studies on group cohesiveness, communication structure or network, leadership, or some other area suggested by your instructor.

Books like the following will give you suggestions on significant studies:

Bass, Bernard M., *Leadership, Psychology, and Organizational Behavior,* 1960.

Hare, A. Paul, *Handbook of Small Group Research,* 1962.

Handbook of Social Psychology, Gardner Lindzey, ed., 1954. Vol. II.

Consult recent issues of these periodicals for first reports of research studies: *American Journal of Psychology, American Sociological Review, Human Relations, Journal of Abnormal and Social Psychology, Journal of Applied Psychology, Journal of Personality, Journal of Psychology, Journal of Social Psychology, Social Forces, Sociometry, Speech Monographs.*

Significant studies appear in collections like these:

Group Dynamics: Research and Theory, Dorwin Cartwright and Alvin Zander, eds. First edition, 1953; second edition, 1960.

Small Groups: Studies in Social Interaction, A. Paul Hare, Edgar F. Borgatta, and Robert F. Bales, eds., 1955.

The Study of Leadership, C. G. Browne and Thomas S. Cohn, eds., 1958.

INDEX